Nature and Society

Nature and Society

Later Eighteenth-Century Uses of the Pastoral and Georgic

RICHARD FEINGOLD

Rutgers University Press
New Brunswick, New Jersey

Permission to quote from the following work is gratefully acknowledged: *Virgil's Georgics: A Modern Verse Translation*, translated by Smith Palmer Bovie; © 1956 by The University of Chicago; reprinted by permission of the publisher and the author.

Publication of this book was partially supported by a grant from the American Council of Learned Societies to the Rutgers University Press in recognition of its contribution to humanistic scholarship. The funds were provided by the Andrew W. Mellon Foundation and are to be applied to the publication of first and second books by scholars in the humanities.

Library of Congress Cataloging in Publication Data

Feingold, Richard, 1938–
  Nature and society.

  Includes bibliographical references and index.
  1. Cowper, William, 1731–1800. The task.
2. Dyer, John, 1700?–1758. The fleece. 3. Pastoral
poetry, English—History and criticism. 4. Great
Britain—Economic conditions—1760–1860. I. Title.
PR3382.T33F4 1978   821'.5'09   77–13418
ISBN 0-8135-0847-9

For Linda and Billy

Contents

Acknowledgments ix

Introduction 1

I. The Good Society and the Bucolic Mode:
Virgil and Pope 19

II. Bucolic Tradition and Virtuous Work:
Arthur Young and Adam Smith 51

III. Two Worlds of Work: John Dyer's
The Fleece 83

IV. William Cowper: State, Society,
and Countryside 121

V. Art Divorced from Nature: *The Task*
and Bucolic Tradition 155

Epilogue 193

Index 201

Acknowledgments

In its first form this book was my doctoral dissertation at Columbia, and I am especially pleased now to express my gratitude to my teachers, Jim Clifford and John Middendorf, for their patience, their hearty encouragement, their scrupulous criticism. In revising and enlarging my work later, I benefited immeasurably from my colleagues at Berkeley. Paul Alpers read the manuscript and offered painstaking criticism over a long period of time, always with firm encouragement. Had I been able to make use of all he taught me about the pastoral, this would have been a better (but a different) book. Ralph Rader took an early interest in my work and has been generous with help and advice on this project and others since I've known him. Josephine Miles's scholarship, especially her *Eras and Modes in English Poetry,* was influential in shaping my thinking about eighteenth-century poetry long before I knew her, and I have been privileged since to benefit from her interest and her friendship. To the reviewers for Rutgers University Press, and to its director, Herbert Mann, I owe thanks for their perceptive and sympathetic criticisms and for the humane efficiency with which the process of review was conducted.

It would be idle for me to try to describe the value of John Paterson's warm and generous friendship over many years and through several difficult times. To my wife and son, I owe the most. This book is for them; without them I could not have done it.

R. F.

Berkeley, July 1977

Introduction

My subject in this study is the use of pastoral and georgic fictions in the poetry of the later eighteenth century; my interest is in the reasons why these ancient and honored forms began to fail as expressive opportunities for poets who found it both natural and delightful to employ them, experiencing in their ease and delight, no doubt, the assurance of authentic expression. Certainly too, the very considerable contemporary popularity of this poetry could only support a writer's confidence. But after 1800 the pastoral was something to be either contemned or rescued, and the georgic simply disappeared. In trying to understand why this happened, I soon saw that the questions I was asking about pastoral and georgic began to include further questions about history—about England's larger life, the agricultural and commercial (even industrial) expansion that surrounded poets who sought to interpret this new national experience within the perspectives offered by pastoral and georgic forms. My argument is that what we perceive today as a failure of art is implicated in the pastoral or georgic poet's way of seeing this new national experience.

The heart of this book is my discussion of John Dyer's *The Fleece* and William Cowper's *The Task*, but these poems alone do not define my subject or describe my purpose. It is perhaps best that I say something here about my material and my procedure, an explanation at the start being preferable to an apology at the end.

I have thought it important to ask about the meaning of the fact, boldly stated by Donald Davie, that the English poets of the later eighteenth century, for whom the literary countryside was so pervasive and compelling a subject, failed as a group to understand what was happening in the actual countryside—the actual countryside that was the first scene of the momentous changes in English life that were so abruptly transforming the nation.[1] My inquiry proceeds on the assumption that what we can learn in the critical process of explication and evaluation resonates with what we can learn about the larger life surrounding the life of an aesthetic object. It seemed obvious and natural to me that my critical work would be connected with the economic and social experience the poetry I study grows from and refers to. This is the experience of political economists, merchants, agrarian capitalists and agrarian reformers—practical men whose work and utterance also are strongly shaped by attitudes that can be called literary and whose intellectual success and failure with their own proper material resembles the success and failure of poets with theirs. What I am concerned with here is an intersection of art and actuality, and in seeking answers about how poems work or fail to work I have seen that their character as poems is mirrored in mundane experience, that what shapes or distorts a poem can also shape or distort an economic treatise, that an economic treatise also has an imaginative identity, a shape of thought reflecting the forces that determine a poem. I emphasize, therefore, that in chapter two my study of Adam Smith, Arthur Young and others is not offered merely as background to my criticism of Dyer and Cowper but is of a piece with it and in places shares with it the same page. It is precisely because the countryside and the farm, actual and literary, have served for over two thousand years as moral ideas, imaginative touchstones for the criticism of social and political life, that the pastoral and the georgic could become so crucially important to men, poets and projectors and political economists, who sought for an understanding of their burgeoning England. If the pastoral and the georgic are forms of social and political understanding, then it

1. "We get the paradox that in literature the Industrial Revolution is recorded almost exclusively in its effect upon agrarian England. The poets saw what was happening to rural England without understanding why it was happening" (Donald Davie, *The Late Augustans* [London: Heinemann, 1965], p. x).

should not be surprising that their attitudinal and expressive habits can be seen, in their strengths and weaknesses, in the imaginative and critical thought of political economists and agrarian capitalists as well as of poets. For such an approach to the poetry, moreover, there is ample support in Raymond Williams's recent and brilliant *The Country and the City* (1973).

Eighteenth-century literature was from the first deeply implicated with history, as obviously enough a great satiric literature will be. Empire, a social order growing with, and perhaps for, an incredibly energetic marketplace, a politics moving with that growth and answering to that energy—these constitute a good deal of the subject matter of the public poetry of the Augustan age, as well as much of our own daily legacy from the history of the eighteenth century. Undoubtedly we have been helped by our understanding of our own history to value correctly the period's satire as its authentic expressive act, its great art. This, and not the art which itself responded positively—as much georgic poetry did—to the rapid and profound changes taking place in eighteenth-century life, has compelled our attention and shaped our understanding of that age and of our own. I mention this only to suggest that the connections between life and art, between a poet's experience of the historical world and the poems he frames to interpret it, call for a criticism which ought not to be glib in its assumption of art's prerogative to transmute facts into significant—Aristotle said philosophical—fictions. Pope's fictions tell enduring truths, John Dyer's do not, though their celebrative, georgic manner is in a simple sense immediately appropriate to what he saw in England's busy life and what he felt about it. We really do not know enough about the generation of authentic art to justify either simply excluding or simply including historical considerations in our efforts to evaluate poetic expression. And yet, we cannot ignore them. In discussing the validity and responsibility of Juvenal's exaggerated satiric violence, for example, Alvin Kernan assures us that the question is really "delusive, for we are dealing with art, albeit highly rhetorical, not history. Rome was somewhat corrupt, and Juvenal constructed his satires in such a way as to reveal that corruption in the most striking manner possible." Yet surely our responses to Juvenal are helped along in their assent to his art by our knowledge of the empire's decline and fall, and how can we say that the authenticity of Juvenal's art is not a function of his very real imaginative apprehension of the feel of disaster? Authentic art is vindicated by history, though I do not think we know just how. In this study I try, I hope tactfully, to probe the pressures history applies to art and to use my sense of these pressures to help me evaluate some poems. My assumption is that if we find *The Fleece* a difficult poem to value now, we are not likely to deny that a passage like this one about factory labor circa 1757 (book 2, lines 79–84),[2] which we can responsibly judge by our own knowledge of subsequent history, contributes to our difficulty:

> . . . the tender eye
> May view the maim'd, the blind, the lame, employ'd,
> And unreject'd age: ev'n childhood there
> Its little fingers turning to the toil
> Delighted: nimbly, with habitual speed,
> They sever lock from lock . . .

Is such a passage not a plain, though very interesting, failure of Dyer's apprehension of history? In making such a statement I am willing to risk judging the poem as more than merely a document of its time; I think we can and often do make such evaluations responsibly, and that the process does not preclude sympathetic reading, even if the result is an adverse one.

Our understanding of the great satiric literature of the Augustan age has been finely exemplified in Maynard Mack's observation that "Pope did not, like Walpole, represent the self-confidence of the English which would one day rule the world. His part of the English temperament was that part which has so filled the national literature with commanding images of a city beyond the existing

2. John Dyer, *The Fleece*, in *The Poems of John Dyer*, ed. Edward Thomas (London: T. Fisher Unwin, 1903). The reference to Kernan is to *The Cankered Muse: Satire of the English Renaissance* (New Haven: Yale University Press, 1959), p. 78.

city that it is likely to remain the nation's glory long after the last
vestiges of empire have disappeared."[3] But Mack's appreciation of
the glory of Pope's art and the moving beauty of the literary role he
created for himself in the 1730s as Walpole's "mighty opposite" is
offered as something of a rebuttal to Samuel Johnson's own observation that for Pope's "intense and repeated reference to a nation in
decay" there was no historical foundation.[4] Mack emphasizes that
Johnson's judgment is that of a man looking back from a distance
of forty years and taking a historian's stance, forgetting that his
own poem, *London*, in its Juvenalian anger, described a city "not
wholly to be discovered on any of John Rocque's maps." The great
poetry of the 1730s, then, a more philosophical thing than any
chronicle or successful merchant's ledger, becomes so by virtue of
fictions which can, all the same, disturb the historian in his stub-
born concentration on the energies of the existing city.

Probably it is no accident that Johnson, while writing his life of
Thomson, would dismiss the image of England created by the
satirists whose attention was on Walpole. Thomson, after all, spent
some energy composing a poetry of praise—praise of power, praise
of commerce, praise of industry, praise, in short, of England's
existing city. This was a poetry no less intimately rooted in contemporary affairs than Pope's, but it presents a very different
version of the English nation. The most notable perhaps of a long
line of Whig panegyrics, as C. A. Moore has dubbed them, some of
Thomson's work has merited, for its celebrative enthusiasm, the
label "propaganda."[5] But the panegyrist, in his celebration of what
was coming to be understood as an enormous growth of English
wealth and power, can more charitably be seen to have been
responding directly to the very palpable and demanding facts of his

3. Maynard Mack, *The Garden and the City: Retirement and Politics in the
Later Poetry of Pope 1731–1743* (Toronto: University of Toronto Press, 1969), p.
231.

4. Mack, *Garden and the City*, p. 230. For Johnson on the satiric climate see
Lives of the English Poets, ed. G. B. Hill, 3 vols. (Oxford: Clarendon Press, 1905),
3:289: "At this time a long course of opposition to Sir Robert Walpole had filled
the nation with clamours for liberty, of which no man felt the want, and with care
for liberty, which was not in danger."

5. C. A. Moore, "Whig Panegyrical Poetry," *PMLA* 41, no. 2 (1926): 362.

day. New forms of commerce, new methods of industrial and agricultural production, new patterns of population, new habits of consumption, new international commitments, new and growing military might—all these features of English national life are the subjects of the poetry of praise, just as they were the subjects of satire, just as they formed the concerns of political economists, journalists, gentlemen, and members of Parliament. Again, that Dr. Johnson should sense the propriety of remarking that in this burgeoning England there were no signs of national decay—and that he should invoke the testimony of history—might remind us of his own developing enthusiasm for the national spectacle, which he expressed on several occasions, most notably when he busied himself at the disposal of Thrale's brewery, perceiving with excitement that in the transaction there lay ready for someone the possibility of growing "rich beyond the dreams of avarice." Nor is it surprising that he should have acknowledged such help as Mandeville could give in opening his eyes to real life. For his mind, early freed from cant, it was possible to recognize how much of the truth about a vigorous and growing nation Mandeville's notorious paradox—private vices make public benefits—was revealing. Yet Johnson could simultaneously recognize how at its heart that paradox was merely a matter of words, that there was no clear reason why those public benefits could not more suitably be recognized as public evils. Without illusions, yet still with honest enthusiasm, Johnson could come to terms with England's national vigor, avoiding the fictions of both the satirist and the celebrant to speak with special authority as a kind of observer, even philosophical historian.[6]

In offering some penetrating speculations about the connection

6. But see Jeffrey Hart, "Dr. Johnson as Hero," *Johnsonian Studies*, ed. Magdi Wahba (Cairo: Société Orientale de Publicité, 1962), pp. 35–36. Hart argues that Johnson's responses to England's commercial vigor emanate from the keen imaginative grasp of contemporary experience shared by the great conservatives of his century and suggests further that Johnson's enthusiastic outburst on the sale of Thrale's brewery is a sign of his early awareness of the Faustian spirit of capitalism. For Johnson on Mandeville see James Boswell, *The Life of Johnson*, ed. R. W. Chapman (1953; reprinted., London: Oxford University Press, Oxford Standard Authors, 1966), p. 948.

between literature and history in the Augustan age, Ian Watt has characterized Augustan literature as defensive in nature, taking "more notice of Virgilian farming methods than of the great agricultural and industrial revolutions that were changing the face of England. More significantly the Augustan writers," Watt says, "often looked back as a way of measuring the deterioration of the present; they were obsessed with decline."[7] These judgments depend perhaps upon how severely we restrict our application of the term "Augustan." Do we, for example, understand it simply to mean "Tory"? A "Whig" poem like Dyer's georgic, *The Fleece*, is certainly conservative in a formal sense, patterned scrupulously on the formal model of Virgil's *Georgics*. Looked at in another way, however, it is strikingly original and anything but defensive. The poem is Dyer's effort to discover in wealthy, commercial (and to some extent industrial) England the very model of a virtuous polity. A good deal of Dyer's poem has to do with sheepherding, but there is even more in it about the wool industry. The poem, indeed, comes out of the countryside to deal with the activities of the city, the wharf, the factory and the counting house, all of which, Dyer asserts, lives in happy harmony with the virtuous pastoral lives of the shepherds who lavish innocent care upon the sheep whose wool is England's treasure. Though the quiet virtues of the pastoral life are conventional touchstones guiding Dyer's judgment of the energetic English nation, the poet simultaneously expresses his exultation over its energy, its imperial power, and commercial wealth. Dyer's model of public virtue is still that of the old agrarian order (celebrated in the rhetorical conventions of the georgic mode), but the energies that fascinate him are those which shape the commercial state. This is a difficult pair of attitudes to affirm simultaneously (which may explain T. S. Eliot's description of the effect of much eighteenth-century Miltonic verse: "What the writers have to say always appears surprised at the way in which

7. Ian Watt, "Two Historical Aspects of the Augustan Tradition," *Studies in the Eighteenth Century: Papers Presented at the David Nichol Smith Memorial Seminar, Canberra 1966*, ed. R. F. Brissenden (Toronto: University of Toronto Press, 1968), p. 82.

they choose to say it"), but it seems to me that Dyer's poem, in its intentions, form, and manner, is a work we might characterize as Augustan, conservative, and enthusiastic—anything, indeed, but defensive. Dyer looks back to his Roman model, not at all obsessed by decline, but rather taken with the possibility that his own age could be appropriately colored by the ancient lustre. Furthermore, some georgic poets in England were using Virgil's literary model to celebrate precisely those features of the agrarian revolution that were part of the long process that since the fifteenth century was putting an end, not only to "Virgilian farming methods," but inevitably also to the feudal structure of rural life.[8] As a body of work, it seems to me that this poetry of praise raises a compelling question of literary value in its blend of formal conservatism with an enthusiasm for those happenings we have come to recognize as revolutionary in industry, agriculture, society, and politics. If we no longer read *The Fleece* we may wonder how much, and in what way, its failure for us is a question of literary form. More precisely, how does our experience of the subsequent course of history influence our response to this literary form, telling us that the georgic writer's conservative and celebrative fictions are inauthentic?

We have been generally accustomed to discover, in the literature of the Augustan age, two different attitudes to the developing course of history, which we label as Tory and Whig. To call that habit into question seems to me not so important as to remember that, whether a man was apprehensive or enthusiastic about what was happening around him in politics and the marketplace, he

8. For example, Robert Dodsley in his georgic "Agriculture" (part of his larger, incomplete *Public Virtue* [London, 1753]) celebrates Jethro Tull's research and innovation; Tull is the "Shelborne Swain" of the following lines and what Dodsley sings of here is Tull's advocacy of drill planting, an important change from the traditional practice of broadcast sowing:

> Thus taught the Shelborne Swain; who first with skill
> Led through his fields the many-coulter'd plough:
> Who first his seed committed to the ground,
> Shed from the drill by slow revolving wheels,
> In just proportion, and in even rows;
> Leaving 'twixt each a spacious interval,
> To introduce with ease, while yet the grain
> Expanding crown'd the intermediate ridge,
> His new machine. . . .

> ["Agriculture," book 2, lines 85–93]

would, as a writer, be drawing upon very much the same body of imaginative literature in his effort to frame the fictions by which he celebrated or attacked what he saw. Everybody knows how the model of Virgil's *Georgics* nourished Pope's imagination; but also for the Whig, Addison, the *Georgics* was the "best poem of the best poet," and Thomson, the patriotic celebrant, was dubbed "the English Vergil." All of this is well known, but we have not much bothered to ask why the conservative fictions which served so well for satire were so entirely inappropriate for celebration— inappropriate, that is, as we now can see, having ourselves rejected them. The question is a compelling one if we consider again how, for a time, these celebrative fictions enjoyed enormous popularity among readers who simultaneously delighted in their bitter satirical literature. Satire obviously was not telling the whole truth about England to the men of the day, though for the most part it has seemed to us to have been telling the most significant truths, not only about contemporary affairs, but perhaps about ourselves as well. So that our own judgments have, for some two hundred years, been confirming the existence of an eighteenth-century dilemma: there was, apparently, no viable form which the age, as we experience it, could discover to celebrate those events and phenomena which, to many observers, were eminently worth more than attack—were, indeed, an exciting stimulus of contemporary wonder and congratulation. In the end, this dilemma is a symptom of a failure of art, and the appearance at the end of the century of new habits of feeling and expression, generally called romanticism, marks the discovery not only of new kinds of psychological and literary experience but necessarily also of new ways of understanding the nature of the public world and the artist's place in it. Clearly to us now there was throughout the eighteenth century a kind of crisis in men's understanding of that world and a necessity for radical choice in the invention of interpretive fictions. And perhaps what is now most clear about the poetry of public praise is its failure to recognize that need for choice. Its characteristic quality is the habit of interpreting, by means of ancient forms of fiction, phenomena which were radically new.

It will be clear from what I have been saying that my thinking has benefited importantly from Raymond Williams's *The Country and the City* (1973), a work which has enhanced our understanding both of eighteenth-century culture and of the pastoral writing which it produced in enthusiastic abundance. Williams's comprehensive study takes him well beyond the generic and historical borders of my work, but his explorations of the intersections (and evasions) of art and actuality across the four centuries of capitalism's history come to an especially critical juncture in his judgments of late eighteenth-century pastoral writing. His sense of its difficulties and of the kind of rescue it required and received from the next literary generation develops from his approach to the pastoral as a keenly sensitive if ultimately evasive response of the imagination to the first major effort of capitalist enterprise, the reorganization of agricultural industry in the actual English countryside, already well under way in the sixteenth century. Williams's judgments are not happy ones; his view of pastoral is of a literary form that worked to mystify that actual countryside into an idealized and lyricized evasion of the harsh actualities of production and exploitation upon which a new economic and political energy was founded.[9]

"Mystification" is Williams's word; its dangers as a category of literary judgment are obvious and I do not intend to review them here. Mystification in one viewpoint may be vision in another. But vision too is a category of literary judgment that can count, perhaps too positively, in critical inquiry. Williams has been right to ask about the *authenticity* of the pastoral and about the adequacy of its vision, and he has been right to put forward as a proper test the actuality that vision is supposed to interpret. What we can judge positively as vision or metaphor may be no more than mystification and perhaps the most significant responsibility of criticism is to feel for the distinction and to recognize in it the test of authentic expression.

It is, of course, a difficult test. Williams, for example, can honor

9. Raymond Williams, *The Country and the City* (London: Chatto and Windus, 1973), p. 31.

Crabbe for the authenticity of his denial of pastoral idealizing and celebration, yet he also recognizes the limitations of Crabbe's response. These limitations he understands as determined by Crabbe's final appeal to a structure of values more consistent with the very pastoral idealizing he attacks than with the harsh criticism he levels.[10] But against this judgment we may place Irvin Ehrenpreis's:

> Crabbe, in *The Village*, pretends to give a faithful picture of a scene falsified by [Goldsmith's "Deserted Village"], but he hardly instills conviction; for he keeps his eye too closely on the poem he is refuting, and simply inverts Goldsmith's representation instead of dislodging it with an independent view. His own congenital pessimism imposes itself too systematically on the details of the landscape. One realizes that one is facing a projection of the poet's character and not an English village fairly observed.[11]

Following this judgment we might conclude that another style of mystification follows upon a failure of a different stamp, but here it can be explained by a more familiar, if less satisfying, formula: lack of genius.

What is required, it seems to me, is that the test for authenticity search for the straining points at which whole poems bend or

10. Ibid., pp. 93–95.

11. Irvin Ehrenpreis, "Poverty and Poetry: Representations of the Poor in Augustan Literature," in *The Modernity of the Eighteenth Century*, ed. Louis Milic (Cleveland and London: The Press of Case Western Reserve University, 1971), p. 27, n. 31. The realism or the lack of it in the period's pastoral writing has been a regular concern of scholarship, though its exploration has not yielded significant results. What has been needed is the definition of a context within which this literary issue can be shown to resonate significantly with the urgent concerns of a culture to which the pastoral was an important form of imaginative thought. It is not simple realism that Williams looks for as the medium for the revival of the pastoral; this is clear from his criticism of Crabbe. What we have had, by and large, are disembodied accounts of the period's pastoral writing and its theories of pastoral writing that have referred to this issue without defining what was at stake in it. For a complete and useful survey of the eighteenth-century pastoral organized in these terms see A. J. Sambrook, "An Essay on Eighteenth-Century Pastoral, Pope to Wordsworth, Part I," *Trivium* 5 (1970): 21–35, and "Part II," *Trivium* 6 (1971): 103–15. J. E. Congleton's *Theories of Pastoral Poetry, 1684–1798* (Gainesville, Fla.: University of Florida Press, 1952) surveys the range of eighteenth-century critical opinion along these lines.

break, those points at which imaginative structures cohere or fail to cohere into the whole shapes that their ideas, attitudes, and metaphors imply. It is the necessary and brilliant comprehensiveness of Williams's purpose and of his argument that precludes such an inquiry and prevents him from attaining at several crucial points the fullest power to convince. It is difficult, for example, to know what to do with Williams's judgments of "To Penshurst." That the poem's celebration of the Sidney estate grows from Jonson's sense of harmony between its economic operation and some larger natural order is for Williams an evasion of the

> insatiable exploitation of the land and its creatures—a prolonged delight in an organized and corporative production and consumption—which is the basis of many early phases of intensive agriculture. . . . [But this makes it] difficult to talk, in a simple way, of a "natural order," as if this was man in concert with nature. On the contrary: this natural order is simply and decisively on its way to table.[12]

But where does this judgment lead us when we find ourselves responding with pleasure and approval to Jonson's poem for reasons comfortable with our regular critical practices of explication and evaluation? Williams has sought to "call the bluff" of these procedures,[13] but we are still left with Jonson's poem, which is for Williams, as much as for us, a delight. This obvious question needs to be asked, but asked in full acknowledgment of Williams's judgments, which call now for new inquiries into Jonson's poem and its kind, inquiries as profound as Williams's "calling the bluff" of a criticism that ignores his considerations. If, as it seems likely, Jonson's poem will survive all inquiry, we need to ask why, and to seek for those breaking points in literary history where similar celebrative efforts fail to hold together against the recalcitrant pressures of actual history. Perhaps Jonson does not talk in a *simple* way of a natural order, but we need to ask for the reasons why any such talk at another time does become simple and imaginatively incomplete, and therefore vulnerable to any style of critical judgment.

12. Williams, *Country and the City*, p. 30.
13. Ibid., pp. 18–19.

What I offer here is a context for and then the close readings of two long, whole poems, Dyer's *The Fleece* and Cowper's *The Task*; my effort is to define their straining points and to judge their power in accommodating the stresses of their own imaginative and intellectual structures. The conclusions I reach are about these poems and about what they tell us of the pastoral and georgic kinds. It seems to me that a view of these poems from the inside of the culture they come from tells us that mystification is not their characteristic vulnerability. Indeed, I have specifically chosen two works which seem to me to struggle against mystification and to look directly at the actual facts of contemporary history, of production and consumption, of political experience, and whose effort is managed by the appeal to the metaphorical and thematic constructs of the pastoral and georgic kinds. In the end my judgments are critical but not unsympathetic, for what is remarkable about Dyer and Cowper is how much of plain actuality they admit into the imaginative ambit of their poems as they try to avoid literary mystification. In these poems we discover a direct effort to see, judge, and feel, the result of which finally is to disturb or disrupt imaginative integrity, but not cheaply or simply. Dyer's poem, in fact, is fully responsive to his perception of the driving intensity of capitalist production and consumption, its rootedness in human desire, its promise of "riches beyond the dreams of avarice." And Cowper's perspective sees into more than he knows how to understand of a social and political order building itself to accommodate those drives. In these poems we see how the pastoral and the georgic in the eighteenth century record an effort of political understanding, fitfully enthusiastic about and frightened by its perceptions into the social order that could organize itself newly and forthrightly in the service of desire, and in that service define its own ends, its own means. It is not a mystification of capitalism that we see in this literature, but a prescient approach towards and bewildered withdrawal from the larger phenomenon of which capitalism is a part—the secularization of life, the divorce between ethics and politics, and the need for these to be acknowledged, named, envisioned, and interpreted.

The straining points in Dyer's and Cowper's poems form around the characteristic structures of thought and feeling of the pastoral and georgic kinds: these are metaphors of virtuous work, of country and city, of nature and art, and my analysis of the poems is deeply indebted to a growing body of criticism which has illuminated the play of these imaginative structures within pastoral expression. Frank Kermode has maintained that the pastoral is found wherever a writer is seeing experience through the perspective created by the paired terms, nature and art.[14] William Empson, in the seminal *Some Versions of Pastoral*, goes so far as to assert that the presence of the pastoral is always implied when a writer's concern embraces the relations between the social classes, and that the genre's characteristic amalgam of lowliness and elegance in the figure of the articulate shepherd figures forth an inherently celebrative idea: by seeing the two social classes combined we are made to think better of each as we respond to a metaphor which asserts the union of the "effective elements of society."[15] Taken together, Empson and Kermode suggest that apart from its formal appearance in eclogues, the pastoral is identifiable by its engagement of man's experiences within the social order—as a citizen, a soldier, a merchant, farmer, and poet.

Following Kermode, Edward W. Tayler has shown how the paired terms nature and art gave shape to the pastoral mode as employed by Spenser, Shakespeare, and Marvell (*Nature and Art in Renaissance Literature*, 1964). Tayler demonstrates how crucial the pastoral was to Renaissance poets as they engaged the urgent concerns of their culture, attempting an interpretation of human life in terms of its possibilities in the several spheres of experience—grace, nature, and civilization—within which man understood his life to be defined. Tayler's study suggested to me that the uses of the paired terms nature and art in the poetry of the eighteenth century would illuminate the uses of the pastoral in that period and the direction in which it was developing. Accor-

14. Frank Kermode, ed., introduction, *The Tempest*, William Shakespeare, 6th ed., The Arden Shakespeare (Cambridge: Harvard University Press, 1958), pp. xxxiv-xxxviii.

15. William Empson, *Some Versions of Pastoral* (Norfolk, Conn.: New Directions Paperbook, 1960), pp. 11–12.

dingly, much of my argument focuses upon those terms, especially in the chapters on Cowper. Harold Toliver has similarly explored the "Augustan balance of nature and art" in his chapter on the eighteenth-century pastoral. Recognizing that the achievement of the pastoral in that period is problematical, he has pointed to the contradictions in its effort to join "an urge to transcendence" in its appeal to nature, with an entanglement in economic and social problems in its celebration of "art," an effort never successfully resolved and finally inherited by the romantic poets. Toliver does not develop his argument with reference to the peculiar stresses created by the pastoral's entanglement with the intensities of capitalist energies; consequently, pastoral writing for him, as it develops away from the eighteenth century and into our own, "more and more links social affairs . . . to epistemological problems and levels of the mind. . . . As one of our more habitual fictions, the pastoral is a vital instrument in taking the measure of reality and proposing new ways of seeing it. Rejected as in any way a mode concerned with literal truths, it may become one of several strategies for placing constructions on reality."[16] These thoughts may be usefully contrasted with Williams's, where the pastoral of Wordsworth and Clare is also seen as a new vehicle for inwardness, but is determined as such precisely by its concern for literal truth, its insistence upon the harsh actualities of the economic and social environment.

The pastoral's continuing presence into the nineteenth century as a vehicle for the interpretation of public experience is the subject of Leo Marx's *The Machine in the Garden: Technology and the Pastoral Ideal* (1964), a study of the sudden impact upon the American mind of man's new "curious engines of speed." Marx has looked closely at the American literature of the past century and a half and his achievement is to show how deeply involved are the habits and conventions of pastoral literature in its representation of social and political experience. Marx distinguishes between the sentimental quality of "spurious" pastoral—what Tayler calls

16. Harold Toliver, *Pastoral Forms and Attitudes* (Berkeley, Los Angeles and London: University of California Press, 1971), pp. 208–9.

"the cotton candy kind"—and the more complex character of
literature that makes use of the pastoral ideal as a "powerful
metaphor of contradiction," resisting the easy formulation of
nature into a primitive or paradisic ideal, but instead welding the
claims of art and of nature into an ironic, sometimes tragic, statement of the human condition. Marx demonstrates the fertility of
what has been developing in criticism as an understanding of pastoral's natural, as opposed to conventional, generic characteristics.

In the variety of their procedure, then, these important studies
support my assumption that purpose and point of view are to be
considered along with conventional formal criteria in speaking of
the pastoral and the georgic as literary kinds.[17] Throughout I have
settled, loosely, for the term "bucolic" to designate works which
express a judgment of the moral quality of civil society by explicit
or implicit reference to rural experience. "Bucolic" is a good word
because it insists upon the literary traditions behind contemporary
interpretations of rural experience and because it allows simultaneous reference to pastoral and georgic writing. I have not been
concerned about the conventional formal distinctions between the
pastoral and georgic, and justification for my loose usage of traditional terms may be based most pertinently on the practice of the
poets I study. Both Dyer and Cowper blend georgic and pastoral
forms to fit their own purposes, creating an amalgam of elements
which, in Virgil's own work, are kept scrupulously distinct. Bruno
Snell has argued (*The Discovery of the Mind*, 1953) that Virgil's
eclogues define a very special imaginative locale, a "spiritual
landscape" where poetry provides the link between man and nature. In the *Georgics*, however, it is labor though which man
experiences nature; in writing about human work, Virgil in the
Georgics created a landscape—very different from that of the
Eclogues—which could be used to express and interpret political as

17. "If there are traditions of pastoral and romance that persist in modern
literature, how must we extend our definitions of these genres to accommodate
them (or can they be called genres in the accepted meaning of the word)? Genre, as
generally defined, admits criteria of form, style, or subject matter. In the light of
contemporary practice we must add purpose or point of view" (Ellen Terry
Lincoln, ed., *Pastoral and Romance: Modern Essays in Criticism* [Englewood
Cliffs, N. J.: Prentice-Hall, 1969], p. 1).

well as poetical experience. Though Brooks Otis has maintained, as have others, that even the *Eclogues* are very much concerned with public issues (*Virgil: A Study of Civilized Poetry*, 1964), it seems clear that for Virgil pastoral and georgic were two very different ways of expressing man's experience of nature, although each may very well have reached out, in its own fashion, to man's experience in state and society. But to the poets I study, and to most others in the century, the careful and precise formal distinctions between the two kinds are of no major concern in practice, though they were all alert to the careful distinction Virgil observed between them. The georgic with its emphasis on work, and the pastoral, taking pleasure and tranquillity for its ambience, do not in our period split apart each into its own generic reserve, the first for the treatment of public, the second of private, experience. Instead we find each coloring the other, quite freely combined within single poems as if to announce an ideal of optimal civilization, a blend of *otium* and *ponos* itself figuring forth an ideal pattern of life in a good social order.[18] This insistence upon the imaginative, practical compatibility of literary forms whose distinctiveness was theoretically felt tells us much about the character of eighteenth-century social thought and the art which contributed to it. This is the subject of my first chapter.

---

18. *Otium* and *ponos* are Thomas G. Rosenmeyer's terms, according to which he distinguishes sharply between the characteristic subjects and coloring of pastoral and georgic (*The Green Cabinet* [Berkeley and Los Angeles: University of California Press, 1969], pp. 22–26 and chap. 4, passim). Rosenmeyer's absorbing study of Theocritus seeks to establish strict generic bounds for the pastoral in line with his reading of Theocritus's *Idylls*, the art of which he sees as devoted entirely to the representation of the sufficiency and the value of *otium*. Rosenmeyer has seen, however, that his argument implies the need for a special definition for eighteenth-century pastoral, which so regularly reaches out toward large public concerns. He therefore distinguishes between Epicurean *otium* and Horatian retirement, which "is regularly found as an object of praise and nostalgia in Augustan poetry. The temper of the Augustan restoration would have frowned on any interpretation of *otium* that completely disregarded the welfare of the commonwealth and the citizens. Hence the stalwart, *and quite unpastoral* [italics added], quality of otium advocated by Horace. . . . [T]his kind of otium is an extension of the [world of civic duty] beyond it, a busman's holiday" (p. 71). For Rosenmeyer, then, eighteenth-century pastoral writing in its most characteristic manner is "quite unpastoral." See below, chap. 3, nn. 5 and 6.

I

The Good Society and the Bucolic Mode: Virgil and Pope

Virgil's *Georgics* is a poem whose social intention is celebrative and whose style is heroic. The poem was Virgil's preparation for the *Aeneid*; it was in the *Georgics* that he learned the diction and developed the narrative art that he was to use in his epic.[1] The celebrative intention and the heroic manner of the poem are evident everywhere in it; we may take two passages, one near the beginning of Book I, the other concluding the entire work, as examples:

> You also we would hail, oh godlike man,
> Octavian Caesar: you will be a god,
> But in what form the gods do not reveal;
> You may become a deity of land
> Protecting towns and fields, a great provider,
> Lord of the seasons, crowned with Venus' myrtle

1. Dryden points out that "Virgil in his fourth Georgic, of the Bees, perpetually raises the lowness of his subject, by the loftiness of his words, and ennobles it by comparisons drawn from empires, and from monarchs" (*A Discourse Concerning Satire* in *Essays of John Dryden*, ed. W. P. Ker, 2 vols. [Oxford: Clarendon Press, 1900], 2: 107). Brooks Otis has argued that in the *Georgics* Virgil developed the narrative art which he was to handle consummately in the *Aeneid*: "Though not a narrative—that is, not a story—[the *Georgics*] is . . . a continuous whole concerned with the most central and serious themes of Augustan Rome. . . . [A]fter writing it, Virgil perhaps was able to see his way clear to a form of epic which could embody his patriotic purpose . . ." (*Virgil: A Study in Civilized Poetry* [Oxford: Clarendon Press, 1964], p. 145).

Whom the mighty sphere of earth receives;
You may come as a god of boundless ocean
Whom distant shores and sailors worship solely
And Mother Ocean seeks for her own daughter;
You may find place among the constellations,
Linked to summer's chain of lazy months
There, between the Scorpion and Virgo—
The scorpion contracts to leave you room—
Whatever form you take, O Caesar, never
Will the underworld have hope of you as king,
For no crude desire for domination
Possesses you, although the Greeks adore
Elysian fields, and Proserpine recalled
Has no desire to stay beside her mother:
Whatever form, O Caesar, you assume,
Smooth my path, condone this enterprise
Of bold experiment in verse, and share
Concern with me for uninstructed farmers:
Grow used to prayers appealing to your name.
. . . .
    All this I've sung of cultivating fields,
Of tending flocks and caring for the trees,
While by the deep Euphrates noble Caesar
Thunders triumph, grants the reign of law
To grateful subjects, clears his path to heaven.
All this time sweet Naples nourished me,
Her Virgil, in the flower of humble peace,
In study: I who played at shepherds' songs
In callow youth, and sang, O Tityrus,
Of you at ease beneath your spreading beech.

                              [1:4–5; 4:111]²

Framing the work, these two passages speak clearly of Virgil's effort to place his imperial theme within the order of nature. We hear of a young emperor and a young empire. The first passage

2. *Virgil's "Georgics": A Modern English Verse Translation*, Smith Palmer Bovie, trans. (Chicago: University of Chicago Press, paper ed., 1956). I have used this text throughout. References are cited by book and page (*not line*) numbers in my text since the line numbers in the text of the translation refer to the Latin original. It seemed appropriate to me to use a modern instead of a period translation because I want my observations about the character of the *Georgics* to be tested and felt independently of a period version.

brilliantly unfolds the cosmic scheme, expressing a sense of enormous promise and possibility while at the same time defining the boundaries within which man's natural life is restrained—the elements of earth (a deity of land), water (Mother Ocean), the heavens (the constellations), and underworld (the Elysian fields). In the passage which concludes the entire poem the promise of Octavius's immortality is again heard; the poet refers to Octavius's triumphs at the Euphrates and in a quiet voice, names himself and honors Naples: Caesar by the Euphrates and Virgil back at Naples express the imperial theme, a poet and an emperor defining Rome's political boundaries. The allusion in the very last lines to Virgil's youthful efforts in the pastoral mode delicately suggests that the growth of the poet proceeds inevitably along with the growth of Rome, which supplies the matter for his new style to grow on. Through his art the poet becomes an integral feature of his polity. The two passages come together to define the nature of optimal civilization, a vision of restrained growth, proceeding in accord with nature, harmonizing its best energies to nature's limits. Rome may grow because the emperor knows no "crude desire for domination" and is "linked"—as the constellation is to the lazy summer months—to nature's contingencies. Consequently his triumphs are quite appropriately accompanied by the singing of a maturing poet.

The poet who takes upon himself the task of writing a public poem with a celebrative purpose will inevitably have to discover the fictions which enable him to commit himself to his subject without violating his integrity. What threatens his integrity is history—the deeds of war, of aggression, the questionable motives and terrible effects of the men who become the heroes of his poetry. Virgil's poem is created from an image of Rome as the center of civilization; it is this vision that generates the fictions which structure the poem. The *Georgics* is about work, and in a bold politicization of Hesiod's subject, its central imaginative idea is the virtuous Roman farmer who comes to represent the health at the heart of Roman life, the source and justification for its imperial energies. It is not surprising that English poets who sought to celebrate the

achievements of a nation most busily at work—to come to terms
with this fact of their history—would discover in Virgil a literary
and a moral model. If England's growing wealth and power could
also be understood to be rooted in virtuous work, then the grounds
for celebration might be clear enough.

Pastoral poetry tends to deal with the subject of human labor in
a mythical way. In the simplest of its forms, the pastoral will
invoke the idea of the golden age as a kind of implied lament for
man's fallen condition, the hallmark of which is his need to work.
What is sometimes known as the "libertine pastoral" is likely to
make much of this idea. More complex forms of pastoral art are
likely to develop the idea in profounder ways, attempting to bring
together the condition of innocence with the condition of labor, so
that a kind of paradoxical resolution may be created in which man
at work is in the condition of innocence, performing innocent
work, in which his original nature is fulfilled, not thwarted.
Adam's work in Milton's Eden is this kind of paradox: Eden is
perfect, Nature in its prime; yet it needs pruning, needs it because
man was placed there, and it is his nature to work.

> Man hath his daily work of body or mind
> Appointed, which declares his dignity,
> And the regard of Heaven on all his ways;
> While other animals unactive range,
> And of their doings God takes no account.
> To-morrow ere fresh morning streak the east
> With first approach of light, we must be risen,
> And at our pleasant labor, to reform
> Yon flowery arbors, yonder alleys green,
> Our walks at noon, with branches overgrown,
> That mock our scant manuring, and require
> More hands than ours to lop their wanton growth.
> Those blossoms also, and those dropping gums
> That lie bestrown unsightly and unsmooth,
> Ask riddance, if we mean to tread with ease. . . .
>   [*Paradise Lost*, 4:618–32][3]

For all of its perfection, Eden can be "unsightly and unsmooth";

3. John Milton, *Complete Poems and Major Prose*, ed. Merrit Y. Hughes (New
York: Odyssey Press, 1957). The passage is cited by book and line numbers.

man has, in some sense, become the measure of nature, and nature, though perfect, needs work because man needs a path. These are paradoxical thoughts; they must be, because toil in innocence is a paradoxical situation. The virtuous work of Adam becomes a kind of prototype of what work might really be: Adam's care for Eden is a kind of prayer. Like the gratitude he owes God, it is a benefit to himself and flows from his own unfallen nature.

The georgic poem, on the other hand, tends to deal with the theme of virtuous labor, not in terms provided by the magical condition of innocence, but rather from the standpoint of the iron age. Early along, Virgil clearly states his subject as the work of men's hands subsequent to the golden age:

> The Father willed it so: He made the path
> Of agriculture rough, established arts
> Of husbandry to sharpen human wits,
> Forbidding sloth to settle on his soil.
> Before Jove, farms and farmers were unknown;
> To mark off or divide the land was wrong,
> For things were held in common, and the earth
> Brought forth her substance then, more generously,
> When none imposed demands upon the ground.
> Jove endowed the serpents with their venom,
> Commanded wolves to prowl and seas to rise,
> Shook honey from the leaves, hid fire away,
> Stopped up the streams of wine, so that mankind
> By taking thought might learn to forge its arts
> From practice: seek to bring the grain from furrows,
> Strike out the fire locked up in veins of flint.
> Then rivers first bore hollow boats, and sailors
> Numbered the stars and named them: Pleiades,
> The Hyades, the radiant Northern Bear.
> Men discovered how to trap and hunt,
> How to circle forests with their hounds;
> Some plunged their casting nets deep in broad rivers,
> While others trailed their dripping lines at sea.
> Harsh iron emerged, and saws with whistling blades,
> (For earlier, men split their logs with wedges);
> Then followed all the civilizing art:
> Hard labor conquered all, and pinching need.

[1:9–10]

Here the history of human labor is the history of civilization, of human growth; labor is not the companion of innocence. Virgil emphasizes the harshness of Jove's edict that man shall work, yet recognizes the human blessing that edict entailed. It is labor that banishes sloth and sharpens human wits. We may ask then about how this labor is controlled. How does it remain virtuous and under what conditions do sharpened human wits continue in their devotion to civilizing toil rather than aggressive greed? Virgil, to be sure, was well aware of the aggressive greed and violence civilization could breed. The deeply moving plea for peace concluding the first book testifies to that.

The answer is to be sought in the vision of optimal civilization which pervades the *Georgics* and invigorates the conventional ideas and attitudes Virgil could apply to his material in order to define it as a literary subject. Among these attitudes there is, first, the disdain for luxury—a great theme of the famous *O fortunatos nimium* passage.

> Oh that farmers understood their blessings!
> Their boundless joys! A land far off from war
> Pours forth her fruit abundantly for them.
> Although no stately home with handsome portals
> Disgorges on its step a wave of callers
> Every morning, gaping at his doors
> Inlaid with tortoise shell, astonished by
> His gold-trimmed clothes and his Corinthian bronzes . . .
>   [2:50]

There is, furthermore, the simple veneration of the countryside—veneration whose first object is the literal countryside, with its rural beauties plain to the senses; the veneration which begins as a simple expression of the love for nature, then grows more fervent as its object grows in complexity to become a poetic idea.

> His rest is sound, his life devoid of guile.
> His gains are manifold, his holdings broad:
> Caves and living lakes, refreshing vales,
> The cattle lowing, slumber in the shade.
> Familiar with the haunts of animals,
> The farmer lives in peace, his children all

> Learn how to work, respect frugality,
> Venerate their fathers and the gods:
> Surely, Justice, as she left the earth,
> In parting left her final traces here. . . .
> Still, let me relish the country, humbly revere
> Streams that glide through glades, the woods, the rivers.
>
> [2:50–51]

Finally, the theme of virtuous work is expressed in the sense of healthy, immediate experience of nature which is the farmer's happy lot: he is close to nature, must be alert to its changes, quick to take his signs from nature, to judge the day, the season, the weather for his proper work. Again and again in the *Georgics* this quality of the rural life is stressed.

> If you observe the fiery sun, and moon
> In systematic phase, tomorrow's hour
> Will never fool you, nor will tranquil night
> Enmesh you in her snares. For if, when the moon
> First gathers her returning fire, she grasps
> Between both horns a field of misty dark,
> For land and sea a heavy rain is in store. . . .
> . . . .
> In short, the sun will give you all the signs:
> What promises the tardy dusk conveys,
> From what direction wind drives tranquil clouds,
> And what the dripping South Wind has in mind.
> . . . .
> Incredibly, when olive trunks are split
> A root will push its way from the dried out stem. . . .
>
> [1:22, 24; 2:30]

The Virgilian farmer is a man whose senses are alive, who inhabits a sacred countryside, who despises luxury. Above all, his work is a perfect expression of human energy, of art in its harmony with nature. He is a man whose labor, therefore, is virtuous. A literary figure, he is created by the confluence of several literary ideas, which, we are made to feel, express an integrated vision of reality— the georgic vision of work as a civilizing force, divinely ordained to create good order out of chaos.

Virgil's great subject is the virtue and the destiny of heroic

Rome. The trick (as Empson would say) of the *Georgics* is to mirror that great subject in the virtuous rural life of the empire, the tough husbandman, whose virtuous work makes him a metaphor of the "effective elements" of his society. Virgil's praise, therefore, of rugged toil is quite naturally followed by his description in military terms of the farmer's tools: "Now I must describe the armaments/Tough country-dwellers use, without which crops/ Could not be sown nor raised; the ploughshare, first,/And the curved plough's heavy stock. Demeter's slow-wheeled/Carts, remorseless heavy hoes, the harrows,/Threshing tables; also, wicker ware/Of the common sort that Celeus used, and hurdles/Of arbutus wood, and Iacchus' ritual fans./All these things you provide for in advance/If you would earn the country's sacred praise" (1: 10–11). The theme of virtuous work, developed along with the theme of moderation and the veneration of the countryside, is thus made to function as an expression of the larger imperial theme, of the virtue of Rome. It is inextricably part of the larger vision of the just power of a virtuous state, which is itself an emblem of civilization. The sacred and the political are thus fused in the fields of the Roman farmer.

> Italian soil has bred a race of heroes,
> Marsians, Sabines, toughened generations
> From the Western Coast, and tribes of Volscians
> Handy with the spear. Great family names,
> Camillus, Decius, Marius, Scipio,
> And, chief of all, Octavianus Caesar,
> Who triumphs now on Asia's farthest shore,
> And defends the hills of Rome from the timid foe,
> All hail, Saturnian Land, our honored Mother!
> For thee I broach these themes of ancient art
> And dare disclose the sacred springs of verse,
> Singing Hesiod's song through Roman towns.
>   Now for the innate qualities of soils . . .
>
> [2: 36–37]

Virgil's politicization of Hesiod's song yields a set of attitudes we can recognize and describe as "classical," amounting almost to an ideology of overwhelming attractiveness; it could offer, as we will see, numerous opportunities for role-playing on the part of agrarian entrepreneurs who, almost two thousand years later, had occasion to see themselves in a Virgilian light, even as they were subverting, as capitalist agronomists, a rural order made up of the labor of tough, though inefficient, husbandry.[4] That art can be joined with nature in the enterprises of a temperate entrepreneur, that these enterprises can be understood as offering a fine blend of the pleasures of rural retirement with the energies of the active life, and that the affairs of this kind of farmer are integral to the larger processes of economic and political life flowing about him—all this can be seen not only in the purely literary writing of the eighteenth century, but also in the nascent social science and in the journalism of the day. The *Georgics* had become more than a model for a certain kind of patriotic poem; it was a most important source of certain habits of thought and feeling which found expression in the works of men whom we are more likely to conceive of as projectors than as poets.[5] A passage from the *Wealth of Nations* is a case in point; its context is Smith's account of the growth of opulence.

> Upon equal, or nearly equal profits, most men will choose to employ their capitals rather in the improvement and cultivation of land than either in manufactures or in foreign trade. The man who employs his capital in land has it more under his view and command, and his fortune is much less liable to accidents than that of the trader, who is obliged frequently to commit it, not only to the winds and the waves, but to the more uncertain elements of human folly and injustice, by giving great credits in distant countries to men with whose character and situation he can seldom be thoroughly acquainted. The capital of the landlord, on the contrary, which is fixed in the improvement of his land, seems to be as well secured as the nature of human affairs can admit of. The beauty of

4. See below, chap. 2.
5. See Raymond Williams, *The Country and the City* (London: Chatto and Windus, 1973), chaps. 6 and 7, and below, chap. 2, n. 12. A. J. Sambrook's "The English Lord and the Happy Husbandman" (*Studies in Voltaire and the Eighteenth Century* 57 [1967]: 1357–75) surveys the literature embodying this idealization of agricultural improvement as well as some early critical responses to it in the nascent radicalism of the next century.

the country besides, the pleasures of a country life, the tranquility of
mind which it promises, and wherever the injustice of human laws
does not disturb it, the independency which it really affords, have
charms that more or less attract everybody; and as to cultivate the
ground was the original destination of man, so in every stage of his
existence he seems to retain a predilection for this primitive employment.[6]

Smith is arguing on behalf of manufacturing and seeking to show
that it poses no necessary threat to the interests of agriculture,
indeed, that there is a complex and happy relationship between the
two. Easily detectable, however, is something more than the theoretical or even polemical concerns of the political economist. One
senses the pressure of the agricultural ideology as something that
the writer must work against in his argument for manufactures and
commerce; but perfectly evident at the same time is the writer's own
familiarity with and respect for the habits of that ideology. We can
see how natural it was for Smith's thinking to shape itself to the
patterns of some familiar attitudes. Like Virgil, Smith is also
writing about the hard work that sustains civil society. And what
begins as a straightforward account of how men calculate the
investment of their capital opens out into a little essay on the
pleasures of country life, a little essay in which we can see the
reflection of much eighteenth-century literature; something that we
might not be surprised to discover in the poetry of, say, Cowper or
Thomson, is all the more striking for its appearance in what is,
after all, a serious tract on political economy and an argument in
behalf of urban industry and commerce. Smith's larger purpose in
that section of his book in which the passage above appears is to
show that the growth of manufactures can result only in the
improvement of agriculture. But that he should slip into the
language of idyllic retreat; that he should point to the charms of
the country life, the beauty of the landscape, the tranquillity it
engenders in the mind; that he should hint at the opposition

6. Adam Smith, *An Inquiry into the Nature and Causes of the Wealth of
Nations*, ed. Edwin Cannan, 6th ed., 2 vols. (London: Methuen and Co., 1950), 1:
357. Cited throughout as Smith; citations are to volume and page numbers.

between nature and art (it is the threat of injustice in *human* laws which may disturb the tranquillity which nature, undisturbed, promises); and that he should conclude the passage with an evocation of a "soft" primitivism; all of this indicates how very intimate a connection there was between a man's literary experience and his more mundane concerns, and how very useful that literary experience could be to him as he looked out on a rapidly changing economic and social situation hoping to understand it.

It hardly needs saying that Smith entertained no sentimental notions about man's just vocation. That the farmer alone is no hero for him is clear from the sentence immediately following the passage cited above: "Without the assistance of some artificers, indeed, the cultivation of the land cannot be carried on but with great inconveniency and continual interruption."[7] And not very many pages later, Smith clearly explains that whatever the quality of country life may come to be, it is certainly "an art to be made good":

> Thirdly and lastly, commerce and manufactures gradually introduced order and good government, and with them, the liberty and security of individuals, among the inhabitants of the country, who had before lived almost in a continual state of war with their neighbors and of servile dependency upon their superiors.[8]

In contrast to the tranquillity and independence for which, quite conventionally, Smith praises the idealized rural life in the earlier passage, it is the violence and servility endemic in the actual countryside which he focuses on here. What is striking is the easy appearance in an unsentimental tract on political economy of certain patterns of thinking quite apparent in Virgil's great poem about Roman civilization: nature and art, country and town, tranquillity and anxiety, independence and servitude, virtuous work. It is not difficult to see that like any other eighteenth-century gentleman, Smith had at his disposal, and perhaps at his command, certain habits of feeling and thought that belong in large part to an

7. Smith, 1: 357.
8. Smith, 1: 384.

enduring tradition in Western literature. What seems clear is that some version of pastoral or georgic was invoked regularly as a perspective on the nation's vigor, and then as a means of defining, with reference to that energy, an appropriate judgment of the character of human social experience in a heady new climate of change felt as progress. Smith, arguing here on behalf of manufacturing, insists that it be recognized as a cause of improvement, a positive achievement of civilization, even as he recognizes the valid resources the gentler countryside possesses for judging that active and risky enterprise. We can sense in Smith's simultaneous appeal to an idealized and actual countryside the kind of moral effort this was: to mark and value properly how much was achieved without losing sight of its radical departure from traditional formulations of private and social virtue.

This was an effort involving peculiar difficulties, difficulties arising precisely from the radical nature of the alternatives men were forced to consider. And it had serious, ultimately decisive implications for the very habits of thought and feeling men relied on to guide them through the dilemmas presented by such well-understood evils as luxury, the growth of cities, the military commitments of empire—evils well understood indeed, were it not for the puzzling and uncomfortable reality of a nation thriving under real improvement. Satire, we know, was one response to this puzzle, and though satire discovered its norms in Virgil's georgic vision, its own invective energy tended to disrupt the resolved tensions of Virgil's representation of civilization as the harmonious, potentially good expression of human energy, of art in accord with nature; in satire those tensions harden as their elements reassert themselves into compelling opposites rather than harmonized energies. If Dyer's *The Fleece* attempts heroic song to celebrate England's new life, Cowper, writing later in the century and trying to avoid satirical expression, still develops a darker response to England's exuberant activity. Adopting the topics and the perspective of the rural moralist, *The Task* develops a response to English public life which leads that familiar figure out to the periphery of his world; nature and art, country and town, retirement and activity come to present themselves to him as absolute choices rather than grounds for mediation. Cowper's failure to fuse these alternatives marks the failure of a vision which could sustain and generate the heroic fictions the writer of celebrative poetry had sought to establish as honest responses to history in the manner of Virgil.[9]

✨

One of the supreme moments in Pope's poetry is the vision that concludes the *Epistle to Burlington*. That poem itself is a concentrated expression of the issues I have been discussing, and one of the finest examples of what the bucolic tradition could mean at this late stage in its history. The poet's concluding vision of a magnificent kingdom describes the building of a civilization which, like the Rome of Virgil's *Georgics*, has its roots in the virtuous life of the land, most particularly, the good estate of the man of sense. The conclusion of the poem is a vision of work—of harbors and highways a-building, of dams and canals. It is georgic blending into epic; we can hear behind it Aeneas's sudden expression of civic enthusiasm evoked in him by the spectacle of the building of Carthage—*"O fortunati, quorum iam moenia surgunt!"*

> You too proceed! make falling Arts your care,
> Erect new wonders, and the old repair,
> Jones and Palladio to themselves restore,
> And be whate'er Vitruvius was before:
> Till Kings call forth th' Idea's of your mind,

9. M. S. Røstvig's *The Happy Man: Studies in the Metamorphosis of a Classical Ideal*, 2 vols. (Oslo: Akademisk Forlag, 1958), vol. 2 is the standard survey of Virgil's influence on the nature poetry of the eighteenth century through 1760, particularly of the shape given to it by the *beatus ille* and *O fortunatos nimium* themes of *Georgics* 2. Røstvig addresses the apparent contradictions in a poetry that simultaneously values an ideal of retirement and an active social commitment; she concludes that the active commitment is undertaken by the nature poet as an intellectual task of a physico-theological character. This task Røstvig sees as a self-imposed "unending marathon among the stars" (2: 408). It seems to me that this view misses the very direct connection pastoral and georgic nature poetry maintains with the more mundane elements of the sublunary active life in agricultural industry and commerce.

> Proud to accomplish what such hands design'd,
> Bid Harbors open, public Ways extend,
> Bid Temples, worthier of the God, ascend;
> Bid the broad Arch the dang'rous Flood contain,
> The Mole projected break the roaring Main;
> Back to his bounds their subject Sea command,
> And roll obedient Rivers thro' the Land;
> These Honours, Peace to happy Britain brings,
> These are Imperial Works, and worthy Kings.
>
> [191–204][10]

The passage is rendered as a prophecy and an exhortation, and has been carefully prepared for throughout the poem's development, which has been establishing all along the justification for this vision of a good polity. I say justification because, like Virgil, Pope needs to answer an implicit question: under what conditions are the works of empire and of power and politics good works and not the result of aggressive greed, luxury, and corruption? To state this more immediately in the poem's own terms, how does this vision of a nature dominated and shaped, commanded and controlled by man—

> Bid the broad Arch the dang'rous Flood contain,
> The Mole projected break the roaring Main;
> Back to his bounds their subject Sea command,
> And roll obedient Rivers thro' the land . . .

how does this vision emerge without clashing with the poem's earlier evocation of a nature itself conceived as the energy and principle guiding human works and demanding proper submission?

> Consult the Genius of the Place in all;
> That tells the Waters to rise, or fall. . . .

It is the achievement of this poem to create the conditions for an

10. All citations from the *Epistle to Burlington* and the *Epistle to Bathurst* are to Alexander Pope, *Epistles to Several Persons (Moral Essays)*, ed. F. W. Bateson, 2nd ed., Twickenham Edition of the Poems of Alexander Pope, 10 vols. (London: Methuen; New Haven: Yale University Press, 1939–67), vol. 3, part 2. All subsequent citations are identified in my text by line numbers.

imaginative apprehension of the essential identity between nature commanded and nature commanding. The expression of that identity is the justification of the vision of the good polity.

We come to apprehend the identity between nature commanded and nature commanding in the poem's fusion of pastoral with georgic feelings. We can be confident of the ethical quality of the civilization Pope envisions because its materials have come from the empire's moral heartland, the good estate of such figures as Bathurst and Boyle:

> His Father's Acres who enjoys in peace,
> Or makes his Neighbours glad, if he encrease;
> Whose chearful Tenants bless their yearly toil,
> Yet to their Lord owe more than to the soil;
> Whose ample Lawns are not asham'd to feed
> The milky heifer and deserving steed;
> Whose rising Forests, not for pride or show,
> But future Buildings, future Navies grow:
> Let his plantations stretch from down to down,
> First shade a Country, and then raise a Town.
>
> [181–90]

This good estate is one "sanctified by use," which implies human purpose and work. But there is a magical quality to the picture which mutes that implication and instead seems to evoke a sense of rest and plenitude. The ample lawns *feed* the livestock; rising forests *grow into* buildings and ships; plantations, as if responding to impulses of their own "stretch from down to down,/First shade a Country, and then raise a Town." The coordination of the verbs "shade" and "raise" expresses the simultaneous presence of pastoral and georgic feeling. We do not see the human toil that ekes its benefits from a grudging nature, as we might expect in a georgic, but instead we see nature giving of itself, as if it were informed by the energies of art.[11] Indeed, the essential compatibility of nature and art is clearly expressed in the "progress" of the good man's

---

11. Maynard Mack, *The Garden and the City: Retirement and Politics in the Later Poetry of Pope 1731–1743* (Toronto: University of Toronto Press, 1969), p. 97.

plantations: they "stretch" to confer their benefits, as if in one continuous impulse, upon both the country which they shade, and then the town, which they raise. This is a complex poetic achievement—its expressive habit belongs to pastoral, whose presence is unmistakable, yet the occasion is one more immediately recognizable as belonging to georgic and epic, into which, indeed, these lines merge as they yield the vision of the closing passage. The final movement of the poem is one of the finest examples of the blending of both pastoral and georgic habits of feeling to communicate the sense of pleasure pervading life in the nation's moral heartland; it is pleasure offered by nature, so that all the magnificence of the imperial city arises still from a countryside seen as a kind of fruitful pleasance:

> Another age shall see the golden Ear
> Imbrown the Slope, and nod on the Parterre,
> Deep Harvests bury all his pride has plann'd,
> And laughing Ceres re-assume the land.
>
> [173–76]

These lines, which dismiss Timon, are the prelude to the vision of the good estate and the good empire it nourishes, and they establish as the sustaining condition for both estate and empire the joyous dominance of a plentiful, not a grudging nature. The pleasing mystery of these lines lies in their simultaneous evocation of feelings belonging to the pastoral and the georgic, feelings that are more usually kept distinct. They describe, after all, the effects of hard labor, but again we are not shown the labor that produces the crops. Instead we are made to relax, to give ourselves up to the joyous but inexorable power of a "laughing Ceres." The goddess of agriculture has been made into a kind of mysteriously powerful dryad, less imposing perhaps than in her full divinity, but more powerful for this, the dominating presence of a field of corn that has been imagined as a pleasance. Her laughter is a pastoral act. This strangely evocative blend of pastoral and georgic feeling is part of the poem's larger imaginative effort to discover the ethical foundation of empire in a world of nature which man relaxes with and which also supplies the energy for his city to grow on. (These wonderful lines mark the point at which the poem itself relaxes, suddenly releasing the nervous intensity created by the visit to Timon. We can, and I think are meant to, sense the shift back into conversation from invective, a shift managed in a laugh directed not only at Timon, but back also bemusedly at the speaker himself, as if he had caught himself having become needlessly agitated about Timon's gross trivialities, having almost forgotten his pastoral obligations to himself. Note how the vowels open out and ask for easy breathing with their pronunciation. And yet, for all this ease, the passage is, in fact, a prophecy.)

Enjoyment and relaxation are central motifs in this poem. From the first lines

> 'Tis strange, the Miser should his Cares employ,
> To gain those Riches he can ne'er enjoy. . . .

on through the devastating portrait of Timon, agonized and agonizing in his incredibly uncomfortable villa, and concluding with the good man who enjoys his father's acres, gladdens his neighbors, and makes his tenants cheerful, the poem has sought to establish the character of life on the good estate as something very much like the tranquil hedonism of pastoral song.[12] No wonder then that it is a "laughing Ceres" who reassumes the land, marking with her laughter the pleasure to be had in nature and the essentially harmless foolishness of Timon's naive and uncomfortable ostentation. Her laughter is at once a social gesture and an impulse of the bower.

The poem's emphasis on enjoyment is felt throughout in evocations of pastoral *otium:*

> Thro' his young Woods how pleas'd Sabinus stray'd,
> Or sat delighted in the thick'ning shade

---

12. Thomas R. Edwards, Jr. in *This Dark Estate: A Reading of Pope* ([Berkeley and Los Angeles: University of California Press, 1963], pp. 62, 66) has pointed out how the madness of the misers and materialists of *To Bathurst* and *To Burlington* is a kind of asceticism, a "mad spirituality." His fine reading of *To Burlington* emphasizes the presence of pastoral feeling pervading Pope's vision of the ideal public order: "The pastoral 'magic' that controls nature becomes literal fact through the sensible creativity of the Augustan genius" (p. 71).

With annual joy the red'ning shoots to greet,
Or see the stretching branches long to meet!
His Son's fine Taste an op'ner Vista loves,
Foe to the Dryads of his Father's groves,
One boundless Green, or flourish'd Carpet views,
With all the mournful family of Yews;
The thriving plants ignoble broomsticks made,
Now sweep those Alleys they were born to shade.

[89–98]

The figure of Sabinus is as close as Pope comes in this poem to the representation of a recognizable pastoral character, but Sabinus, we must not forget, is a landowner, not a shepherd. Still, despite his unpastoral status, Sabinus's experience—he strays, he sits delighted, he greets with joy, he sees his "stretching branches long to meet"—is the tranquil enjoyment of a bower and the ambling relaxation of the shepherd. His son's failure to share in this ease not surprisingly results in the destruction of the pleasance. He is "Foe to the Dryads of his Father's groves" and is thus an agent of social instability, in pointed contrast to figures like Bathurst and Boyle, whose ability to delight in their land is linked to their sense of their patrimony. Unlike the destructive efforts of Sabinus's son, what Boyle builds can be trusted, precisely because he is open to delight, and, relaxing with Nature, able to fall in with its spontaneity:

To build, to plant, whatever you intend,
To rear the Column, or the Arch to bend,
To swell the Terras, or to sink the Grot;
In all, let Nature never be forgot.
But treat the Goddess like a modest fair,
Nor over-dress, nor leave her wholly bare;
Let not each beauty ev'ry where be spy'd,
Where half the skill is decently to hide.
He gains all points, who pleasingly confounds,
Surprizes, varies, and conceals the Bounds.
    Consult the Genius of the Place in all;
That tells the Waters or to rise, or fall,
Or helps th' ambitious Hill the heav'n to scale,
Or scoops in circling theatres the Vale,

Calls in the Country, catches opening glades,
Joins willing woods, and varies shades from shades.
Now breaks or now directs, th' intending Lines;
Paints as you plant, and, as you work, designs.
  Still follow Sense, of ev'ry Art the Soul,
Parts answ'ring parts shall slide into a whole,
Spontaneous beauties all around advance,
Start ev'n from Difficulty, strike from Chance;
Nature shall join you, Time shall make it grow
A Work to wonder at—perhaps a STOW.

[47–70]

I have quoted this passage at length because it epitomizes the imaginative design of the poem's celebrative intention. The passage begins as a georgic in miniature; we hear this in its didactic address. But the didactic address is not designed to teach; Boyle, the listener, knows all of this, it is his doctrine. We are closer to the lines if we recognize their celebrative quality; Pope is rehearsing Boyle's doctrine as a means of honoring it. And as the passage proceeds we recognize that its georgic manner celebrates a relationship with nature very different from the grudging struggle which Virgil had delineated in the passage I quoted earlier. Here nature cooperates with the efforts of art, and the theme throughout has to do with the spontaneity (a pastoral value) demanded of the man who would cooperate with Nature. His skill as an architect—a very unpastoral occupation—is entirely dependent upon his capacity to enjoy his land, and the lines virtually describe the relaxed ambling of an afternoon's walk through one's property, a walk like Sabinus's. The architect's designs result from such ambles, during which, completely at ease in nature, his own receptive spontaneity makes him alive to her graces and forms.

This merging of pastoral and georgic attitudes helps to express the poem's imperial theme. An empire is good if it has, living in its countryside, men who delight in their estates. What makes a good estate makes a good kingdom, and the tranquil hedonist is the same man as the builder of cities. His pastoral pleasure in his estate is his qualification for commanding nature in the projects adumbrated in the poet's epic command: "You too proceed! make falling

Arts your care. . . ." And that command itself signifies the poet's own commitment to the city which is to be built, imperial engineering understood as virtuous work. The *Epistle to Burlington* shows us under what conditions a poet becomes a celebrant: it is a role he undertakes when his imagination has been able to encompass simultaneously the vision of pastoral and of georgic, a vision that expresses the union of the ethical and the political.

But *To Burlington* is a difficult poem to account for: its celebrative intention distinguishes it sharply from Pope's largely satirical work, which, from 1728 on, absorbed almost all his energy. Upon what resources did he draw to produce that concluding vision? Certainly that vision is implicitly behind all of his satire, but the discovery of a vehicle for its positive expression, indeed the development of the positive statement out of the satiric movement of the Timon passages, identifies the remarkable achievement of the poem.

Maynard Mack and others have recognized in the celebrative vision of *To Burlington* the presence of attitudes that can be traced as far back as Rome, but of which Pope had more immediate experience in his reading of seventeenth-century poetry, especially works like Jonson's *To Penshurst*. The "picture of the country gentleman living on his estate, and so far as possible by it, seeking no city gain or court preferment, radiating through the land practices of provident abundance, occupying a great house 'rear'd with no man's ruin, no man's groan,' caring for his tenants and . . . loved by them . . . this is Pope's picture, too, wherever in the satires he allows the positive ideals underlying his satire to emerge . . . ."[13] I have tried to suggest, however, that *To Burlington* brings the country gentleman into the city, basing its confidence in his public benefactions on the quality of his life on his estate, adding a public dimension to the pastoral experience of retired ease. *To Burlington* enters the domain of history, both by its attack on Timon and its vision of empire, elements not contributing explicitly to the poetic world of *To Penshurst*. But it enters that domain obliquely by means of a vision or a prophecy the quality of which demonstrates,

13. Mack, *Garden and the City*, p. 96.

perhaps, the conservative or defensive nature of Augustan literature of which Ian Watt has written. A good close look, such as Dyer
was to take, at the commercial vigor of the industry on the Thames
would have yielded a realistic picture of the city as it was, the basis
of the actual empire that was to be, but this was a scene in which
Pope could have had little positive interest. What we miss in this
very great poem, finally, is that peculiar merging of an "almost
absolute degree of realism . . . with an almost absolute degree of
myth"[14] which Sir Kenneth Clark defines as the distinctive achievement of Virgil's *Georgics*.

Mack has pointedly described the celebrative movement of *To
Burlington* as belonging "in outlook, though not in phrasing, to
the Renaissance."[15] There is something uneasy in the implications
of this judgment. In it lies the suggestion of strain between meaning and language, between what a poet believes or wants to believe,
and the imaginative resources he draws upon for the poetic embodiment of that belief. Simply put, Mack's perception raises a question about the wholeness of Pope's imaginative response to his
subject. Still, in *To Burlington* this is not a troublesome question,
because the normative attitudes which inform the poem's outlook
serve at once to provide the basis for the satiric attack on Timon
and the concluding vision of optimal civilization. The poem is
self-consistent. Henceforth the direction of Pope's art in its confrontation with the history of his day was, however, to point away
from the celebrative purpose so well expressed in that poem; it was
to point toward the very different visions of the *Epilogue to the
Satires* and finally *The Dunciad*, the norms of the Renaissance
outlook finding their fittest expression in invective and apocalypse.
It is as if Pope came to realize that his art could no longer retain its

14. Kenneth Clark, *Landscape into Art* (London: J. Murray, 1949), p. 54, as
quoted in Mack, *Garden and the City*, pp. 235–36. Mack feels, however, that
Pope's satires of the 1730s taken as a whole do achieve this characteristic georgic
effect. I would argue though that Pope's celebrative intention in *To Burlington*
could not be realized except by dissolving the tension between realism and myth,
substituting instead a movement between two different orders of idealism—the
pastoral and georgic kinds.
15. Mack, *Garden and the City*, p. 97.

wholeness and simultaneously discover a positive fiction in which
the ideals of *To Burlington* could be embodied. The perfection of
To Burlington is understandable, finally, in its substitution of a
vision for a realistic appraisal of the commercial and political facts
which were actually sustaining an imperial power of a very different quality from that celebrated in that splendid poem.[16]

During the eighteenth century those conditions were developing
which were calling in question the attitudes which inform the
outlook of *To Burlington*. What was happening was to be better
understood much later as a radically new statement of the meaning
and purpose of man's social experience. The debate (occupying the
energies of many writers and moralists over the course of many
years) about "luxury" can, for example, be seen easily enough now
as essentially a debate about the nature of society: do the effects of
wealth possibly accompany and perhaps generate real benefits to
human life; or is a society given to foreign luxury and founded
upon a money economy nothing but a corrupt creature of nature's
ape, art? Is society part of a larger order, and are its workings
consonant with that order, Nature; or is it a thoroughly secular
institution, with no purpose other than that of perpetuating itself
as the stage for a morally purposeless, but very active human
existence, doomed by its mad, dull energy to an apocalyptic death?

> At length Corruption, like a gen'ral flood,
> (So long by watchful Ministers withstood)
> Shall deluge all; and Av'rice creeping on,
> Spread like a low-born mist, and blot the Sun . . .
>
> [137–40]

These lines from Pope's third moral essay, portraying the vision
granted to Blunt by a wizard and parodying the lesson of the Flood,
contain in them that image of the apocalypse later to be fully

16. Cf. Edwards, *This Dark Estate*, p. 72 and Ian Watt, "Two Historical Aspects
of the Augustan Tradition," *Studies in the Eighteenth Century: Papers Presented
at the David Nichol Smith Memorial Seminar, Canberra 1966*, ed. R. F. Brissenden
(Toronto: University of Toronto Press, 1968), pp. 79–84; Watt's article "The
Georgian Background" (*The Listener*, 13 April 1967, esp. p. 491) is also pertinent
to what I am saying here.

developed in *The Dunciad*: spiritual death in chaos and murk. And it is, of course, in the *Epistle to Bathurst* that the paradigm of social order implied in the pastoral domains of the Man of Ross is the norm against which the corruption, the purposelessness of a society founded upon finance, are measured.

But the *Epistle to Bathurst* stops short of the *Dunciad*. The wizard's vision is only part of the poem which opens out into an affirmation of the moral nature of society. As the poem moves through instance after instance of the madness and corruption of a society whose motive force is money—as it moves into the clearer air of the fields of the Man of Ross, the verse expresses itself in a suddenly changed rhythm. The rushed narrative rhythms telling the story of the steps in the ruin of stingy Old Cotta's prodigal son, later to be heard again in the progress of Sir Balaam's ruin, give way to the longer periods, the easier breathing of the address to Bathurst:

> The Sense to value Riches, with the Art
> T' enjoy them, and the Virtue to impart;
> Not meanly nor ambitiously pursued,
> Not sunk by sloth, nor raised by servitude;
> To balance Fortune by a just expense,
> Join with Economy, Magnificence;
> With Splendour, Charity, with Plenty, Health;
> O teach us, BATHURST! yet unspoil'd by wealth. . . .
>
> [219–26]

Significantly, Pope has achieved the transition from satire to celebration in rhythms and phraseology reminiscent of the opening lines of Dryden's translation of the *Georgics* and has put us in the same poetic environment as in *To Burlington*. The poem moves out to the country in order to celebrate the art of properly enjoying riches, and inevitably, the poet's mind associates the change in moral perspective with a very special change in expression; it seems clear that a certain category of feeling has asserted itself, and been appropriately announced by an echo of Virgil.

The bucolic echoes in the *Epistle to Bathurst* accompany the depiction of the decent alternatives Pope establishes to the corruptions of men and manners wrought by the depredations of misdirected abundance. But the terms of the poem's attack on corruption are not derived solely from the implicit values of the pastoral domains of the Man of Ross or the georgic echoes in the address to Bathurst; these, in fact, are only inevitable components of a larger view of the character of the social order. There is "philosophy" in this poem, much of which can be found in the *Essay on Man*, a project with which Pope was occupied at about the same time that the *Epistle to Bathurst* was published. In the *Essay*, Pope propounds a theory of the social order which locates the institution of civil society in the natural drive of the human creature to establish bonds of fellowship with his kind, harmonizing his egoism with his social instincts; human society, in Pope's view, is thus a natural order, and its workings are admirably adapted to blend those two sources of energy in the natural man—self-love and social generosity. These are the attitudes which inform the *Epistle to Bathurst* as it probes the nature of a social order many steps removed from the golden age primitivism of the state of nature depicted in book three of the *Essay on Man*. And, of course, these attitudes belong to the classical and renaissance outlook Mack spoke of in defining the manner of *To Burlington*.

That the order of nature and the order of society are not at radical odds with each other is, it may be maintained, the assumption of what we may call the bucolic attitude. That conflicts may arise, that society may grow corrupt, that man may lapse from moral health—these possibilities provide, of course, subject matter for moralists or poets, and their perspective for studying these problems can be, as it is in part in the *Epistle to Bathurst*, the perspective of the pastoral domain. But *To Bathurst* directs its attention to the contemporary details of a commercial society in a way that *To Burlington* does not. And already in *To Bathurst* we can detect a strain in Pope's art caused by his attempt to explain the blatant corruption rampaging through society as an aspect of the overarching moral harmony of the cosmic order. This third moral essay of Pope's, to be sure, concludes happily enough that all partial evil is universal good: Old Cotta is a miser; therefore his son is a prodigal;

and thus, in time, the old man's gold gets into circulation. In this way self-love and social good eventually come to be the same. But Pope's poem betrays some uncertainty: towards the end of the dialogue the question that must be posed is posed: is virtue in this corrupt world its own reward? And, as a corollary, can society be a fit environment for the worthy man? The answer is the parable of Sir Balaam, and it is a neatly ambiguous one, for from it we learn only that in this world (and the next) vice, at least, is certainly its own reward. About virtue we can only draw our own conclusions. Nor can we be too sanguine about the social order, which encourages Sir Balaam's vices as part of the process leading to his ruin and casting out. How good is the mechanism which tempts, traps and kills, all in order to cleanse? (It is important to note here that when this harsh ethical calculus is proposed again in *To Burlington* with reference to Timon, it is rejected and replaced by the better answer of the visionary conclusion.) Furthermore, Pope's readers have sometimes found themselves uneasy in the presence of *To Bathurst*'s optimistic resolution of the problem posed by the corruption in the social order, and have sensed that the poem's imaginative energy pulses more forcefully through those sections which detail the very real life of corruption and prodigality than in those parts in which the cosmic vision is asserted as a counterweight. Reuben Brower, for example, has justly praised the poem's achievement while noting as a flaw the imaginative discrepancy between the elements of grotesque fantasy in the images and allegories of venality, and the plainer, less energetic statements supporting the fitness of things seen in the long view, from the epicycle of Mercury, as Diderot would say.[17] And indeed, the

17. Reuben Brower, *Alexander Pope: The Poetry of Allusion* (Oxford: Clarendon Press, 1959), pp. 259–60. A searching examination of the strain between the rhetorical and ideological elements of *To Bathurst* is Paul J. Alper's "The *Epistle to Bathurst* and the Mandevillian State," *ELH* 25, no. 1 (March 1958): 23–42. Alpers shows how the realism of *To Bathurst* commits Pope to precisely that close observation of the economic facts which we do not find in *To Burlington*. Alpers emphasizes that, at its heart, *To Bathurst*'s formal and rhetorical difficulties are rooted in Pope's refusal to split the political and moral imagination. This might be said to be the great effort of all eighteenth-century poems of society, a hallmark of which is their continuing reference to pastoral and georgic forms and attitudes.

pastoral landscape managed by the Man of Ross on five hundred a
year is somewhat tame, and is, perhaps, merely a *topos* when
juxtaposed with the fantastic achievement of filthy lucre in its
modern form:

> Blest paper credit! last and best supply!
> That lends Corruption lighter wings to fly!
> Gold imp'd by thee, can compass hardest things,
> Can pocket States, can fetch or carry Kings;
> A single leaf shall waft an Army o'er,
> Or ship off Senates to some distant Shore. . . .
>
> [69–74]

Whereas Pope's universe in this poem, and its social component, are
assuredly stated to be ordered and ultimately beneficent, it is difficult to avoid the conclusion that the poet's real attention, and
therefore the main force of his imagination, is beguiled by the
possibility that things may not come round at the end. Between
this possibility and its contrary statement there has occurred a
failure of art. What is resolved in the dialogue is left suspended in
our response to the total effect of the poem. Are we so certain, after
reading this poem, that self-love and social good are the same, that
the good man can live in both country and town, that society is
harmoniously conjoined with nature? Or does society answer
chiefly to the demands of art and of corruption as its modern
instruments (blest paper credit) most assuredly do? And if society
does not share in the order of nature, what are the implications for
the bucolic vision which had generated the celebrative fictions of
To Bathurst? Are the Man of Ross and his celebrant in verse going
to be part of or alienated from the vigorous life, the questionable
urban activity, of his world? Much that is so confidently and
flawlessly concluded in *To Burlington*'s prophetic vision is left
unresolved in our responses to this poem's doctrine and its art.

That Pope could, from such similar material, create two such
different structures of feeling as the third and fourth moral essays,
is not perhaps unusual; the history of the imagination contains
many similar examples of attitudinal uncertainty. What I would

emphasize here is the radical nature of that uncertainty, of the alternatives that present themselves. At issue is not so much the poet's decision about the nature of the social order, but rather the categories of judgment by which the social order may be understood. It is not a matter of submitting the actual workings of the economic and social mechanism to moral or transcendental norms according to which that mechanism may be positively or adversely judged; it is a matter of the applicability of those norms, of their reference to actuality, and finally of the stance remaining to the poet or moralist who would continue to subscribe to them. One is reminded of Diderot's *Rameau's Nephew* (1773), which, much later in the century, records an afternoon's conversation between a rogue and a moralist; they range over topics similar to those in Pope's poems, and their debate on society is organized along similar thematic lines. It is an inconclusive debate, recording only the moralist's melancholy sense that his commitment to his view of things will edge him over to the periphery of society where he must stand as its scornful and bitter conscience, like Diogenes, to whom he pointedly likens himself. But when the conversation had begun, the moralist had eagerly welcomed it, had, indeed, accepted the rogue's own playful self-identification with Diogenes, and had been willing to entertain whatever views he could hear from such a corner: it would be a useful resource for self-examination, and no more. But in the good man's uneasy movement from the center to the social periphery we can see those forces at work which create the strain between satire and celebration in the poems I have been discussing. In this strain the issue to be discerned is not whether the rogue or the moralist is right, but rather how the moralist *feels* about being right.

What this signals is the transformation of an ethical attitude from a form of experience variously diffused in the poet's system of apprehension and response to an idea, valuable perhaps, but vulnerable, too plainly open to the processes of skeptical recognition and judgment. What we may call a form of being becomes in this process only a form of thought, as vulnerable as it is recognizable.[18]

---

18. This is a formulation of John F. Danby in his *Shakespeare's Doctrine of Nature* (London: Faber and Faber, 1949), p. 216.

The attitude undergoing this transformation within Pope's system of apprehension and response is the Virgilian feeling for the union of the ethical and the political to which the Roman poet gives imaginative body in his *Georgics,* a poem whose language and structure are able to reconcile an "almost absolute degree of realism . . . with an almost absolute degree of myth." Mandeville, who had settled simply for an absolute degree of realism, produced in his notorious formula—private vices are public benefits—a parody of that feeling for the union of the ethical and the political, a parody that is really a joke, the ultimate mode of skeptical scrutiny and play.

What Mandeville could so breezily offer as a formula for the criticism of politics and society—breezily, because we do not sense in him that darkness of response to the implications of his own idea that we feel in Pope—may well stand as the attitudinal underpinning for what Thomas Edwards has dubbed "the decline of politics" in the eighteenth century. Edwards means by this the disappearance of significant moral energy from political experience, leaving among serious men a sense that "the human purposes of political activity [were difficult to associate] with any existing partisan cause." And, though Edwards accepts Namier's point that such political quietude offered to the nation a valuable period of reconciliation and consolidation, he emphasizes the "aimless indulgence and moral inertia" dominating that long age of commercial energy and political comfort, "when the great attachment was not between a man and his principles or his leaders but, in a good Lockeian way, between a man and his property."[19] Edwards goes on to argue wittily that the dominant poetic mood accompanying this politics of property leaves "you with a depressing picture of a rural landscape crowded with lugubrious figures, none of them seeming to know the others are there too, busily writing poems called 'A Hymn on Solitude,' 'Ode to Evening,' or 'The Pleasures of Melancholy.' By the testimony of their verses, at least, these poets never read newspapers, went to parties, or held a steady job, and it

19. Thomas R. Edwards, Jr., *Imagination and Power: A Study of Poetry on Political Themes* (New York: Oxford University Press, 1971), p. 105.

is hard to think of an age whose literature . . . shows less contact with public experience."[20] Commenting on an M.P. who, sitting for Ripon from 1721 to 1781, enjoyed sixty years of parliamentary comfort and of whom his biographer could write that "the contemplation of the beauties of nature, and rural occupations, formed his chief and unceasing delight," Edwards says, "When politicians assume the sensibility of poets, what in the world shall poets do?"[21]

But Edwards recognizes another of Namier's judgments—that "there is something to be said for a Parliament whose members, for whatever dubious reasons, have a strong interest in commerce and finance and surprising expertise about the technical details of economic questions." This was, after all, a period which one historian labels "the classical age of the constitution."[22] A casual survey of the names of those whose careers were linked to the rotten boroughs, Burke only most notably, must tell us that something creative was happening in all this yeasty corruption. And this brings me back to my subject—that bucolic poetry of public affairs in which the Augustan tone is dominant, but not in its satirical (or lugubrious) register. I am using "Augustan" as Edwards, following Leavis, does: a term denoting the serious, insistent social interest, the vigorous imaginative engagement with public affairs, that we recognize as the characteristic quality of significant eighteenth-century expression, whether in satire or not.

The bucolic poems I study here are often reflective, and sometimes in solitude, but never lugubrious. They can be distinguished from each other by the complexity in which they interpret public experience, but the countryside they see, create, and transform into their vehicle for social, economic, and political understanding is not that melancholic scene Edwards rightly jibes at for its familiarity to the "reluctant readers of period anthologies." It is the country-

20. Ibid., p. 119. Cf. Williams on the melancholy note in the poetry of the countryside from Thomson through Goldsmith (*Country and the City*, chap. 8).

21. Edwards, *Imagination and Power*, p. 105.

22. David Lindsay Keir, *The Constitutional History of Modern Britain*, 9th ed. (London: Black, 1969). "The Classical Age of the Constitution" is Keir's chapter heading (chap. 6, pp. 289–364) for his discussion of the constitutional history of the eighteenth century.

side of those M.P.'s, so vigorous and alert to gain, yet so ready to celebrate their energies in Virgilian terms. It is an Augustan countryside, an imaginative as well as economic resource, as Augustan as its proprietors. We hear this note in figures like Lord Kames, literary man and agricultural enthusiast, whose *Gentleman Farmer* can be called a "georgic in prose," linking its detailed instructions on farm management, on profit and loss, to those moral and public concerns that bucolic tradition had engrafted to the rural scene for two millenia. The Augustan note is to be heard in Kames's georgic-like celebration of the modern gentleman, who formerly "led the life of a dog, or of a savage; violently active in the field, supinely indolent at home. . . . How delightful the change, from the hunter to the farmer, from the destroyer of animals, to the feeder of men."[23] It is no source of embarrassment to Kames that this transformation yields a politics of property and is supervised by an alert eye for profit and loss.[24] This new gentleman is, after all, advancing the Augustan enterprise of civilization, with its peculiar and often wonderful joy in a modernity whose essential identity is yet rooted in moral and literary tradition. Lord Kames can express, therefore, his enthusiastic sense that agriculture is on the verge of a great scientific push forward, can note its need, for example, of a new and precise vocabulary,[25] and at the same time judge the value of this enterprise in conceptual terms he had to learn from literature. I

23. [Henry Home, Lord Kames], *The Gentleman Farmer*, 5th ed. (Edinburgh, 1802), p. xix.

24. Some of Kames's chapter headings: "Feeding Farm Cattle"; "Fences"; "The Proper Size of a Farm, and the Useful Accommodations it ought to have"; "What a Corn-Farm ought to yield in Rent."

25. "Earth, land, ground, soil are not synonymous; and therefor, in correct writing, their meaning ought to be ascertained. . . . [To] fix a precise meaning to each will probably require a century or two more" (Kames, *Gentleman Farmer*, p. xxiii). Kames also insists, for example, on the need to distinguish between such terms as "furrow" and "furrow-slice" (*Gentleman Farmer*, pp. xxii–xxiii). It is interesting in this connection to note John Arthos's observation that the diction regularly employed in the eighteenth-century didactic-descriptive poem serves a scientific end: the classification according to types of the observed phenomena of the natural world. Arthos suggests that the ultimate development of familiar "stock diction" (e.g. "the finny brood") is the system of classification established by Linneaus (*The Language of Natural Description in Eighteenth-Century Poetry* [Ann Arbor: University of Michigan Press, 1949], esp. chap. 3).

want to turn now to some "practical" writers, who, in engrafting their Augustanism to the politics of agricultural property, were engaged in an effort of imaginative understanding linking their work in its success and its failure to the bucolic poetry that sought to fashion a contemporary criticism for a powerful new world. Arthur Young and Adam Smith are the subject of the next chapter.

II

Bucolic Tradition and Virtuous Work: Arthur Young and Adam Smith

Nobody responded with greater enthusiasm than Arthur Young to the technological and commercial development of agriculture in the second half of the century. Young's work as editor of the *Annals of Agriculture* was a natural consequence of his enthusiastic and extensive observation of the changing rural scene; he was a kind of Augustan Johnny Appleseed, disseminating news of what was being done in the land, encouraging technological laggards to learn the new ways, promising them the rewards of riches and the assurance that those riches were the wages of virtue and public honor. It would be difficult to imagine a mind more pliantly receptive to England's new wealth as the fulfillment of an Augustan promise; to Young it was all so tangible, so palpably real, this countryside which the hard work of the georgic would so easily, inevitably transform into the national pleasance. Shrewd, intelligent, and practical, Young fashioned for himself a career thoroughly in tune with the commercial energy of the age at the same time as he drew upon the period's literary resources to seek for explanations of what that energy could signify. Deeply interested in the commercial potential of a vigorous agricultural industry, Young was at the same time taken with those attitudes toward rural life that are products of literary tradition. Young and the contributors to his journal, in investigating the relations between agricultural practice and the national economy, find themselves dealing at length with the very topics of bucolic poetry—city and country, luxury and simplicity, rural virtue and urban sophistication—and their achievements and difficulties are of a piece with those we discover in the thought—and the art—of poets for whom bucolic tradition provided a way of seeing and understanding England's new life.

The implicit conflicts between the values embodied in bucolic tradition and Young's commercial enthusiasm are obvious enough. We can easily see now, for example, that the enclosure movement, whose effect was to decrease the rural population even as it enhanced the efficiency of agricultural industry, could not be easily squared with an attitude that held the countryside to be the seat of the virtuous life itself.[1] Young, who enthusiastically supported enclosures, could face such an issue when he encountered it directly, and, in those circumstances, could resolve it directly in a way that placed him squarely on the side of commercially efficient practice. It would be wrong to conclude, however, that Young's commercial enthusiasm was a simple matter, dictating to him in terms of profit and loss only, his ultimate standards of value.[2] Consider, for example, this small passage from his *Travels in France*:

> The poor people seem poor indeed; the children terribly ragged, if possible worse clad than if with no cloaths at all; as to shoes and

1. Kenneth MacLean points out, for example, that Young's praise for the rural life, which was the tack he took as a propagandist for reform, was at odds with the actual effects of reform, which brought "an end to rural living for that part of the population which probably derived most benefit from a life on the land—the yeomen, small farmers and country laborers" (*Agrarian Age: A Background for Wordsworth* [New Haven: Yale University Press, 1950], p. 12). And John Middendorf writes that "we have only to realize that the urbanization of nineteenth-century England was in large measure due to eighteenth-century changes in agriculture to understand how complex and far-reaching was the movement of which Young was a part ("Arthur Young, Traveller and Observer" [Ph. D. diss., Columbia University, 1953], p. 196). I want to emphasize my indebtedness to MacLean's and Middendorf's studies; they pointed me to those places in the work of Young and Adam Smith that were directly pertinent to my own interest in the bucolic poetry I study. Their importance to me will be evident throughout this chapter.

2. Raymond Williams, *The Country and the City* (London: Chatto and Windus, 1973), p. 67.

stockings they are luxuries. A beautiful girl of six or seven years
playing with a stick, and smiling under such a bundle of rags as
made my heart ache to see her: they did not beg, and when I gave
them any thing seemed more surprised than obliged. One third of
what I have seen of this province seems uncultivated, and nearly all
of it is misery. What have kings, and ministers, and parliaments,
and states, to answer for their prejudices, seeing millions of hands
that would be industrious, idle and starving, through the execrable
maxims of despotism, or the equally detestable prejudices of a
feudal nobility.[3]

There is in this passage the sound of rich political feeling; in it we
can hear the positive possibilities hidden away in that M.P. from
Ripon who found his chief and unceasing delight in the contemplation of the beauties of nature and rural occupations. Here too
we can sense just what was of value in all those English M.P.'s
who, as Namier showed, had "for whatever dubious reasons . . . a
strong interest in commerce and finance and surprising expertise
about the technical details of economic questions." Young sees
those poor French people precisely—their bare feet, the beautiful,
wasted child, her pathetic toy, the smile from under a bundle of
rags that makes his heart ache. His observation and his judgment
join to draw the political and moral connection between the
uncultivated land and the human misery, misery presented as an
image of human possibilities thwarted and destroyed. The beautiful child does it, determines the passage's development towards the
angry indictment of "the execrable maxims of despotism," the
"detestable prejudices of a feudal nobility" that starves and makes
idle those millions that "would be industrious." The feeling here is
real and directly expresses Young's sense of the moral implications
of politics. We can see easily how his response to this scene is
determined by his commitment to a very different political economy, one in which commercial and industrial energies are released
rather than restrained. And we can sense the moral value Young
attributes to a politics which permits the release of those energies.

3. Arthur Young, *Travels in France during 1787, 1788, and 1789*, 3rd ed.
(London: G. Bell and Sons, 1890 and 1912), p. 125. The entry is for 5 September
1788.

The positive possibilities of a vigorous capitalism are in Young's mind here, and the passage demonstrates the genuine resources of feeling that could support an authentic rhetoric of commercial and political celebration. Such a rhetoric could grow from a writer's imaginative apprehension of the union of "the ethical and the political" in the release of vigorous commercial activity, itself understood as an aspect of a politics freed from the dead hand of the "detestable prejudices of a feudal nobility, the execrable maxims of despotism." For such a rhetoric and such a vision, indeed, a century of English political history could provide an authentic basis.

In fact, though Young was no systematic thinker, it is possible to trace in the development of his attitudes toward economic activity a shift from a mercantilist to something of a free trade position, a development in outlook fully in accord with the political attitudes implied in his attack on the "maxims of despotism."[4] But it is equally clear that this intellectual effort was an ambiguous one, tempered and inhibited by the pervasive presence of another set of attitudes whose moral and literary authority was both powerful and attractive. These are the attitudes of bucolic tradition, literary attitudes, whose moral force, as we can see in Virgil and in Pope, would support an economy of restraint and contentment, not the economy of energy and gain. To Young the economy of contentment is as appealing as it is ideologically off-base, at once a resource and a hindrance to the fullest statement of his own preferences.

We can see why in a piece he wrote for his journal on the subject of "The Pleasures of Agriculture"; here Young set out to praise the rural life and at the same time to present, in plain terms, its financial requirements and possibilities. He defines his subject clearly at the outset and is particularly careful to note that it is not his purpose "to draw parallels between the pleasures supposed to reside in retirement, and the anxieties hidden beneath the blare of capitals."[5] This is an interesting disclaimer: Young emphasizes his

4. John Middendorf, "Arthur Young, Traveller and Observer," p. 196.
5. Arthur Young, "The Pleasures of Agriculture," *Annals of Agriculture* 2 (1784): 457.

intention *not* to seek an advantage from the ancient, perhaps too familiar, topic of town and country, with its formulaic preference for rural retirement as the situation of virtue. He seems to be looking for a way to "naturalize" nature, to free it from its literary reputation so that its real advantages can be seen and valued for what they are without being implicated in a habit of imaginative and moral thought that would celebrate those advantages only at the expense of the economic ones he is so committed to demonstrating. He develops his argument, therefore, as a response to a question he formulates plainly, as if such a question could be explored without reference to a deeply ingrained set of literary attitudes: "What are the essentials of a life both useful and amusing?" And he organizes his answer to show how the life of the gentleman farmer offers "freedom from anxiety, duration of pleasure, and views sufficiently interesting to command the attention of the cultivated mind."[6] (It seems clear that there was no easy escape from Virgil.)

Young's argument is, finally, no different from what even a casual reader of the *Georgics* might have expected, but his manner deserves attention. In part it embodies the rapturous praise of the landscape common in the didactic-descriptive poem, expressed in prose like this:

> [In the springtime] the orchard's loaded branches bid streams nectareous warm the peasant's heart and the rifled sweets of *incense-breathing* spring flow from the labours of the industrious bee. . . . [In the winter] *sliding through the sky* pale suns unfelt at distance roll away. . . . [Then] the planter appropriating the right soil for the beauties of landskip, marks his barren spots, and the *prophetic eye of taste* sees refreshing shades thicken over the bleak hills while the sturdy woodman provides for the hearth. . . . [7]

We should note how easily his representation of the "pleasures of agriculture" discriminates between the "planter" and the "sturdy woodsman"; the first is, indeed, occupied with the tasks of pleasure: it is his "prophetic eye of taste" which sees into the genius of the place and can envision, even in the bleak winter hills, the thickening shades of his summer groves. For him, land is land-

6. Ibid., p. 458.
7. Ibid., pp. 476–78.

scape; only the "sturdy woodsman" inhabits in mind and body the wintry moment, an image of labor, providing for the hearth. But we should also note how the adjective "sturdy" pastoralizes that image, just as the hearth, understood as the object of the woodsman's labor, softens it to bring it into accord with the aesthetic imagination of the planter-proprietor. The same tendency is obvious in Young's description of the springtime, where the only suggestion of work is "the industrious bee," so that even the peasant is represented as a figure of leisure, the beneficiary of the pastoral will of the "orchard's loaded branches [which themselves] bid streams nectareous warm the peasants heart." As Young's italics indicate, much of this has been influenced by bucolic poetry. Furthermore, his use of literary tradition is perfectly clear in another context when, arguing that agriculture has sufficient intellectual riches to reward enlightened minds, Young cites as examples the figures of Xenophon, Cicero, and Virgil—who wrote on husbandry—and Horace, "who with a taste for dissipation, and experienced in all the gaiety of a court, preferred his farm so much to both, that the united persuasions of Augustus and Maecenas could not draw him from it."[8] It is obvious here that despite his initial disclaimer of any intention to draw invidious literary distinctions between town and country, Young's dependence on literary tradition draws him inevitably into that *topos*, just as his acquaintance with pastoral literature inevitably surfaces to dominate his representation of the economic landscape.[9]

When we contrast this prose with what he could write on France's rural poverty, a passage whose directness is so adequate to

8. Ibid., p. 471.

9. John Barrell argues that Young was ill at ease in the face of the appeal of the sublime or picturesque landscape, as if he discerned an implicit conflict between its aesthetic appeal and the economic value of the cultivated and improved countryside. As evidence Barrell notes Young's habit of capping his descriptions of a sublime prospect with references to a cultivated field nearby: "[T]he more one looks at his language, the more one speculates about the precise nature of Young's guilt at having a taste for the sublime. . . . No real reconciliation of course is possible between the interests of the practical farmer and the picturesque writer, although this technique of Young's does allow them to coexist, and indeed insists that they do" (*The Idea of Landscape and the Sense of Place 1730–1840: An Approach to the Poetry of John Clare* [Cambridge: At the University Press, 1972], p. 83).

the political and moral feeling Young develops from it, we must sense a regrettable loss. What is lost is precisely that realism Young himself sought, a realism appropriate to his sense of the landscape as potentially a scene of virtuous work, of actual industry that ennobles and liberates even as it provides and enriches. But if Young's essay, despite his initial intention, finds its way, regrettably, into some familiar topics and attitudes, there is another side to it and another style as well. His demonstration that the gentleman farmer lives free from anxiety is managed not only through rapturous reminiscences of landscape poets. Answering the objection that the financial risk involved in running a farm introduces a measure of anxiety into the life of retirement, Young points out that "with a proper capital [and here he adds a footnote: "Five pounds an acre"] the losses upon livestock are well known to amount to no more, on an average of several years, than four or five per cent of the value. Calculation, when founded upon knowledge of the subject, prepares a man for losses, and puts anxiety, in a rational mind, at great distance."[10]

Here is another voice. It reminds us that the major end of Young's instruction, after all, has to do with making the farm pay. That the title of the article immediately following "The Pleasures of Agriculture" is "Queries on the Irrigation of Land Answered" demonstrates plainly the presence of two voices structuring, not only a single essay, but the larger character of his journal itself: one is borrowed from literature, one from the exchange. But there is only one concern: to promote agricultural efficiency and thereby raise the farmer's profits, the national wealth, and the public good. The rhetoric of rural praise, adequate or not, is the celebrative accompaniment to the didactic and commercial enterprise. There is an artlessness, even a kind of innocence, in the mingling of the two forms of writing. It is the work of an enthusiast and a projector. A flourishing farm is, after all, wealthy virtue, the owner's good and England's too. And the economy of contentment and the economy of gain join to support this sense of things.

"On the Pleasures of Agriculture" was written in 1784. By 1784

10. Young, "Pleasures of Agriculture," p. 461.

the gentleman farmer—that is, the wealthy, large landholder, seriously devoted to agricultural improvement and agricultural profit—no longer needed exhortation to cultivate his lands. Statistics and parliamentary records very clearly indicate that years before the publication of Young's essay the process of enclosing the land was well accepted and inexorably changing the face of English rural experience.[11] Nobody in 1784 needed convincing that money was to be made from the land. Young's essay, it would seem, is in large part written in acknowledgment, not in anticipation, of great changes taking place in the practice of farming. It becomes possible to read an essay like Young's, therefore, as a reflection of social experience, expressing as it does a candid recognition of the extension into agriculture of the commercial energy pulsing through English life, a sense that this is good, and at the same time, some uncertainty about how to promote the effort, how to praise it, how to understand it. If the traditional attitudes of bucolic literature were not finally adequate to this enterprise, nevertheless, for their prestige and their provenience, they were enthusiastically adopted. Clearly the economy of contentment was sought out as the moral foundation for the economy of gain. One writer has remarked that the classical praise for the rural life perfectly suited the purposes of a landholding class that was unusual in its ability to shift from an older sense of the meaning of proprietorship—the feudal ideology with its disdain for commerce—to the active cultivation of the land in the spirit of the developing capitalism of the day. "More and more it became possible to retain proprietorship over the land only by candid recognition of the new commercial nature of society and complete adaptation of farming practices to

11. Just who was dispossessed, and just how many, by the enclosures of the late eighteenth century are difficult questions. MacLean provides a useful summary of conflicting opinions. The complexity of the question arises in part from uncertainty about the meaning of the term "yeomanry," the class who suffered most from the enclosures. Were they small freeholders or long-established tenants? There is, though, little argument that in absolute numbers some 180,000 small farmers—freeholders and tenants—had disappeared into the cities by the end of the century. Though not undertaken on a massive scale until the nineteenth century, the enclosure movement, especially on sheep lands, was well underway in the years 1760–80. See MacLean, *Agrarian Age*, p. 14.

meet the new conditions. Sometimes older landowners changed their ways; sometimes they lost their lands to burghers or successful tenants. English agriculture was the first to be widely penetrated by the capitalist spirit."[12]

If, then, a large part of Young's praise of agriculture comes directly from classical literary tradition, it is obvious that his thinking about the land is not determined simply by literature's identification of the country as the seat of contentment. Certainly though, the classical view of rural life as the embodiment of virtue was an enormous ideological comfort to enterprising farmers as their interests clashed with those of the merchants of the towns, as they did, for example, well into the nineteenth century over such issues as the Corn Laws. Not a few instances can be cited where "specific encouragement was given to the artistic treatment of rural subjects by spokesmen of the agrarian interest."[13] The relationship between rhetoric and reality appears, then, to have been more than a literary issue.

It is probably impossible to define the appropriate uses of literature. What is appropriate is what is successful, and the creative imagination has generally pushed back the limits that have tended in one way or another to define the forms and purposes of literary art. That certain aspects of bucolic tradition were used to advance certain new interests in agriculture itself neither condemns the practice nor precludes the possibility that a significant art might grow from it. But surely Young's use of bucolic tradition in support of his commercial enthusiasms raises a question about the integrity, the wholeness, of his vision of the rural life and the authenticity of his appropriation of the ideology connected with it. How well did he maintain his classical sense of rural virtue, of the meaning of rural life, when he turned his attention to the economic as well as the moral components of agricultural industry? When, for example, he had to think about the city as a consumer of rural

12. Paul H. Johnstone, "Turnips and Romanticism," *Agricultural History* 12, no. 3 (July 1938): 249–50.

13. Ibid., p. 254. Arthur Young himself sponsored the publication in England of a German treatise called *The Rural Socrates,* in which the virtues of the golden age are seen to be embodied in a contemporary Swiss peasant.

produce at good prices, did he continue to think about the relations between town and country in terms of the classical literary *topos*? Did the terms of imaginative literature fully explain to him the meaning of rural experience and its implication with the larger economic life of the land?

For example, if we consider Young's use of the country-city *topos* when the subject of cities comes up in a nonliterary context, we discover that despite his rhetorical assertion of the countryside as the seat of the virtues, Young was quite well aware of the importance of the big city to the agricultural industry he envisioned. He has something to say about the mundane as well as the literary relations between town and country, and it is worth considering carefully Young's common sense observations, very clearly derived from his first-hand experience. As we might expect, when it came to evaluating a market, Young could discount the evils of great cities and thus ignore for the moment their rhetorical reputation. In a short article he wrote for his journal in 1795 he noted in some detail the benefits accruing to the agricultural industry of Norfolk from the proximity of the London market. He points out that

> besides supplying all her own consumption, and supporting immense flocks of sheep . . . [Norfolk] sends, all winter through, great herds of fat oxen to London, as I am a weekly witness of numbers that pass my door in their way thither. This not only shows how exceedingly productive the husbandry of that county is, but it is also a proof of the importance of a great capital city; very contrary to the reasoning of many modern speculative politicians. If London was divided into many provincial towns, Norfolk would be entitled to about 15 or 20,000 souls, added to those of the towns she possesses already, which would not be felt in the county in supplying a demand in lieu of the market which the capital is at present. . . . A city with 7 or 800,000 people in it forms a far more extensive demand than 7 or 8 cities each of 100,000. . . . When these circumstances are considered . . . I believe it will be found that the capital (always supposing it safe from foreign attacks) *cannot be too large; and that its being an active market for every branch of distant industry, increases the national wealth, and quickens the population of the*

kingdom to a vastly greater amount than all the destruction we read of from abuses, ill health, &c. &c.[14] [Italics added].

There is no effulgent prose here; this is the second style, which, with considerable ease, Young had placed beside the rapturous voice in his praise of the virtues of rural life. Here the statistics speak eloquently for themselves, the voice of the projector heard in the countryside. There is nothing here that can be called sentimental; Young does not, for example, deny the "destruction we read of from abuses, ill health, &c. &c." But he does dismiss these observations of "modern speculative politicians," not troubling to disguise his contempt for such men, and obviously much more concerned for the health of the agricultural economy of Norfolk than for the miseries of London, its benefactor. It is worth noting here that it is not simply the city that Young approves of, but the big city, the metropolis. It is not merely the size of the market, but its concentration that offers the farmers of Norfolk their opportunity. We discover little enough here of the rhetoric of rural praise— the praise of rural tranquillity over urban anxiety—which marked his earlier essay on the pleasures of agriculture. Indeed, in another place, writing about the elimination of the small farmer subsequent to enclosures, he baldly admits that life on the land is not essential to human happiness.[15] Which did he believe—his rhetoric or his statistics?

※

Young's recognition of the role of the big city is not the most thoroughgoing statement of that point of view. A more detailed argument had been presented, again in Young's *Annals of Agriculture*, five years earlier by one Paolo Balsamo, professor of agriculture in the University of Palermo. This writer agrees with Young that the concentration of the populace, not merely its size, makes the city a fine market for the produce of the countryside. But

14. Arthur Young, "Importance of London to the National Husbandry," *Annals of Agriculture* 23 (1795): 272–73.
15. MacLean, *Agrarian Age*, p. 19.

Balsamo states his position more boldly, attacking yet another foundation of the ancient rural ideology—that simplicity is to be preferred over luxury. "It is evident that 100,000 people . . . scattered into many villages, consume much less than if they were gathered into one town, *for the reason of luxury* which increases in proportion to the number of individuals united together; and which, giving so the strongest impulse to circulation, in spite of all the loud complaints of the moralists against it, must be acknowledged very useful to society"[16] (italics added). We may note here the same disdain for "the moralists" as Young expressed for the "speculative politicians." Among the moralists Balsamo had in mind were, perhaps, writers like Oliver Goldsmith. But the extent to which Balsamo had adapted his Mandevillian thinking to his concern for the health of agriculture becomes clear as the argument is pursued. Noting that wealthy men living outside of cities tend to hoard, while the urban environment encourages them to spend their wealth, Balsamo argues that the farmer is, in the process, allowed to have the whole profit from his industry instead of having to compete with the prodigal were the prodigal to reform, return to his farm, and become a competitor.[17] It is to the best advantage of agriculture that this race of urban spendthrifts, all in close proximity to one another, able to urge each other on, spend all their property in the consumption of the farmer's products. An observation, we may note, that places the farmer also well outside the economy of contentment, defining him as a shrewd benefactor from the hyperactive urban economy, heating itself, like a critical mass, into an explosion of consumptive, economic desire.

Not only do great cities provide the best kind of market, but they also consume in the way most profitable to the farmer. The many buyers constitute a market without "monopolies"; the flurry of demand sets up a kind of competition among buyers which tends

16. Paolo Balsamo, "Thoughts on Great Cities," *Annals of Agriculture* 13 (1790): 466. MacLean points to Balsamo as an example of the "increasing inconsistency [which appeared] in the literature on progressive farming as the enthusiasts for the plow and country life became as well the advocates of the big city" (*Agrarian Age*, pp. 18–19).

17. Balsamo, "Thoughts on Great Cities," p. 467.

to raise the farmer's prices in the city *and* in the country; products that would ordinarily be of little value in the country sell well in the city, for example, straw for fodder; furthermore, certain produce—fruits, herbs, flowers—grown near and specifically for the urban market constitute an industry that otherwise simply would not exist. All of these facts Balsamo assures us are well known to the farmer: "Farmers understand profit better than logic, crowns and guineas better than syllogisms and philosophical essays."[18]

Somehow a new image, a new character, seems to be forming in these observations; neither the gentleman farmer of fact nor the *vir bonus* of an honored rhetorical tradition, Balsamo's and Young's farmer is a man who values money and cultivates this interest as a virtue. He cares little for the literary reputation of his vocation, and he has recognized, perhaps better than the moralists, poets and speculative politicians who value the countryside for something else, that it is a part of a larger society whose nature is simply commercial. To find Mandeville in the countryside, openly proclaiming the social virtue of urban luxury, is indeed to discover that the social vision, as well as the moral vision, of pastoral and georgic tradition has fled, has become merely rhetoric, perhaps merely propaganda.

The argument, after all, is plain and simple: the farmer thrives on the vices of the town. Balsamo is perfectly clear that the vices of the town are, in fact, vices. Farmers, for example, are not to live in cities lest they pick up the bad habits of that life. Let a farmer take a town house and "dissipation and laziness" must follow. Great proprietors who are absentee owners and who spend their money on luxury instead of improving their estates do themselves injury. Therefore they should not participate in, only benefit from, the socially useful vices of the town. This is a doctrine which, however shrewd it may be, splits apart the integrity of the pastoral and georgic vision, making the rhetoric of that tradition, at most, a kind of decoration. We may note here that Balsamo, in encouraging the new industry of the kitchen gardens—those flowers and fruits

18. Ibid., p. 470.

grown specifically for city markets—quite openly goes after the opportunity offered by the urban market for luxury. However, he anticipates an objection from those who tend to look toward agriculture as an industry with more than merely a commercial identity: "I am aware that some of your readers will laugh at this argument [that is, in favor of kitchen gardens]; those, I mean who despise every mode of husbandry which produces no corn, or feeds no cattle; and who, for this reason, will rather detest than praise great cities, as what diverts the farmer from the *sacred* purposes of sowing wheat or clover, or the like. But this opinion certainly is not political."[19] Balsamo refers with some impatience to a well-established position, both among economists and moralists, which held that there is a kind of superior virtue (as well as economic soundness) in the cultivation of the staple crops.[20] He dismisses the notion that there is a sacred purpose in sowing and sets up another standard of judgment by asserting that the objection to kitchen crops is not "political." By "political" he means the systematic organization of life in civil society for the purpose of procuring human happiness; happiness, moreover, he defines simply as the satisfaction of ever-increasing desires. We see in these thoughts that city and country, luxury and simplicity, the sacred and the political, are not understood as they had been before. The sacred purposes of sowing no longer belong to the same world as the political, and the

19. Ibid., pp. 472–73.
20. A good example is Dr. Johnson's observation that "Agriculture . . . and agriculture alone, can support us without the help of others in certain plenty and genuine dignity. . . . [W]hile our ground is covered with corn and cattle we can want nothing; and if imagination should grow sick of native plenty, and call for delicacies or embellishments from other countries, there is nothing which corn and cattle will not purchase. . . . The pineapple thrives better between the tropics, and better furs are found in the northern regions. But let us not envy these unnecessary privileges. Mankind cannot subsist upon the indulgences of nature, but must be supported by her more common gifts." Johnson had no doctrinaire objections to luxury, quite the contrary in fact; yet the diction of this passage seems to express more than an argument for the economic soundness of the basic crops. He calls the delicacies and exotic crops "unnecessary privileges," and seems to understand them as nutriments for the jaded imagination. It was the jaded and driving imagination to which Balsamo looked as a source of income for the prudent farmer who would supply its needs. The quote from Johnson is from his "Further Thoughts on Agriculture" (1756) in Samuel Johnson, *Political Writings*, ed. Donald J. Greene, Yale Edition of the Works of Samuel Johnson, 10 vols. to date (New Haven and London: Yale University Press, 1958—), 10:124.

other terms—city and country, luxury and simplicity—are now merely topics for a literature that may, and may as well not, have anything to do with the practice of tilling the soil for profit.

Of Young's rapturous essay on the pleasures of agriculture, Kenneth MacLean has said that its spirit is that of classicism, or at least that aspect of classicism which we customarily recognize as the pursuit of the golden mean, the exaltation of moderation.[21] Paolo Balsamo, however, whose thoughts on great cities were prompted by some similar thoughts of Young's and were published in Young's journal, offers some philosophical observations *against* moderation in support of his endorsement of great cities. We have noted that Balsamo, in general, was not eager to have the farmer pick up the habits of the town. Yet, though he recognized urban vices for what they were, he apparently felt the need to offer a kinder view of them than one might infer from his advice to the farmer to stay on the farm. He extends his argument beyond the limits necessary to his chief subject—whether great cities are beneficial or hurtful to agriculture—into a brief consideration of the psychology of excess. Admitting that great cities increase the wants of men and thus their anxieties, he maintains that cities also increase the means of satisfying these new desires. He then makes a thoroughly unclassical observation: "To satisfy *more wants* increases man's happiness." Furthermore, he senses something of the spirit of his day in his assertion that "the people of the present age [have an] unbounded ambition of extending always their enjoyments, and [their] happiness improves in proportion as fresh or new pleasures take place." "It follows that political bodies, and with more reason great cities, are better calculated . . . to procure man's happiness than deserts and petty villages." Of the notion that moderation is one road to happiness, Balsamo simply says that this "may be good for the people of the moon."[22]

These thoughts certainly were not new in 1790. Yet, even now, two centuries later, it is possible to feel their dissonant connection with different habits of feeling that still survive in us and that prompt us to respond with uneasy questions. If happiness is the

21. MacLean, *Agrarian Age*, p. 11.
22. Balsamo, "Thoughts on Great Cities," p. 480.

definition and subsequent satisfaction of constantly new desires, then in what way is the good farmer, taught by Balsamo to remain away from the great city where such happiness is found, to earn his share of it? Is the happy man of bucolic literary tradition, satisfied in moderate measure, to be recognized as mere rhetoric? (The uncertain status of pleasure in Balsamo's conception of the farmer's life suggests, in literary terms, a thorough split between pastoral and georgic attitudes. Yet, it is clear that in ideological terms it was just such a union of attitudes that agrarian spokesmen asserted or sought, as we see in even Young's essay on the *pleasures* of agriculture.) In short, Balsamo's remarkable little essay has loose edges, as we might expect in an effort which forthrightly speaks on behalf of the energies of commerce, argues for the application of these energies to agricultural enterprise, and all the while, quite innocently, is encumbered with some of the remnants of what we may call the classical agricultural ideology. Moderation is still a rural virtue, but it operates in Balsamo's thought as a means, a rather shrewd means, by which the farmer may grow very rich. Happiness, no longer that tranquil state of soul to which the virtue of moderation contributes, is now the boon to be won by the urbanite's hyperactive pleasure seeking as he helps contribute to the farmer's treasure. This is just one of the anomalies we encounter as we watch the spirit of commerce in the eighteenth century trying to realize itself at the same time as it resists its own proper energies in its attempt to reconcile itself to an ancient habit of thought. The anomaly here is the more striking for the fact that the conflict between two opposing senses of proper human fulfillment takes place on familiar literary ground—the countryside, now however not a metaphor for virtue but rather those very literal fields which are to be understood as merely one kind of natural, economic resource.

The strain between what Balsamo would recognize as the moralist's view of a proper economy and a shrewd farmer's is obvious.[23] Equally obvious is the difficulty of imputing to this farmer's

23. Ibid., p. 479. Here he expresses his impatience with the moralist's familiar suspicion of the city as the seat of unhealthy labor.

enterprise the designation of virtuous work, at least insofar as that term is linked to such values as moderation, temperance, contentment, and through them, with the countryside in a configuration of attitudes that can be responsibly, if loosely, labeled as classical. That label describes a habit of feeling and judgment in which the economic life—production, finance, commerce, consumption—is placed within a larger ethical context than that provided by the marketplace itself. A loose but responsible application of the label could be made to the Christian prohibition of usury, for example, which was part of a system of thought whose tendency was to value those economic activities that served obvious and limited and real human needs. Production rather than finance is the valued activity here, the "virtuous work" of the marketplace. As late as this century, indeed, Thorstein Veblen drew a distinction between those actively engaged in the production of goods and those who finance and market them. Veblen saw the producers as the virtuous workers of the marketplace; consumers and financiers come in for little of his praise. Wherever the life of the marketplace is judged within a larger order of activities and values, it seems that some particular form of economic activity is likely to be designated as virtuous work. When, however, the marketplace is looked upon as a self-justifying process or organism, producing goods, services, and profits all answering to man's propensity for increasing his desires and sources of pleasure—and this is Balsamo's sense of the exchange—then the economist of desire and profit is likely to look with scorn on the moralist's notion that some kinds of work (or crops) are invested with a peculiar virtue. Perhaps one way to define the significance of Mandeville and Balsamo is to say that they pointed to that tendency of the marketplace to serve no other purpose than that of aggrandizing itself. By pointing to this facet of reality Mandeville and Balsamo call into doubt the notion that work is virtuous only as it contributes to an economy of moderation and contentment. The term virtuous work is, perhaps, insufficient to define an attitude toward the economic life that is pervasive enough to include Virgil and Veblen, but it will work to designate that set of expressive habits taking rural labor as the foundation and emblem of the economy of contentment.

Now, it is difficult to think of Young's or Balsamo's countryside in these terms. Instead they give us a picture of the farmer and his toil which indeed fits into a larger pattern of social and political observation, but surely it is the Mandevillian pattern. Balsamo, indeed, with Mandevillian impatience, identifies his opponent in argument as "the moralist," and shrugs off his objections as "not political." Clearly the idea of virtuous work, the classical idea with its emphasis on moderation and its metaphorical assertion of the countryside as the scene of that good work, was not easily harmonized with a sophisticated understanding of the economic processes that created wealth, the nation's good, from the impulse to excess, from the pleasures of luxury, from the "useful" vices of the social order. Balsamo and Young are not poets, and we should not expect of them that integrated, imaginative sense of the meaning of social experience that we expect from poets. But we shall see that the heroic rhetoric of Dyer's georgic poem also founders on the rocks of the economic fact so well, if unembarrassedly, expressed in the thinking of Balsamo. For Balsamo the countryside was just one element in the total market; to think of it as the seat of the virtues was occasionally convenient, and sometimes just habitual, but never serious. Balsamo's essay is really a kind of answer to the unresolved questions of Pope's *Epistle to Bathurst*: in a society based upon money, there is really no such thing as virtuous work. The only evil is idleness, and the entrepreneur, in the country and the city, is always busy.

✿❀✿

During the eighteenth century as the recognition of the nature of commercial society began, fitfully, to form in men's minds, the classical idea of virtuous work had somehow to be worked into the expansive spirit of developing capitalism: a sense of moderation fitted to an enthusiasm for expansion, a disdain for luxury accommodated to a new recognition of the public utility of private desires, ever growing. In Virgil, to be sure, a similar pattern is apparent in that the growth of imperial Rome is somehow understood to be founded on the virtues of the rugged husbandman, the simple man who represents all that is good in Roman tradition. There is not, however, in Virgil any attempt to assimilate the evils of war, of luxury, of imperial expansion, to his vision of Roman rural virtue, which is allowed to remain as the controlling metaphor of the poem. Above all, the *Georgics* is marked by a sense of limits; the order of nature, the gods—these are the controlling forces of the poem. They impose the limits within which the empire may justly grow. To be sure, these limits may be breached, a recognition that tempers the enthusiastic celebrative mode of the poem by a tragic sense. Book one ends with a lament and a prayer—a lament for the wars Rome has fought, a prayer for the peace that empire may bring.

In the eighteenth century the sense of limits which in Virgil tended to create a tragic tone wherever certain recalcitrant facts like luxury, war, and bloodshed needed to be brought within the celebrative ambit of the poem—this sense of limits begins to disappear. A simple kind of excitement leading to a simple sense of optimism was one kind of response to the palpable fact of England's growing wealth and power. Though the imagination would call upon the old idea of virtuous work in its effort to celebrate and understand the abundance spreading over the nation, there was no way to come to grips with the evils of abundance except to deny that they were evils—unless, of course, one wrote satire. Replacing the tragic sense we discover in the *Georgics* was the extraordinarily useful idea of the public good as Mandeville understood it, and, as we have seen, Young and Balsamo expressed it. Since the public good was understood to thrive on many private evils, one could be duly enthusiastic about the workings of the political economy of abundance. It is not difficult, however, to see that the old idea of virtuous work is not to be easily worked into the Mandevillian notion of the public good. Poets and projectors went ahead and did so, of course, but not without considerable strain upon the art of the one and the integrity of the other.

Adam Smith is an important figure to consider here. Perhaps the leading theme of *The Wealth of Nations* is the argument that productivity, not treasure, is the real source of a nation's wealth and power. Again and again in *The Wealth of Nations* it is the shrewd, productive acquisitiveness of the independent, freely competing entrepreneur—both in agriculture and in manufactures—that comes in for Smith's special praise. Furthermore, the free and open system of political economy under which such a man best functions Smith describes as "just," "generous," and "liberal."[24] Nevertheless, the crucial further step of attributing virtue to the efficient work of the entrepreneur and to the system as a whole, Smith does not take.[25] Throughout his great work his personal predilections are clear enough—the disdain for luxury, the respect for productive efficiency—but Smith is extraordinarily careful to refrain from introducing into his thought any attempt to support his praise for productive efficiency by asserting the superior value of that style of work. It is not virtue, but the public good, which is its justification, and nowhere is he clearer about this than in his discussion of the breakdown of large feudal estates, a process which contributed to the public good, but, as the following passage makes sufficiently clear, resulted from the play of the vicious, vain, ridiculous, shrewd, mean, and selfish energies that men bring into the perilous marketplace of the public happiness. Smith writes:

> [W]hat all the violence of the feudal institutions could never have effected, the silent and insensible operation of foreign commerce and manufactures gradually brought about. . . . For a pair of diamond buckles perhaps, or for something as frivolous and useless, [the great barons] exchanged . . . the price of the maintenance of a thousand men for a year, and with it the whole weight and authority which it could give them. The buckles, however, were to be all their own, and no other human creature was to have any share of them. . . . [T]his difference was perfectly decisive; and thus, for the gratification of the most childish, the meanest and the most sordid of all vanities, they gradually bartered their whole power and authority. . . .

24. Adam Smith, *An Inquiry into the Nature and Causes of the Wealth of Nations*, ed. Edwin Cannan, 6th ed., 2 vols. (London: Methuen and Co., 1950), 2: 176. All citations are to this edition and identified as Smith. References are to volume and page.

25. In the *Theory of the Moral Sentiments* (1759) Smith does, however, dispute Mandeville's choice of the word "vice" to describe the self-interest or "self-love" which Smith saw motivating the economic behavior of men as producers and consumers (Smith, 1: xliii).

[Where a rich man] can spend the greatest revenue upon his own person, he frequently has no bounds to his expence, because he frequently has no bounds to his vanity, or to his affection for his own person. . . .

A revolution of the greatest importance to the public happiness, was in this manner brought about by two different orders of people, who had not the least intention to serve the public. To gratify the most childish vanity was the sole motive of the great proprietors. The merchants and artificers, much less ridiculous, acted merely from a view to their own interest, and in pursuit of their own pedlar principle of turning a penny wherever a penny was to be got. Neither of them had either knowledge or foresight of that great revolution which the folly of the one, and the industry of the other, was gradually bringing about [1:386–87, 389–90].

Quite as obvious as Smith's moralizing in this passage is the control he maintains over it. It is no edifying picture that emerges here of the play of forces which, ultimately, redounds to the public happiness. But the breakdown of large estates is fortunate; the pedlar principle is shrewd; the great proprietor is ridiculous, and the public happiness is greater. But surely the machinery of the public happiness is ethically dubious if not disastrous: one rises on another's fall. Pope could perceive no public happiness in such events, and Smith, for all of his perception of the greater good, does not pretend to see virtue in them. The productivity of the merchant and manufacturing classes he plainly admires, but, as we have seen, he also perceives and can label their virtues as "pedlar principles," recognizing the mean role they play in the production of the greater good. The point is that Smith avoids the cast of thought which would apply only to the productive skills the designation of virtuous labor; he seeks to dissociate any such habit of judgment from his consideration of the workings of political economy. The pedlar principles are generated by acquisitive shrewdness rather than temperance, and they contribute to a system equally dependent upon profligacy for its workings. They constitute no virtuous work in the old sense of that idea.

An important example of Smith's reluctance to attribute virtue to the processes of production and consumption is to be found in the course of his critique of the doctrines of the physiocrats.

Physiocratic thought leaned leavily on the idea that agriculture was the only genuinely productive industry; but this economic doctrine was buttressed by an attitude toward agriculture that expressed more than an interest in profit and loss. Leaning on ancient prejudices, the physiocrats found a superior virtue, as well as the only genuine productivity, in the occupation of tilling the soil. The economic argument was that agricultural industry annually provides a "neat produce" over and above what was required for the subsistence of the farmer: this was realized in the rent he paid to his landlord. On the other hand, artificers, manufacturers, and merchants annually reproduced nothing beyond the funds needed for their own subsistence. The burden of Smith's critique of physiocratic thinking is his refutation of this notion of productivity; he shows how the labor and produce of the manufacturer or merchant is "not at any one moment of time . . . greater than the value he consumes, yet at every moment of time the actually existing value of the goods in the market is, in consequence of what he produces, greater than it otherwise would be" (2:174).

The line of physiocratic reasoning on this point, furthermore, led to the conclusion that the farmer, because his labor uniquely produced more than he required for subsistence, could enjoy a style of life more easy, open, and generous than could the merchant or manufacturer. Since their annual work produced no real increment of value over the cost of their subsistence and materials, merchants or manufacturers could augment the wealth and revenue of their society only by parsimony, "that is, by depriving themselves of a part of the funds destined for their own subsistence" (2:166). From this line of reasoning, physiocratic thought ventured a step further to make a judgment of the character of men and of nations on the basis of the kind of industry they principally engaged in. As Smith represents the physiocrat doctrine on this point, it proceeds in this fashion: "Nations, therefore, which like France or England, consist in a great measure or proprietors and cultivators, can be enriched by industry and enjoyment. Nations on the contrary, which, like Holland and Hamburgh, are composed chiefly of merchants, artificers and manufacturers, can grow rich only through parsimony

and privation. As the interest of nations so differently circum-
stanced, is very different, so is likewise the common character of the
people. In those of the former kind, liberality, frankness, and good
fellowship, naturally make a part of that common character. In the
latter, narrowness, meanness, and a selfish disposition, averse to all
social pleasure and enjoyment" (2:166–67).

Smith responds to this argument, which is based more on literary
prejudice than economic analysis, by demonstrating that the only
means of increasing the real revenue of a society is by increasing
the efficiency of the workman or his machinery and the capital
which employs him. This, Smith maintains, holds true of both
agriculture and the industries of the town, sharply denying the
physiocratic effort to discover a happy accord between ethical and
economic value in terms of the virtue of the countryside.[26] Indeed,
Smith goes on to argue—on the principle of the greater efficiency of
those industries amenable to the division of labor—that the industries of the town must have the advantage over the industry of the
land in productivity. It thus comes about that the town is more
likely to enjoy the pleasures of consumption than is the countryside, or the primarily agricultural nation. But what is most important here is that Smith refuses to pursue his argument a step further
to assert the moral superiority of one form of work over another, as
did the physiocrats. His reasoning rejects the economic basis of the
physiocratic position that agricultural societies are happier than
commercial ones; but, interestingly enough, he does not even
bother to make the counterargument, which he could have sustained precisely in the terms put forth by the physiocrats: that the
economy of gain *is* the economy of contentment. He notes, certainly, that the inhabitants of an industrial or commercial nation
are likely to "enjoy a much greater quantity of subsistence than

26. "[Farmers] and country labourers can no more augment, without parsimony, the real revenue, the annual produce of the land and labour of their society,
than artificers, manufacturers and merchants [since] the annual produce of the
land and labour of any society can be augmented only in two ways: either first, by
some improvement in the productive powers of the useful labour actually maintained within it; or, secondly, by some increase in the quantity of that labour"
(Smith, 2: 174).

what their own lands, in the actual state of their cultivation, could afford," but that is his last word on the subject. About the greater happiness that might result from this "greater quantity of subsistence" he has nothing to say.

If, then, Smith rejects that tendency of physiocratic thought which attributes a peculiarly virtuous character to agricultural industry, he equally resists making the same kind of claim for the industry of the towns. There is, however, another and very interesting side to Smith's thinking about the nature of human work which we see in various observations he makes about the debilitating effects of the daily work experience of the town laborer. Kenneth MacLean shows that though Smith emphasizes the efficiency to be won from the division of labor, he also expresses considerable concern for the quality of life imposed upon the workman.[27] Yet nothing is clearer in *The Wealth of Nations* than Smith's advocacy of the division of labor as the very means of achieving the industrial efficiency which creates the real wealth of nations. Between the productivity of human industry which Smith so much admires, and the nature of the daily labor which creates it, there is, in Smith's thought, a kind of conflict which he himself defines, as we shall see, by falling back upon some notions about virtuous work that come from literary tradition, not from economic analysis.

Taking note of the debilitating effects of the routine daily labor of the factory worker, Smith proposes that the state may properly enter into the lives of its people by providing for the laboring poor the education that might yet make them decent citizens as well as adjuncts to their machines. One of the miserable effects of the division of labor he points to is the torpor it introduces into a man's soul, rendering him incapable of judging "of the great and extensive interests of his country . . . and . . . equally incapable of defending his country in war. The uniformity of his stationary life naturally corrupts the courage of his mind, and makes him regard with abhorrence the irregular, uncertain, and adventurous life of a soldier. It corrupts even the activity of his body, and renders him

27. Smith, 2: 267. See also MacLean, *Agrarian Age*, pp. 80–81.

incapable of exerting his strength with vigour and perseverence in any other employment than that to which he has been bred. *His dexterity at his own particular trade seems, in this manner, to be acquired at the expense of his intellectual, social, and martial virtues"* (2:267, italics added).[28]

Smith goes on to offer some observations on the manner in which the Greeks and Romans maintained, through publicly provided gymnastic instruction, the martial spirit of their people, a project which even were it "of no use toward the defense of the society, yet to prevent that sort of mental mutilation, deformity, and wretchedness, which cowardice necessarily involves in it, from spreading themselves through the great body of the people, would still deserve the most serious attention of government. . . ." (2:272). It seems clear that some sense of the public good more complex than that created by the play of economic self-interest is making itself felt here. The good citizen Smith seems to have in mind in these observations is very much like Virgil's rugged husbandmen, whose rural work, as we have seen, Virgil could describe in martial terms; whose alertness contrasts so clearly with the torpor Smith sees resulting from the division of labor; and whose identity as a Roman was somehow deeply involved in his rural work, developed as a poetic idea which could represent the meaning of Roman virtue. In short, the classical literary subjects of the georgic poem— virtuous work, the virtuous citizen, and the virtuous state—assert themselves as habits of judgment, even as controlling thoughts, at certain points in *The Wealth of Nations*—this despite the thrust of Smith's thought toward an understanding of political economy which would free itself of the inhibiting attitudes associated with classical tradition. But most important, Smith seems to have recog-

28. Samuel Hollander has pointed out the significance to Smith of "various extra-economic objectives" for public policy and notes as one of them the education of the poor "as a countervailing measure" to the "dehumanizing effects upon the labourer of one of the key requisites for [economic] growth, namely specialization." Hollander adds, however, that "there is no suggestion that economic growth should be slackened on these grounds" ("Adam Smith's Approach to Economic Development," *The Varied Pattern: Studies in the 18th Century*, ed. Peter Hughes and David Williams, 2 vols. [Toronto: A. M. Hakkert, 1971], 1: 293–94.

nized some fundamental conflict between, on the one hand, a system of work whose productive efficiency he admires and recognizes as the source of a nation's wealth, and, on the other hand, a set of desirable characteristics that are, simply, not likely to flourish in a people occupied in the production of a nation's wealth. It seems fair to conclude that while the major tendency of Smith's economic thought is to reject the attitudes I have been labeling as classical, their echo is still to be heard when the public good arises for consideration in terms more complex than a ledger can record.

It is in the context of his concern for the moral quality of daily labor that Smith's thinking about agriculture displays certain topical resemblances to bucolic literary tradition. In the first chapter of *The Wealth of Nations*, in the course of his discussion of the division of labor, Smith explains why agriculture, not easily adapted to that style of work, progresses in productive efficiency at a slower rate than manufactures. We have seen also that this line of argument is useful to him in his critique of the physiocratic doctrine of the superior productivity of agriculture. Now Smith, though he rejected the grounds of the physiocratic position, nevertheless expressed in several places considerable respect for agriculture. John Middendorf points out that "Smith attacked the Physiocrats for overstressing agriculture but nevertheless asserted its importance as an economic force and gave voice to many of the cliches praising agricultural life as more natural, secure, calm and independent than industrial life. . . . Moreover, Smith lauded the farmer as better informed, more intelligent, and morally and physically superior to the city worker."[29] These clichés, of course, are the very thematic substance of bucolic literary tradition. A very interesting intersection between Smith's economic thought and that tradition occurs in Smith's thinking about the small farmer, a matter over which he splits with Young and the physiocrats. Middendorf shows that Smith's praise for agriculture is centered in his admiration for the small farmer, not the improving and enclosing large holder. For Smith bigness in agriculture was as deplor-

29. Middendorf, "Arthur Young, Traveller and Observer," pp. 251–52.

able as bigness in industry. MacLean, too, has dealt with this aspect of Smith's thought, showing how the same admiration for the efficiency of the small and ambitious entrepreneur in manufactures and commerce is carried over to Smith's attitude toward the small farmer. As MacLean puts it, "the persistent agrarian image in *The Wealth of Nations* is not the leisurely country gentleman but the peasant, the dirt farmer, the man who makes his living on the soil with the labor of his own hands. Thinking in values other than those of profit and loss, Smith interprets fully the virtues of peasant life as he compares this type, not with the gentleman farmer, but with his fellow laborer in manufacturing."[30]

The dirt farmer enters Smith's discussion in that section where he delivers an attack against the monopolistic spirit, in this case its appearance in the industries of the town where the formation of guilds and the institution of apprenticeship come under Smith's scrutiny as obstacles to free competition. A major theme of *The Wealth of Nations* is Smith's argument that the industries of the town inevitably have a beneficial effect on the industry of agriculture and the life of the country; but in this place, arguing against one of the evils of town industry, Smith proposes an image of the country and of the country laborer which produces a contrast with the labor and character of the town—a contrast familiar from its regular thematic appearance in bucolic literature. It is worth quoting this passage at length:

> The inhabitants of a town, being collected into one place, can easily combine together. The most insignificant trades carried on in towns have accordingly, in some place or other, been incorporated; and even where they have never been incorporated, yet the corporation spirit, the jealousy of strangers, the aversion to take apprentices, or to communicate the secret of their trade, generally prevail in them and often teach them, by voluntary associations and agreements, to prevent that free competition which they cannot prohibit by bye-laws. . . .
>
> The inhabitants of the country, dispersed in distant places, cannot easily combine together. They have not only never been incorpor-

30. MacLean, *Agrarian Age*, p. 78. My discussion in the following pages is heavily indebted to MacLean, pp. 78–86.

ated, but the corporation spirit never has prevailed among them. No apprenticeship has ever been thought necessary to quality for husbandry, the great trade of the country. After what are called the fine arts, and the liberal professions, however, there is perhaps no trade which requires so great a variety of knowledge and experience. The innumerable volumes which have been written upon it in all languages, may satisfy us, that among the wisest and most learned nations, it has never been regarded as a matter very easily understood. And from all those volumes we shall in vain attempt to collect that knowledge of its various and complicated operations, which is commonly possessed by even the common farmer. . . .

The man who works upon brass and iron, works with instruments and upon materials of which the temper is always the same or very nearly the same. But the man who ploughs the ground with a team of horses or oxen, works with instruments of which the health, strength and temper, are very different upon different occasions. The condition of the materials which he works upon too is as variable as that of the instruments which he works with, and both require to be managed with much judgment and discretion. The common ploughman, though generally regarded as the pattern of stupidity and ignorance, is seldom defective in this judgment and discretion.... How much the lower ranks of people in the country are really superior to those of the town, is well known to every man whom either business or curiosity has led to converse much with both. In China and Indostan accordingly both the rank and wages of country labourers are said to be superior to those of the greater part of artificers and manufacturers. They would probably be so everywhere if corporation laws and the corporation spirit did not prevent it [1:127–29].

It is difficult to miss here the almost excessive length and the familiar rhetorical quality of his praise of the country, praise which goes quite beyond the immediate demands of Smith's argument. It is worth noting that at the end of book four, in his critique of the physiocrats, Smith points out that the economic development of China and Indostan was probably needlessly hampered by the excessive esteem and emphasis those nations placed upon agricultural industry; here, however, where he is out to score a point against the "corporate spirit" of the towns, he cites with approval the regard for agriculture demonstrated by those eastern nations. Once again we have, I think, an example of the ease with which the rhetoric associated with the countryside found its way into some rather strange corners. In this case Smith's praise of the simple farmer provides him with a rhetorical model of virtuous work, useful to him for the moment in the context of his argument for free trade. Smith has read through those "innumerable volumes" on agriculture he mentions and has clearly picked up their influence.

Furthermore, we may find in the foregoing passage another statement of Smith's concern for the quality of work done under the system of the division of labor. MacLean suggests that Smith's praise for the farmer's work—its varied nature, its tendency to engender alertness, the demands it makes upon a man's judgment—looks ahead to Wordsworth, who, in his worry over the barren experiences of the urban worker, saw a contrasting virtue in rural experience, whose rich variety sharpened a man's senses making of him a sensitive being, alive to the world and able to experience the world richly in his well-nourished imagination.[31] Certainly there is much in Wordsworth to support this suggestion, but it is equally true that Wordsworth was capable of a realism which, at this moment in Smith's argument, Smith wishes to ignore. These lines are from the *Excursion* and (remarkably) follow just such a lament for the blight of industrial town labor as Smith himself expressed. They are spoken by the "pale Recluse" as a response to his own attack on factory work. Now he directs his attention to the country laborer:

> Stiff are his joints;
> Beneath a cumbrous frock, that to the knees
> Invests the thriving churl, his legs appear,
> Fellows to those that lustily upheld
> The wooden stools for everlasting use,
> Whereon our fathers sate. And mark his brow!
> Under whose shaggy canopy are set
> Two eyes—not dim, but of a healthy stare—
> Wide, sluggish, blank, and ignorant, and strange—
> Proclaiming boldly that they never drew
> A look or motion of intelligence. . . .

31. Ibid., p. 80.

What penetrating power of sun or breeze,
Shall e'er dissolve the crust wherein his soul
Sleeps, like a caterpillar, sheathed in ice?
This torpor is no pitiable work
Of Modern ingenuity; no town
Nor crowded city can be taxed with aught
Of sottish vice or desperate breach of law,
To which (and who can tell where or how soon?)
He may be roused. This Boy the fields produce: . . .
In brief, what liberty of *mind* is here?

[8:402–12, 417–25, 433][32]

Against this realism Adam Smith's argument must strike us as peculiarly "literary." His fear for the martial and civic virtues of the urban worker is more easily understood with reference to Virgil's vision of virtuous rural labor than as an anticipation of Wordsworth.

To Smith's image of the virtuous labor of the dirt farmer, we may contrast the gentleman farmer of Arthur Young. He is a large landholder, and one of his chief projects is to increase his holdings so that farming in his domains may proceed more efficiently. We have seen already that Young could call upon the rhetorical traditions of bucolic literature in his advocacy of large-scale farming, just as certain features of the same rhetorical tradition help to fill out Smith's image of the virtuous labor of the small farmer. As MacLean has shown an interesting opposition begins to emerge between Young's enthusiasm for large-scale farming and Smith's praise of the small farmer. Young, of course, is thinking in terms of productive efficiency; Smith is thinking about the moral character of the laborer and his work. Young takes a striking further step in his thought when he applies Smith's thinking on the division of labor to agriculture, seeking to achieve for agriculture that productivity which the manufacturing industries obtain from the specialization of tasks. In an article published in 1804 Young concedes that by its very nature agricultural work is not easily adapted to the

32. William Wordsworth, *The Poetical Works of William Wordsworth,* ed. Thomas Hutchinson, 2nd ed. rev. (1936; reprinted, London, New York, Toronto: Oxford University Press, 1953), p. 686. The quotation from *The Excursion* is identified by book and line numbers in my text.

division of labor: "Agriculture will not admit of this . . . *but the nearer we approach to this the better: which can only be on a larger farm*"[33] (italics added).

Young's suggestion that the division of labor be in some measure applied to farming rests on Smith's argument for the efficiency of this style of work. Indeed, Young's article introduces the suggestion by quoting the famous account of the manufacture of pins. Interestingly enough, Young shows no interest in Smith's reservations about the quality of work so performed and its effects on the character of the workman. All of which is to say no more than that in Young's thinking about agricultural efficiency, as in Smith's thought on industrial productivity, there arises a conflict between the character of work and its simply economic results. A writer who called upon bucolic literary tradition to support his schemes for agricultural improvement and a writer for whom bucolic tradition provided the model of virtuous labor to contrast with his model of productive labor—both fail to bridge the gap between what is good and what is profitable. Yet each of them works with the same *rhetorical* definition of virtuous labor. It is perhaps not injudicious to conclude that the real countryside was beginning to bear little enough resemblance to the literary one and that the literary countryside, insofar as it still remained in men's imaginations as an emblem of virtuous work and the virtuous society, had little enough to do with any kind of reality, urban or rural. What effect this state of affairs had on the poetry of social criticism has long been recognized in Goldsmith's *Deserted Village:* as MacLean and, later, Williams point out, Goldsmith simply fails to locate the actual source of the evil he sees infesting English rural life. Obviously he ought to have leveled some of his attack at rural enthusiasts like Young, for whom at times the countryside was just another corner of the national market. But this gap between rhetoric and reality is to be seen in the art of those who took a more optimistic view of the rural situation, as well as in the art of a man like Cowper, whose use of bucolic rhetorical tradition is more complex than that of any other poet of his time.

33. Quoted in Paul Mantoux, *The Industrial Revolution in the Eighteenth Century*, trans. Marjorie Vernon, rev. ed. (London: Jonathan Cape, 1961), p. 177.

In this sketch of the thinking of Young, Balsamo, and Smith, I
have pointed to some of the ways in which contemporary economic
and social concerns intersected with some of the habits and attitudes of bucolic literary tradition as men struggled, inconclusively,
to frame an understanding of what was happening to English
society and the English countryside under the pressure of capitalist
expansion. What we discover mainly is the unsuccessful search for
standards of moral and political judgment adequate both to the
celebration of the positive possibilities of capitalist industry and to
the criticism of its depredations. For how could men so wrench
their habits of sight and judgment as to define and value the
positive possibilities in an order of production and consumption
whose special power to respond to energies and desires exceeding
all limit must have seemed to them to place it beyond good and
evil? In the end even Adam Smith could not steadfastly face the
necessary and melancholy restriction of moral concern now to
man's inner and private life only. Smith's thought resembles in
this the period's bucolic poetry, with its fitful approach toward and
withdrawal from that difficult recognition. It is no wonder that the
reconstitution of bucolic writing in the next century is also a
reconstitution of lyric expression. Much was gained in this, but
what was lost was irrecoverable: that blend of public and personal
expression so characteristic of the eighteenth century's wish for the
union of the ethical and the political. In the later establishment of
a new pastoral lyric, the georgic was lost, inevitably so, its vision of
good work and public virtue at odds entirely with the private,
implicitly critical lyric, whose pastoral force, as Raymond Williams has shown, absorbs nature into the private self where both
become antagonists of culture and its economy of desire and gain.[34]

34. Williams, *The Country and the City*, pp. 140–41. "What we find in Clare is
not Jonson's idealisation of a landscape yielding of itself, nor Thomson's idealisation of a productive order that is scattering and guarding plenty. There was a
conscious reaction to this [already] in Goldsmith, in Langhorne, and in Crabbe.
But there was also an unconscious reaction, to a country from which any accept-
able social order had been decisively removed. Clare goes beyond the external
observation of the poems of protest and of melancholy retrospect. *What happens
in him is that the loss is internal.* It is to survive at all, as a thinking and feeling
man, that he needs the green language of the new Nature" (italics added).

III

Two Worlds of Work: John Dyer's *The Fleece*

English wealth and English power are the subjects of Dyer's georgic on the wool industry, and we have noted already the celebrative tone his poem assumes as it contemplates its subjects. Enthusiasm for the spectacle of wealth and power, however, was not unusual, even among those who were able to view it with a critical eye. Spectacle is the appropriate word here, because England's might presented itself to the eye, and although the judgment may have had its reservations, the eye could not deny the expansive activity it saw. Henry Fielding, for example—whose *Journal of a Voyage to Lisbon* (1755) is in some part a log of the corruption that had begun to creep into the lives of even the simplest proprietors as they grasped for their share of the wealth they sensed lying about them—also acknowledges the spectacle his eye encounters as his boat begins to move out of London harbor: sailing down the Thames he tells us that "there is nothing to equal it in all the rivers of the world."

> The yards of Deptford and of Woolwich are noble sights; and give us a just idea of the great perfection to which we are arrived in building those floating castles, and the figure which we may always make in Europe among the other maritime powers. That of Woolwich, at least, very strongly imprinted this idea on my mind; for, there was now on the stocks there the Royal Anne, supposed to be the largest ship ever built, and which contains ten carriage guns more than had ever yet equipped a first rate . . .
> We saw likewise several Indiamen just returned from their voyage.

These are, I believe, the largest and finest vessels which are any where employed in commercial affairs. The colliers, likewise, which are very numerous, and even assemble in fleets, are ships of great bulk; and, if we descend to those used in the American, African and European trades, and pass through those which visit our own coasts, to the small craft that ly between Chatham and the Tower, the whole forms a most pleasing object to the eye, as well as highly warming to the heart of an Englishman, who has any degree of love for his country, or can recognize any effect of the patriot in his constitution.

Lastly, the Royal Hospital of Greenwich, which presents so delightful a front to the water, and doth such honour at once to its builder and the nation, to the great skill and ingenuity of the one, and to the no less sensible gratitude of the other, very properly closes the account of this scene; which may well appear romantic to those who have not themselves seen, that, in this one instance, truth and reality are capable, perhaps, of exceeding the power of fiction.[1]

Fielding emphasizes the visual effect of the harbor, with its bustling activity, its ships, its shoreside edifices standing as monuments to England's skill, power, and wealth. He excuses himself from appearing to be "romantic" in his enthusiasm for the scene, and maintains that truth and reality, in this case, exceed the power of fiction. The effect of the harbor spectacle is to evoke a rapturous response from even one of its most critical observers. Much of what preceded and will follow this description of the busy Thames depicts the miserable plight of Fielding as a passenger on board one of the very boats which made up the river scene: his dependence upon the captain, the captain's arrogant greed, and the passenger's uncomfortable awareness that he had, for the duration of his voyage, become a commodity to be exploited, first by the captain, and later by some miserable innkeepers as they try vigorously to extract some coin from him, their share of the busy activity in the harbor. And yet, despite his awareness of the seamy side of commercial vigor, Fielding cannot help responding to the simple and stunning surface it presents, the visible energy of England's

1. Henry Fielding, *The Journal of a Voyage to Lisbon*, ed. Harold E. Pagliaro (New York: Nardon Press, 1963), pp. 53, 55.

wealth. At the same time, the passenger's dismal experiences in the midst of so much gain getting make a judgment of all this very visible commercial energy a difficult matter.

Dyer's poem, too, has its enthusiastic vision of the harbor, which he links with his praise for the bountiful English countryside. Celebrating the fields, crops, and flocks of rural England, he joins his praise of the countryside to his enthusiasm for London's commercial vitality.

> To these thy naval streams,
> Thy frequent towns superb of busy trade,
> And ports magnific, add, and stately ships
> Innumerous. But whither strays my Muse?
> Pleas'd, like a traveller upon the strand
> Arriv'd of bright Augusta, wild he roves,
> From deck to deck, thro' groves immense of masts;
> 'Mong crowds, bales, cars, the wealth of either Ind;
> Thro' wharfs, squares, and palaces, and domes,
> In sweet surprise, unable yet to fix
> His raptur'd mind, or scan in order'd course
> Each object singly, with discoveries new
> His native country studious to enrich.
> . . . .
>
> See the silver maze
> Of stately Thamis, ever checker'd o'er
> With deeply-laden barges, gliding smooth
> And constant as his stream: in growing pomp,
> By Neptune still attended, slow he rolls
> To great Augusta's mart, where lofty Trade
> Amid a thousand golden spires enthron'd,
> Gives audience to the world; the strand around
> Close swarms with busy crowds of many a realm.
> What bales, what wealth, what industry, what fleets!
>
> [1:172–84; 3:622–31][2]

Fielding responded to the harbor scene with a kind of enthusiasm that he felt to verge on the "romantic," and which seemed to move

2. John Dyer, *The Fleece* in *The Poems of John Dyer*, ed. Edward Thomas (London: T. Fisher Unwin, 1903). All subsequent references to *The Fleece* are cited in my text by book and line numbers.

his journal from critical reporting over the line to fiction; he needed to reassure his reader that his account of the harbor was true and real. But in *The Fleece* the harbor *is* seen by a poet—the line has been crossed from reporting to fiction, and the poet's enthusiasm is of the same order as the reporter's. It is likely that these few lines from *The Fleece* may strike us immediately as examples of a rhetoric grossly exaggerated, a rhetoric which imitates the forms of Virgil's and Milton's verse, and falsifies experience in doing so. Yet it seems not too much to suggest that this rhetoric is the result of an honest search for a mode of expression adequate to represent the feelings and experiences of the poet, raptures felt even by a critical observer of commercial progress like Fielding. Dyer's poetry, successful or not, is trying to tell us the truth about what the poet sees and understands of his wealthy and powerful England. The rapturous rhetoric serves to express the poet's enthusiasm, just as Fielding, writing as a reporter, also gave way to expansive feelings at the same spectacle. Apparently, to be moved by the vision of commercial plenitude was something of a national experience, and both the reporter and the poet express their patriotic pride quite openly after seeing the busy harbor of England's capital. Celebration asserts itself over criticism, for the moment at least in Fielding's journal, and for the duration of Dyer's poem.[3]

The strain of London rapture we discover in the first of the above

3. Josephine Miles has offered the richest insights into the stylistic character of poems like Dyer's, which she sees as "the prevailing eighteenth-century poem . . . risen from sources in English efforts at heroic poetry, [and] strengthened by new versions of classical practice. . . . For one whole century it dominated the world of English poetry . . . an exceptionally panoramic and panegyric verse, emotional, pictorial, noble, universal, and tonal, rising to the height of heaven and of feeling in the style traditionally known as grand or sublime" (*Eras and Modes in English Poetry* [Berkeley and Los Angeles: University of California Press, 1964], pp. 56–57). John Chalker in his *The English Georgic: A Study in the Development of a Form* (London: Routledge, and Kegan Paul, 1969), similarly emphasizes the enthusiastic and heroic character of this poetry, but Chalker seems to reflect a modern unease with their grand rhetoric, which he interprets throughout as a vehicle capable of "a saving element of self-mockery," itself a sign of the georgic poet's "fondness for the exploration of multiple viewpoints." See pp. 51–55, 123–39, 210–11. Other modern criticism on *The Fleece*, all of it very brief, is to be found in Ralph M. Williams, *Poet, Painter, Parson: The Life of John Dyer* (New York: Bookman Associates, 1956), pp. 136–37; Bonamy Dobrée, "The Theme of Patriotism in the Poetry of the Early Eighteenth Century," *Proceedings of the British*

passages of *The Fleece* emerges as if accidentally and quite suddenly from a section devoted to the praise of the English countryside, rapturous praise of the sky, the meadows, the brooks, and the sheep. To these elements of the pastoral landscape the poet adds the towns and ports and stately ships of England's commercial enterprise. The great theme of *The Fleece*—England's wealth through wool—of course demanded that the husbandry of the pasture, the industry of the factory, and the trade of the merchants be brought together to form an integrated vision of virtuous work; the poem's theme necessarily brings together shepherd and merchant, country and town, nature and art into a union emblematic of that virtuous work which sustains English power. And throughout *The Fleece* the union of nature and art in England's sheep and textile industry is simply asserted; this ancient category of judgment, nature and art, is easily adapted by Dyer to his celebrative purpose in his poem written in praise of English power and wealth. That power and that wealth are thus placed within the order of nature, and once there, understood as aspects of English virtue.

The praise of art, of civilizing toil, is, of course, a regular theme of georgic tradition, and we have seen how Virgil's treatment of human labor asserts the fortunate aspects of Jove's harsh edict which ushered in the iron age and with it human civilization. Dyer restates this old idea:

> Ev'n Nature lives by toil:
> Beast, bird, air, fire, the heav'ns, and rolling worlds,
> All live by action: nothing lies at rest
> But death and ruin: man is born to care;
> Fashion'd, improv'd, by labour.
>
> . . . .

Academy 35 (1949): 49–66; O. H. K. Spate, "The Muse of Mercantilism," *Studies in the Eighteenth Century: Papers Presented at the David Nichol Smith Memorial Seminar, Canberra 1966,* ed. R. F. Brissenden (Toronto: University of Toronto Press, 1968), pp. 119–32; A. J. Sambrook, "The English Lord and the Happy Husbandman," *Studies in Voltaire and the Eighteenth Century* 57 (1967): 1357–75; and also Sambrook's "An Essay on Eighteenth-Century Pastoral, Pope to Wordsworth, Part II," *Trivium* 6 (1971): 103–15.

> What simple Nature yields
> (And Nature does her part) are only rude
> Materials, cumbers on the thorny ground;
> 'Tis toil that makes them wealth. . . .
>
> [3:22-25, 35-38]

The terms nature and art pervade the poem not only as categories of thought but, perhaps more importantly as habits of feeling and of imagination. The terms structure Dyer's approach to his subject and recur again and again in various forms, explicitly and implicitly. For example, in a brief glance at some new machines used in spinning, Dyer sees them as "curious instruments of speed" which

> obtain
> Various advantage, and the diligent
> Supply with exercise, as fountains sure
> Which ever-gliding feed the flow'ry lawn. . . .
>
> [3:91-94]

The language here compresses the worlds of nature and art: first there is the simple simile likening the spinning machinery to fountains: the image is one of bounty, for the rivers nourish the "flow'ry lawn." But beneath the simple analogy lies the metaphor implied in diction which identifies rivers with fountains and fields with lawns. The landscape here is the bucolic middle ground— nature civilized by art, not the primitive wilderness lying beyond the cultivated fields, nor the sophisticated city at the other boundary of experience. Machines are like rivers, but rivers are fountains and fields are lawns. The entire scene asserts the virtue of human toil in its partnership with nature: the industrial and bucolic scenes merge to benefit the diligent. The diligent, of course, are the proprietors of the machines and the hands who run them. The language succeeds in placing both classes metaphorically into the countryside, workers and owners become swains, and an early moment in the industrial revolution is seen as anything but revolutionary—seen, indeed, within the timeless bucolic vision of the virtuous and bountiful countryside, which retains its rhetorical status as the normative center of the poem: if machines are good things, then they are transmuted into rural images. And this rhetorical habit pervades the poem: the industry of the loom harmonizes with the music of rural nature:

> . . . let the sounding loom
> Mix with the melody of every vale. . . .
>
> [3:398–99]

The action of the loom's shuttle and frame is like the ocean's waves: "the thready shuttle glides along the lines,"

> And ever and anon, to firm the work,
> Against the web is driv'n the noisy frame,
> That o'er the level rushes, like a surge
> Which, often dashing on the sandy beach,
> Compacts the traveller's road. . . .
>
> [3:137–41]

The growing of the woven web is like the spread of light across the skies at dawn:

> . . . the web apace
> Increases, as the light of eastern skies
> Spread by the rosy fingers of the morn. . . .
>
> [3:143–45]

The labor of the fuller, the clothier and the burler—engaged in the industry of cloth making—is likened to the labor of the farmer, and put into rhetorical juxtaposition with it:

> Soon the clothier's shears
> And burler's thistle skim the surface sheen.
> The round of work goes on from day to day,
> Season to season. So the husbandman
> Pursues his cares; his plough divides the glebe;
> The seed is sown; rough rattle o'er the clods
> The harrow's teeth; quick weeds his hoe subdues;
> The sickle labours, and the slow team strains,
> Till grateful harvest home rewards his toils.
>
> [3:175–83]

The narrator's enthusiasm—which we see in the harbor vision—for London's commercial energy and activity is thus an aspect of the poem's larger theme, the harmony of nature and art in human industry. Adapting this familiar topic of bucolic literature to the contemporary experience of a burgeoning industry and a growing commercial enterprise, Dyer's poem seeks to identify England's new growth as a product of the virtuous work sustaining human civilization, the virtuous work established by Virgil as the subject of the georgic genre.

Dyer's rhetoric, then, manages to assert without much difficulty a vision of human work and human society that was increasingly difficult to maintain, whether one had misgivings about the new wealth, as did Pope, or whether one was enthusiastic about it, as was Balsamo, and to some degree Smith. And if today we see an eighteenth-century georgic poem like *The Fleece* as a dead end, a failed form of expression, it surely must be because we sense that Dyer, untroubled by the doubts and uneasy insights of the less exuberant of his contemporaries, could compose his poem in a celebrative mode with a rhetoric surging blindly past some discomfiting facts. I have already pointed to a passage which sings delightedly about the happy toil of the factory hand and must strike us today as an unfortunate triumph of rhetorical habit over plain experience:

> . . . the tender eye
> May view the maim'd, the blind, the lame, employ'd,
> And unreject'd age: ev'n childhood there
> Its little fingers turning to the toil
> Delighted: nimbly, with habitual speed,
> They sever lock from lock . . .
>
> [2:79–84]

Adam Smith, the proponent of the division of labor, never expressed such unchecked enthusiasm for the healthy joy of industrial work; indeed, as we have seen, he rather feared its moral consequences. Dyer's picture of two weavers working together

> While friendly converse, prompted by the work,
> Kindles improvement in the op'ning mind . . .
>
> [3:151–52]

glaringly contrasts with Smith's frightening sense of the dispiriting torpor of such labor.[4] The attempt to understand new experiences in old terms is a feature of parts of Smith's work too, and Balsamo's and Young's and Pope's. Essentially, this is Dyer's effort also, and we may expect his poem to show the strain of his effort in unresolved problems or in conflicting attitudes toward the subject matter of the poetry.

As Leo Marx has shown in his study of the impact of expanding commerce and technology on early nineteenth-century American thought, one major response to the new machines and their produce was strongly optimistic. It was easy for some men to bring the machine into the garden and to respond to its new energy not with misgivings but with a kind of enthusiastic faith that these engines of power would fit in with, not render obsolete, the pastoral virtues thought to be embodied in the American nation. Dyer's georgic displays a similar response to the experiences that were changing the nature of English life. Bringing the machine into the garden was simple enough for Dyer: he simply put it there and declared, in terms appropriate to bucolic literature, that it belonged. The young women who earned their livelihood by spinning thread were, understandably, upset at the sight of that product of "patient art," the spiral engine:

> But patient art,
> That on experience works, from hour to hour,
> Sagacious, has a spiral engine form'd,
> Which on an hundred spoles, an hundred threads,
> With one huge wheel, by lapse of water, twines,
> Few hands requiring, easy-tended work,
> That copiously supplies the greedy loom.

[3:79–85]

4. Although Dyer is thinking here of cottage industry, whereas Smith's fears arose from his observations of factory labor, the point holds. Dyer consistently responded with simple enthusiasm to the prospect of mechanized industry, and his poem contains several exuberant passages on the rudimentary engines around which factory production began to be organized prior to the steam engine. For a detailed account of the happy labor of a factory hand, an account emphasizing the spirited vigor of the worker, see *The Fleece*, 3: 263–85. See also *A Book of English Pastoral Verse*, John Barrell and John Bull, ed. (New York: Oxford University Press, 1975), p. 298.

But Dyer reassures them:

> Nor hence, ye Nymphs! let anger cloud your brows;
> The more is wrought the more is still requir'd:
> Blithe o'er your toils, with wonted song, proceed:
> Fear not surcharge; your hands will ever find
> Ample employment.
>
> [3:86–90]

Yet how much comfort might the girls have been expected to take from such rhetoric when we consider the poet's subsequent delighted astonishment at another new device,

> A circular machine, of new design,
> In conic shape: it draws and spins a thread
> Without the tedious toil of needless hands. . . .
>
> One, intent,
> O'erlooks the work. . . .
>
> [3:292–94, 297–98]

This new machine has, in its efficiency, relegated the domestic spinning of the angry nymphs to the category of "tedious toil." Was Dyer telling the truth, then, or was he merely using rhetoric, when he earlier characterized the traditional domestic spinning of the village nymphs in rather different terms:

> Come, village Nymphs, ye Matrons, and ye Maids!
> Receive the soft material; with light step
> Whether ye turn around the spacious wheel,
> Or, patient-sitting, that revolve which forms
> A narrower circle. On the brittle work
> Point your quick eye, and let the hand assist
> To guide and stretch the gently lessening thread;
> Even, unknotted, twine will praise your skill.
> A diff-rent spinning every diff-rent web
> Asks from your glowing fingers; some require
> The more compact and some the looser wreath;
> The last for softness, to delight the touch
> Of chamber'd delicacy; scarce the cirque
> Need turn around, or twine the length'ning flake.
>
> [3:51–64]

No tedious toil, the work here is rhetorically raised: it is "brittle" work, requires skill, and that skill is supplied by "glowing fingers" and a "quick eye." Which, then, is Dyer's model of virtuous toil: the heightened picture of the skillful girl at the spinning wheel, or the single operator of the circular machine? The first has been praised rhetorically, the second, literally, and by implication. Internal consistency is, perhaps, the first victim of the strain imposed by new experiences on old habits of thought. The world was ready to make the choice between the labor of village nymphs and the more efficient production of the circular engine. Dyer does not acknowledge the necessity for that choice.

It is, finally, difficult to discern in *The Fleece* an awareness of any strain between the old and the new, and perhaps that is the very meaning of the poet's choice of the georgic mode for his celebration of England's new power and wealth. To choose the georgic mode is to assert that these new energies and engines are not incompatible with the old virtues and institutions celebrated in the georgic mode. It is for this reason that the poet can express astonished delight in the machinery of England's new industry; at the same time, in his heroic fable of the fashioning of a loom, he can declare that no needful art is new. The weaver's loom,

> The curious engine, work of subtle skill;
> Howe'er in vulgar use around the globe
> Frequent observ'd, of high antiquity
> No doubtful mark: th' adventurous voyager,
> Toss'd over ocean to remotest shores,
> Hears on remotest shores the murm'ring loom,
> Sees the deep-furrowing plough and harrow'd field,
> The wheel-mov'd wagon, and the discipline
> Of strong-yok'd steers. What needful art is new?
>
> [3:121–29]

Yet, scarcely thirty lines later we encounter the aphorism "Modern invention; modern is the want" to explain the development of more sophisticated kinds of looms designed to weave new kinds of cloth, newly demanded by the awakened desires of the consuming population. Thus, despite his obvious receptivity to the new wonders of industrial technology, and despite his enthusiasm for the wealth created by the new commerce, Dyer seems to lack any clear sense of being at a crossroads in human history, a sense of choice or of crisis. His rhetoric denies the widening gulf between the old and the new, permitting him to express his enthusiasm for the new without critically examining its implications for the bucolic vision which that rhetoric springs from, and for the kind of social order it celebrates.[5]

❧❧❧

The picture Dyer gives us of London harbor expresses the poet's enthusiasm for the world of wealth and power that is the new England. Enthusiasm becomes rapture in Dyer's rhetoric: he is taken by "sweet surprise, unable yet to fix/His raptur'd mind" upon the harbor spectacle. He cannot "scan in order'd course" each object of trade he sees before him. "Wild he roves" among the ships, and the ships are "innumerous," "groves immense of masts." This rhetoric, if we were not told its subject, would immediately suggest some wild landscape, and a possessed narrator: it is the rhetoric of the sublime. The poet tells us quite clearly that his state of mind is far too excited to order his observations; in the throes of an experience that does not submit to order, he roves wildly, his muse strays. The rhetoric seeks to convey an experience that defies common limits as it moves into a realm where things present themselves under the aspect of the infinite, not the ordered. So we have "ships innumerous," and "groves immense"; rhetorically the simple list is the only adequate means to express the disordered profusion of wealth the narrator sees in excitement:

5. Patricia M. Spacks discusses the similar pattern of Thomson's conflicting enthusiasms for the energies of the English nation on the one hand, and the beauties and sublimities of nature on the other; she sees this conflict, insofar as it distorts *The Seasons*, as evidence of Thomson's general limitations as a poet as well as of the extraordinary diversity of ideas and attitudes available to an alert citizen of Thomson's age (*The Varied God: A Critical Study of Thomson's "The Seasons"* [Berkeley: University of California Press, 1959], pp. 167–75). Chalker traces this attitudinal conflict back to Virgil, whose *Georgics* he understands to contain the similarly contradictory enthusiasms for rural retirement and Augustus's Rome. John Barrell and John Bull (*A Book of English Pastoral Verse*, pp. 295–97) comment efficiently on this matter.

> 'Mong crowds, bales, cars, the wealth of either Ind;
> Thro' wharfs, squares, and palaces and domes . . .

and later

> What bales, what wealth, what industry, what fleets! . . .
>   [1:179–80; 3:631]

The enraptured rhetoric is, however, only one of the expressive patterns of *The Fleece*. It belongs to London's harbor and England's international trade, and expresses the sense of infinite possibility—of wealth and of experience—inherent in that harbor and its trade. Dyer's vision of the city *is* romantic in that sense, and is like F. Scott Fitzgerald's view of the white buildings that make up Manhattan island; seen from a sufficient distance and a proper perspective, the buildings represent wealth in its "good" aspect— the magic substance that opens the doors of new possibilities, strange experiences. Fitzgerald calls this magic substance "non-olfactory money." When he views its effects from the Fifty-ninth Street Bridge at the right time of day, the money does not smell.

There is, though, another range of experiences portrayed in the poem, another rhetoric, and another center of value: the experience, rhetoric, and norms of the pastoral countryside. We hear it, for example, in such set pieces as the celebration of the small cottager's work, his care for the land:

> I knew a careful swain . . .
> . . . oft with labour-strengthened arm he delv'd
> The draining trench across his verdant slopes,
> To intercept the small meandring rills
> Of upper hamlets. Haughty trees, that sour
> The shaded grass, that weaken thorn set mounds,
> And harbour villain crows, he rare allow'd;
> Only a slender tuft of useful ash,
> And mingled beech and elm, securely tall,
> The little smiling cottage warm embower'd;
> The little smiling cottage! where at eve
> He meets his rosy children at the door
> Prattling their welcomes, and his honest wife,
> With good brown cake and bacon slice, intent
> To cheer his hunger after labour hard.
>   [1:108, 111–24]

This passage belongs to the line of rural praise set out in Virgil's *O fortunatos nimium* theme. The immediate context of the passage is a didactic discussion of trees: the decorative as opposed to agricultural virtues of various kinds of landscaping. The passage is nicely turned into an emblematic account of modesty and order. Certain spectacular trees, whose size harms the land, come to be called "haughty"; and the modest cottager who is also, perforce, the good farmer ("careful swain"), selects only "slender," "useful," and "securely tall" trees to embower his cottage—"the little smiling cottage." His skill in husbandry, his taste in landscape, his cottage, and his supper—"good brown cake and bacon slice"—are all of a piece. They portray the virtues of modest possession, not infinite riches. We come back here to the linking of temperance with the quality of virtuous work. As we might expect, the appropriate expressive framework for this set of attitudes is the idyll, the little picture, a mode quite distinct from the sublime vein Dyer uses for his London rapture.

The small cottager's virtues—his associated modesty and skill—are thus part of an appropriate landscape: the trees of modest height, the humble, embowered cottage are literary ideas as well as aspects of an actual landscape. Even if we knew nothing of bucolic tradition it would not be difficult to recognize the praise of modesty and temperance implied in the landscape surrounding the humble cottage. But, in fact, *The Fleece* is pervaded by those familiar attitudes of bucolic tradition, of which the humble cottager is only one representative. Perhaps the most curious instance of the author's use of that tradition comes as the conclusion to the first book of *The Fleece*, not many lines past the set piece on the humble cottager. The conclusion to the first book is, in fact, an exact replica of an eclogue. Book one of *The Fleece* is devoted to the care of sheep: the pasture they flourish on, the climate they prosper in, the diseases they sicken from. The other three books are concerned with the wool industry: weaving, dyeing, clothmaking and trade. Since the subject of book one is, in fact, about country labor, the poet's decision to conclude with a brief eclogue is, in one sense, appropriate. It raises, however, some interesting questions.

Moderation is the theme of Dyer's treatment of the small cottager. However, the cottager is seen as a workman; Dyer makes no attempt to romanticize or to heighten the quality of his work, which is the virtuous, very real, and difficult work characteristically the subject of the georgic form; it is described in some detail, and with a specific didactic purpose. Furthermore, it is set within a real segment of the landscape: we read of trenches there, and crows. The land needs hard work. But between the lines on the humble cottager and the eclogue concluding book one, the poet makes a survey of the earth's geography: this permits him to work into his poem the set pieces that the contemporary reader might have come to expect since Thomson's *Seasons*. Dyer gives us the Lapland scene, the torrid zone, and a few intervening areas that, for one reason, or another, he wishes to fit into the poem. But throughout this journey the centrally developed theme has to do with the special virtue of England's climate for the sheep raiser. "Sheep no extremes can bear," Dyer tells us, and therefore the temperate quality of England's climate enters into the poem in a way that suggests a bountiful middle ground, a kind of magic landscape within which the fortunate swain enjoys something of the condition of the golden age. The poem shifts from its emphasis on the real toil of the hardworking farmer to the magical, emblematic labor of the golden age; and, therefore, the mode of social celebration shifts as well: England becomes the new Arcadia, and its shepherds accordingly become like the swains of Virgil's eclogues, not the husbandmen of his *Georgics*.

> With grateful heart, ye British Swains! enjoy
> Your gentle seasons and indulgent clime . . .
> Ye, happy at your ease, behold your sheep
> Feed on the open turf, or crowd the tilth,
> Where, thick among the greens, with busy mouths
> They scoop white turnips: little care is yours. . . .
> [1:462–63, 481–84]

Dyer has shifted from a mode of celebration based upon the real, hard work of the English farmer to one based upon the golden age, echoes of which are heard on England's greens.

> At shearing-time along the lively vales
> Rural festivities are often heard;
> Beneath each blooming arbour all is joy
> And lusty merriment. While on the grass
> The mingled youth in gaudy circles sport,
> We think the Golden Age again return'd,
> And all the fabled Dryades in dance:
> Leering they bound along, with laughing air,
> To the shrill pipe, and deep remurm'ring-cords
> Of the ancient harp, or tabor's hollow sound,
>
> While th'old apart, upon a bank reclin'd,
> Attend the tuneful carol, softly mix'd
> With every murmur of the sliding wave,
> And every warble of the feather'd choir,
> Music of Paradise! which still is heard
> When the heart listens, still the views appear
> Of the first happy garden, when Content
> To Nature's flowery scenes directs the sight.
> Yet we abandon those Elysian walks,
> Then idly for the lost delight repine;
> As greedy mariners, whose desp'rate sails
> Skim o'er the billows of the foamy flood,
> Fancy they see the lessening shores retire,
> And sigh a farewell to the sinking hills.
>
> [1:601–24]

This is a curious passage. Having shifted from the realistic vein of the georgic, with its emphasis upon the toil that sustains civilization, the poem now gives itself over to the contemplation of innocence. Not the busy harbor of London, not the virtuous moderation of the humble cottager, the normative center is now the first happy garden, where men knew content. And, *mirabile dictu*, the ethically contrasting image is that of the "greedy mariners" and their "desperate sails." Yet these greedy mariners were presumably in the throes of an energy that, earlier in the poem, excited raptures in the poet's breast as he surveyed, breathless, the ships of the London harbor!

The poet then tries to remember, to

> recall those notes which once the Muse
> Heard at a shearing, near the woody sides
> Of blue-topp'd Wreakin! Yet the carols sweet

Thro' the deep maze of the memorial cell
Faintly remurmur. First arose in song
Hoar-headed Damon, venerable Swain!
The soothest shepherd of the flow'ry vale,
"This is no vulgar scene; no palace roof
Was e'er so lofty, nor so nobly rise
Their polish'd pillars as these aged oaks,
Which o'er our Fleecy wealth and harmless sports
Thus have expanded wide their shelt'ring arms
Thrice told an hundred summers. Sweet Content,
Ye gentle shepherds! pillow us at night."

"Yes, tuneful Damon, for our cares are short,
Rising and falling with the cheerful day,"
Colin reply'd; "and pleasing weariness
Soon our unaching heads to sleep inclines.
Is it in cities so? where, poets tell,
The cries of Sorrow sadden all the streets,
And the diseases of intemp'rate wealth.
Alas! that any ills from wealth should rise!"

"May the sweet nightingale on yonder spray,
May this clear stream, those lawns, these snow-white lambs,
Which with a pretty innocence of look
Skip on the green, and race in little troops;
May that great lamp which sinks behind the hills,
Recall them erring! this is Damon's wish."

"Huge Breaden's stony summit once I climb'd
After a kidling: Damon, what a scene!
What various views unnumber'd spread beneath!
Woods, tow'rs, vales, caves, dells, cliffs, and torrent floods,
And here and there, between the spiry rocks,
The broad flat sea. Far nobler prospects these
Than gardens black with smoke in dusty towns,
Where stenchy vapours often blot the sun:
Yet, flying from his quiet, thither crowds
Each greedy wretch for tardy-rising wealth,
Which comes too late, that courts the taste in vain,
Or nauseates with distempers. Yes, ye rich!
Still, still be rich, if thus ye fashion life;
And piping, careless, silly shepherds we,
We silly shepherds, all intent to feed
Our snowy flocks, and wind the sleeky Fleece."

[1:625–69]

The song of the shepherds in this eclogue has for its theme the common topic of city and country, expresses the familiar praise of innocence over sophistication, identifies innocence with the countryside and sophistication with riches, and concludes, pointedly, by contrasting the pastoral pleasure of the shepherds—careless, accompanied by song—with the urban intensity of self-deluded and inevitably anxious ambition. The plain statement within this eclogue of the city-country *topos* is especially noteworthy when considered in relation to the poem's treatment of this subject in other places. Here, in the eclogue, the country is quite simply asserted as the term of value: the rural prospect is "far nobler" than the towns: they are "dusty," their gardens are "black with smoke," their air is filled with "stenchy vapours," and their streets are overrun with crowds of greedy wretches. This picture of the city contrasts certainly with the rapturous and wholly favorable prospect of London harbor, but it also contrasts with another approach Dyer makes use of in his handling of the city-country theme. Here, for example, are his lines on Leeds:

> Wide around
> Hillock and valley, farm and village smile;
> And ruddy roofs and chimney-tops appear
> Of busy Leeds, up-wafting to the clouds
> The incense of thanksgiving: all is joy;
> And trade and bus'ness guide the living scene,
> Roll the full cars, adown the winding Aire,
> Load the slow-sailing barges, pile the pack
> On the long tinkling train of slow-pac'd steeds.
> As when a sunny day invites abroad
> The sedulous ants, they issue from their cells
> In bands unnumber'd eager for their work,
> O'er high o'er low they lift, they draw, they haste
> With warm affection to each other's aid,
> Repeat their virtuous efforts, and succeed.
> Thus all is here in motion, all is life. . . .

                                                                    [3:306–21]

This rhetoric is not in the rapturous vein. Activity more than excitement is its theme, and the poet has chosen to depict the busy industrial town of Leeds in happy harmony with its rural out-skirts. The rooftops and chimneys of the town are settled into the hills and valleys: we hear nothing of dust or smoke or stench. The crowds at work are not greedy wretches; rather, they are sedulous ants, and they perform their work—"their virtuous efforts"—"with warm affection to each other's aid." Their work is an expression of the cohesive force of the social bond, not aggressive greed. The portrait of Leeds thus belongs to that pattern of observation we have noted already—in which the values of country and city are understood to be happily blended in the operations of industry and commerce. In the eclogue concluding book one, however, Dyer has put the country-city *topos* to different use, exploiting its potential as a critical perspective from which to judge the active lives of men in pursuit of wealth and engaged in commerce.

There are, then, in *The Fleece,* at least three ways of treating the subject of work: the raptures of the poet arising from his glimpse of London; the moderate but wholly approving tone of his praise of the industrial town of Leeds; and the attack on the city, on wealth, and on greedy strife expressed in a thoroughly conventional liter-ary mode, the pastoral eclogue fitted into the poem at the end of book one. But since *The Fleece* is, after all, dedicated to the praise of industry, commerce, and wealth, it is this last treatment of the subject of work which raises the most interesting questions. What, after all, is the relation between Dyer's criticism of industry, wealth, and power and his enthusiasm for it? How did Dyer intend his reader to understand the intrusion of the conventional critical perspective of the pastoral eclogue into a work otherwise dedicated to industry, commerce, striving, and wealth.

We can pursue an answer by considering the end of the eclogue, which gives us a picture of the pastoral environment—the moun-tains, rivers, and fields, the birds and men—as the harvest festival proceeds:

> . . . the mountain-woods
> And winding valleys with the various notes
> Of pipe, sheep, kine, and birds, and liquid brooks,
> Unite their echoes: near at hand the wide

Majestic wave of Severn slowly rolls
Along the deep-divided glebe: the flood,
And trading bark with low contracted sail,
Linger among the reeds and copsy banks
To listen, and to view the joyous scene.

[1:712–20]

Dyer's inclusion of the trading bark in this scene is especially interesting. The ship does not really belong to the pastoral landscape; it comes from that other world of work the shepherds have been deprecating in their song. It belongs to the sublime spectacle of London harbor, not the rural scene of the eclogue. Dyer, however, has acknowledged this in the manner he has chosen to depict the vessel. Unlike the adventurous ships in the harbor with their full billowing sails, this ship "lingers," "listens," and "views." Its sails are at rest: "low," "contracted." A representative of the busy world, the trading bark trims its sails, decorously, appropriately, as it rests for the moment, a witness of the pastoral scene. Dyer's control over his material at this point is admirable. In effect, the trading bark seen at rest is a reminder of that world of experience outside the happy valley; at the same time it serves to identify the happy valley of the eclogue as a literary locality, a place where work can be seen in terms of song, where man's relation with nature is like his relation to his work. With its sails struck the trading bark can be a witness of the scene, even a part of the picture. But its very presence serves to limit the authority of that picture. The pastoral scene is indeed an image of innocence, but the trading bark is there to remind us of the world of experience.[6] It is a major effort of the poem to set these two worlds—innocence

6. Dyer's eclogue demonstrates his understanding of the generic demands of pastoral—its emphasis on pleasure, its insistence upon a childlike consciousness in the shepherd—and his almost total inability to express an authentic pastoral movement. His shepherds possess precisely the self-consciousness Professor Rosenmeyer denies to pastoral characters, and the proximity of the trading bark (1: 718) supports Rosenmeyer's assertion that if there is *otium* in the experience of the eighteenth-century literary shepherd, it is the Horatian brand, the busman's holiday kind. Dyer's shepherds are capable of outlining the demands of pastoral song, even of remembering them, but they are entirely incapable of singing them. Yet undoubtedly Dyer thought he was composing a pastoral movement here, and obviously wanted it for this place in his poem.

and experience—together so that they do not clash but rather mesh properly somewhere in the work of active, public men—improvers, projectors, industrialists, merchants, and farmers. But this effort is also a major source of the poem's flaws, both intellectual and rhetorical. Imposing itself upon the reader is the problem of the idea of innocence in *The Fleece*: its relation to the other ideas in the poem and the rhetorical form of its appearance. This is a problem with no satisfactory solution.

For one thing, the idyll of innocence expressed in the pastoral eclogue belongs, as we might expect, to no identifiable moment of historical time. This is unlike the scene of London harbor, which the poet presents to us as a feature of contemporary England; similarly the following lines on Manchester, Sheffield, and Birmingham express a sense of current experience, of the present historical moment:

> Such was the scene
> Of hurrying Carthage, when the Trojan chief
> First view'd her growing turrets: so appear
> Th'increasing walls of busy Manchester,
> Sheffield, and Birmingham, whose reddening fields
> Rise and enlarge their suburbs.
>
> [3:335–40]

Although the current scene is likened to an ancient one, England's Manchester and ancient Carthage are not juxtaposed in such a way as to suggest timelessness. Quite the contrary, the poem frequently works with the "progress" motif as it traces the history of trade from mythological times to the present historical moment in England. The effect is to bring the present historical moment in line with the ancient past in a way which claims for contemporary England the dignity of a valued precursor. This is quite unlike the sense of history appearing at the crucial, apocalyptic moments of Pope's satire when, as in *The Dunciad*, the poetry seems to become overwhelmed with the sense of the terrible uniqueness of the present historical moment. But in each case, Pope's satire and Dyer's celebration, the matrix of events is history. In the eclogue, however, which concludes the first book of *The Fleece* we are

moved out of the realm of historical time into that area of literary
experience set aside as the locale, the dwelling place, of innocence.
Thus, the poet in introducing the songs of the shepherds in the
eclogue makes it clear that they do not belong to the present
moment: he tries to "recall" their notes, which "thro' the deep
maze of the memorial cell/Faintly remurmur." The eclogue is
presented as the account of events or feelings, now faint in the
memory, which the poet had experienced long ago. It is not of a
piece with his very vivid present experience of London or Manchester or Leeds. Nor does it belong to history; the leap of the memory
back to these remembered songs of the shepherd is not a leap across
historical time but rather across a literary landscape. Not surprisingly, the music accompanying the shepherds' songs is the "music
of Paradise"; it is heard "when the heart listens," not the ear. It
brings with it the "views . . . of the first happy garden"; watching
the harvest festival "we think the Golden Age again return'd." The
garden walks are "Elysian." And, as we noted earlier, the entire
scene is all about the state of the innocent soul when it knows
content, "when Content/To Nature's flowery scenes directs the
sight." It is a "lost delight" the poet writes about here (1:620), and
the contrasting experience is that of the "greedy mariners" and
their "desp'rate sails." Thus, the image of action which the narrator
values in the world of historical time—London harbor—is the
image of an experience which, within the rhetorical and moral
framework of the pastoral eclogue, can only be a cause of regret.

Another instance of Dyer's attempt to incorporate the attitudes
and conventions of the pastoral mode into his celebration of
industry and commerce comes near the beginning of book three,
where his subject is the clothmaking and dyeing industries. The
book opens with an invocation of the Arcadian muse and a critical
glance at the kind of libertine poetry that has too often been written
in her name:

> Proceed, Arcadian Muse! resume the pipe
> Of Hermes, long disus'd, tho' sweet the tone,
> And to the songs of Nature's choristers
> Harmonious. Audience pure by thy delight,

> Tho' few; for every note which Virtue wounds,
> However pleasing to the vulgar herd,
> To the purg'd ear is discord. Yet too oft
> Has false dissembling Vice to am'rous airs
> The reed apply'd and heedless youth allur'd;
> Too oft, with bolder sound, inflam'd the rage
> Of horrid war. Let now the Fleecy looms
> Direct our rural numbers, as of old,
> When plains and sheepfolds were the Muses' haunts.
>
> [3:1–13]

Neither the theme of love nor the theme of war is to be the subject of this poem, Dyer tells us. The subject rather is industry—dyeing and weaving—and the commerce growing out of it. Why then the invocation of the Arcadian muse? In fact, Dyer is describing his own poem, and, more precisely, the effort it, in part, embodies: to understand the new industrial energies of his age in terms of well-respected traditional attitudes and modes of writing. So that if, on the one hand, Dyer disclaims any interest in the erotic fantasies of the libertine pastoral, he nevertheless recognizes that love has always been an important component of the pastoral mode and must, somehow, be worked into his industrial song. This effort to implant the new world of work into the fields of Arcady seems at least to account for such peculiar passages as the following, in which the poet addresses the village girls at work washing down the newly sheared wool:

> . . . in the brook ye blanch the glist'ning Fleece,
> And th'am'rous youth, delighted with your toils,
> Quavers the choicest of his sonnets, warm'd
> By growing traffic, friend to wedded love.
>   The am'rous youth, with various hopes inflam'd,
> Now on the busy stage see him step forth,
> With beating breast: high-honour'd he beholds
> Rich industry. First he bespeaks a loom. . . .
>
> [3:103–10]

This prospect of amorous industry surely springs from that kind of originality which uses familiar forms to express new ideas. The impassioned youth of the pastoral eclogue is here, but he seems to awaken his sexual energy from the spectacle of his girl busily at work washing wool, and from the prospect of "growing traffic." Although he quavers his choicest sonnets to his assiduous help-meet, it does seem as though the loom he is building, and not the girl, is the focus of his attention and his energy. Certainly this industrious lover experiences no amorous torpor. And, in any event, we hear no more about his amorousness once the loom is built. A few lines later he is "the industrious youth," and he is employing all his care "to store soft yarn." Dyer makes no further effort to fuse the worlds of industry and love. For a fitful moment a new version of pastoral was laboring to be born; whether the poet abandoned the effort because of his better judgment or because of his impatience to get on with his account of the dyeing industry is impossible to say. The passage is an amusing indication of the length to which Dyer's ingenuity could go in his effort to place the new world within the old: the factory owner as shepherd swain.

These sections of the poem—the eclogue concluding book one and the industrial idyll opening book three—are, in one sense, peripheral to the poem, and, in another, central to it. They do indeed illustrate the imaginative effort which underlies the poem: to understand the new world of work and wealth within the familiar normative attitudes which had helped men judge the public world around them. At the same time, one senses that the impulse to write *The Fleece* is most apparent, not in those parts which rely upon pastoral conventions, but in those sections devoted to the poet's enthusiastic and straightforward celebration of commercial and industrial activity. We must wonder how such an interlude as the eclogue, with its vision of innocence and the golden age, is to be squared with the experience and the rhetoric of London rapture—or even, indeed, with the vision of hard work and virtuous moderation presented by the humble cottager. There are two worlds of work in Dyer's poem: the real and the mythical. The mythical with its pastoral vision of rural innocence, with its fabulous garden, and with its praise of content, is allowed to serve, momentarily, as the measure of the real. Yet one cannot help feeling that the authority of that measure is spurious, that the center of interest in *The Fleece* is man striving, not man content, and that the narrator is truest to his immediate experience when he reports in rapture his response to the magnificent ships whose sails are full in the wind in London harbor, not contracted, lingering, at rest as in the eclogue. It would be difficult to find a plainer example of the strain a writer could experience in his effort to understand and express the meaning of the energy he saw pulsing through the nation. The appeal to familiar habits of judgment and of expression—which we see in the eclogue closing book one and in the attempt to write about the weaving industry in terms of pastoral love—has an obligatory ring to it. These habits of judgment and expression—the praise of country over city, the preference for simplicity over sophistication, the attack on wealth—forced themselves into a poem which is otherwise concerned to express a strikingly unqualified excitement over the spectacle of wealth, power, and limitless abundance.

The formal and the moral aspects of Dyer's poem are therefore implicated with each other. The decision to write about the harvest in the pastoral mode reflects the decision to include the theme of innocence within the poem. As we might expect in a poem modeled on classical forms, the composition is governed by the ideal of decorum; thus, the poet's control over his material will be evident in such fine touches as the limp sails of the trading bark: a merchant ship in full sail would be utterly inappropriate to the scene Dyer has composed in his eclogue. The vision of innocence that scene conveys, therefore, is one in which the active image and energies of commerce have no place; their inclusion would have been an artistic blunder. But the narrator is deeply interested in, and openly enthusiastic about, the active energies of commerce and, in other places in the poem, attributes great value to them. The scrupulously maintained decorum of the eclogue begins, therefore, to take on the appearance of a perfectly executed part of a seriously flawed larger design.

Thus, Dyer's celebration of trade contrasts sharply both in theme

and manner with his celebration of the pastoral innocence of the
harvest. In place of innocence and content, the life of trade exhibits
desire, acquisition, and activity:

>   To censure Trade,
> Or hold her busy people in contempt,
> Let none presume. The dignity, and grace,
> And weal of human life, their fountains owe
> To seeming imperfections, to vain wants
> Or real exigencies; passions swift
> Forerunning reason; strong contrarious bents,
> The steps of men dispersing wide abroad
> O'er realms and seas. There, in the solemn scene,
> Infinite wonders glare before their eyes,
> Humiliating the mind enlarg'd; for they
> The clearest sense of Deity receive
> Who view the widest prospect of his works,
> Ranging the globe with trade thro' various climes;
> Who sees the signatures of Almighty Pow'r,
> That warn the wicked, and the wretch who 'scapes
> From human justice; who, astonish'd, view
> Etna's loud thunders and tempestuous fires;
> The dust of Carthage; desert shores of Nile;
> Or Tyre's abandon'd summit, crown'd of old
> With stately towers; whose merchants, from their isles
> And radiant thrones, assembled in her marts. . . .
>
>   [2:617–39]

In the eclogue we heard of greedy mariners and their desperate
sails; here, the narrator approves of the impulses driving men across
the oceans. The eclogue praised simplicity and content; here, the
narrator acknowledges with Mandevillian sophistication how much
of civilization flows from "seeming imperfections," "vain wants
or real exigencies," "passions swift/Forerunning reason." Men exert
their energies, not in the environment of pastoral content, but rather
in response "to strong contrarious bents"; irritability, not placidity,
emerges from this passage as the defining trait of civilized man.
And, most interesting, the energies of the seafaring trader are given a
religious sanction quite different from that implied in the eclogue
where the innocence of the first happy garden was the desirable state.

Here, instead, it is the world-roving merchant (the greedy mariner of the eclogue) who imbibes the truest sense of God's almighty power because his voyages provide him with more first hand evidence of God's effects, both natural, like Etna, and moral, like the destroyed Carthage. Consequently, like the poet in his awed response to London harbor, the seafaring merchant participates in the experience of the sublime: he sees "infinite wonders"; these "humiliate" and "enlarge" his mind; Etna "astonishes." His world of work is the world of expansive, even romantic, exotic experience and, like the scene of London harbor, finds its expression in rapturous rhetoric. It cannot be squared with the normative pretensions and rhetorical style of the eclogue, which celebrated entirely different values. Certainly, within this passage commerce seems subordinate to religion; yet as the lines develop, it becomes clear that the various effects of divine power, astonishing and humiliating the minds of the voyagers, are examples of the wages of commercial sin: Carthage, Tyre, Egypt, Arabia, Damascus, each one an object lesson in the evils of pride gone to seed in luxury, "A monument to those who toil and wealth/Exchange for sloth and pride" (3:655–56). The religious lessons of trade are not, after all, designed to teach content and simplicity; instead, the sublime effects of divine wrath go to show that wealth can be a virtue when it arises from toil. Taken in its entirety, the passage is very much about the world of experience, and shows how strenuous commitment to that world need not conflict with higher duties, and indeed, may embody them. Rhetorically, the passage is cast in the style of the sublime, the style used throughout *The Fleece* to celebrate the strenuous energies and infinite perspectives of the world of commerce. A remarkable intuition of the romantic, or perhaps Faustian, possibilities of the spirit of capitalism emerges from this poem modeled on an ancient form.

Despite its homiletic quality, then, the passage seems to express a kind of unreserved delight in the spectacle of human energy and power, delight which suggests a fundamental split in attitude on the part of the poet toward his subject. If the eclogue praises innocence, this passage celebrates experience; if the shepherds know how to limit their desires, the seafarers cross the globe to satisfy them; if the pastoral scene tells of placidity, this tells of power. Of course, power was not an easy subject to deal with; it needed to be tamed, to be placed in comfortable contexts, to be understood in terms other than itself, and to be critically examined. In part, Dyer's eclogue, in very conventional fashion, does this; yet, remarkably, one feels in *The Fleece* the poet's simple infatuation with the undeniable spectacle of man's increasing power over the world he bestrode.

Despite the eclogue, despite the homily implanted within the celebration of trade, *The Fleece* expresses joy in the challenge of limits to be breached:

> Why to the narrow circle of our coast
> Should we submit our limits, while each wind
> Assists the stream and sail, and the wide main
> Woos us in every port? See Belgium build
> Upon the goodful brine her envy'd power,
> And half her people floating on the wave,
> Expand her fishy regions: thus our Isle,
> Thus only may Britannia be enlarg'd.—
> But whither, by the visions of the theme
> Smit with sublime delight, but whither strays
> The raptur'd Muse, forgetful of her talk?
>
> [3:545–56]

Unqualified, uncomplicated, unambiguous, these lines express a delight in the possibilities open to British energy. As he did when he saw the ships in the harbor, the narrator admits to experiencing the romantic emotions associated with the sublime: he is smit with delight, his Muse enraptured, astray. The prospect of British trade thus has much the same effect on the narrator as did the first-hand experience of divine power upon the seafaring merchants. But in these lines there is no mention of the divine; no such stimulus is needed to stir up the poetic faculties to a fevered pitch. The thought of a flourishing merchant marine is enough. And for its conclusion, *The Fleece* devotes its last book to an enraptured journey spanning the trading routes of the earth—those of antiquity, those of the present, those to be established, by British ships carrying British wool. Both the rhetoric and the theme come together to express the poet's simple, almost sensual, pleasure in the spectacle of limits broken, of power imposed, of wealth abounding.

Book four is a wholly secular celebration of secular energies and secular possibilities. To be sure, Dyer had much earlier in his poem called down divine blessings on the improvers of the earth. In book four, however, religion is not one of the poet's subjects; this section of the poem is remarkable for the unmingled enthusiasm it expresses for the great secular projects of humanity. The poem embraces man's projects for improvement, for expansion, for dominion, and for wealth, without explicitly referring these human efforts to any circumambient measure for sanctioning. Here, for example, is a description of a merchant ship moving out past the Channel ports into the open Atlantic:

> Now, with our wooly treasures amply stor'd,
> Glide the tall fleets into the wid'ning main,
> A floating forest: every sail unfurl'd
> Swells to the wind, and gilds the azure sky.
> . . . .
> An hundred op'ning marts are seen, are lost;
> Devonia's hills retire, and Edgecumb Mount,
> Waving its gloomy groves, delicious scene!
> Yet steady o'er the waves they steer; and now
> The fluctuating world of waters wide,
> In boundless magnitude, around them swells,
> O'er whose imaginary brim nor towns,
> Nor woods, nor mountain-tops, nor aught appears,
> But Phoebus' orb, refulgent lamp of light,
> Millions of leagues aloft: heav'ns azure vault
> Bends overhead, majestic to its base,
> Uninterrupted clear circumference . . .
> Again, and oft, the advent'rous sails disperse. . . .
> [4:1–4, 25–36, 39]

Trade is raised by the rhetoric to heroic dimensions: the picture is one of action, sails unfurled, swelling to the wind; the sails are "advent'rous"; and the setting for adventure—the open sea and sky—is described to suggest a sense of limitless expanse. Once again the infinite rather than the bounded is the subject of the rhetoric: thus the oceans swell in "boundless" magnitude; the horizon is an "imaginary brim" from which our gaze is directed upward, "millions of leagues aloft" to find the sun; and the expanse of sky is seen as an "uninterrupted clear circumference."

We may rightly expect to find the narrator imagining human projects commensurate in their daring with this sublime spectacle of the infinite expanses of man's environment. Thus, pondering why the lakes and rivers of the Canadian north freeze in winter while, at the same latitude, Europe's rivers and valleys "blush with clust'ring vines," the narrator wonders whether human art might not yet someday learn to control the climate of the frozen polar regions:

> Must it be ever thus? or may the hand
> Of mighty Labour drain their gusty lakes,
> Enlarge the bright'ning sky, and, peopling, warm
> The op'ning valleys and the yellowing plains?
> Or rather shall we burst strong Darien's chain,
> Steer our bold fleets between the cloven rocks,
> And thro' the great Pacific every joy
> Of civil life diffuse. Are not her isles
> Numerous and large? have they not harbours calm,
> Inhabitants, and manners? haply, too,
> Peculiar sciences, and other forms
> Of trade, and useful products, to exchange
> For woolly vestures?
>
> [4:573–85]

The prospects of a canal through Panama and a fertile Arctic are so easily articulated. Once mentioned, their commercial possibilities are immediately examined. The exuberance and the extravagance of these passages are self-evident. The heroic rhetoric, the delight in strenuous human activity, the sense of mastery over the environment, the faith in civilizing toil—all of these come together rather simply in the final book of Dyer's georgic to assert the poet's innocent pleasure in the new world of work to which the English nation had committed itself. In book two Dyer had told the story of Jason and the golden fleece as an adventure of exemplary stature, well worth the English merchant's attention. In book four the

world-roving ships full of British woolen goods are the modern
argonauts. The power and the wealth created by this expansive
activity are cause only for exuberant optimism in Dyer's poem.
That Jason had a poor reputation in some quarters—Jason was,
after all, a thief and a cad—is not evident in Dyer's version of the
old story.

🙖

Like Arthur Young, Dyer was enthusiastic about new possibilities of wealth and new means of producing that wealth. The real
countryside reported on by Young and by Dyer is an economic
resource intimately related to the industry and the life of the city.
But, both for Dyer and for Young, as we have seen, there is also a
rhetorical countryside, the domain of innocent retirement and
content, the antithesis of the town. The real and the literary
countryside are never brought together satisfactorily by either
writer, a failure which may indicate some serious inconsistency
between their enthusiasms, on the one hand, and their habits of
judgment, on the other. Young's praise of the pleasures of agriculture and Dyer's pastoral eclogue express an attitude sharply in
conflict with the rapturous praise of wealth and worldly activity we
also find in both authors.

Certainly in *The Fleece* there are warnings against political
corruption, laments over war, and many attacks on luxury. But
Dyer distinguishes between luxury, which he despises and cites
again and again as the chief cause of the fall of states, and wealth,
which he encourages his British swains to strive after and which he
understands to be the very foundation of the happy nation. That
corruption, war, and luxury might be the inevitable companions of
political power and great national wealth is not a possibility that
comes up for consideration in Dyer's poem, although, for a brief
Mandevillian moment, he suggests that vanity and imagined, as
well as real, needs are valuable spurs to commerce (2:619–24). This
remains, however, an undeveloped thought; it makes its appearance and is not heard again. In another place, as his rapturous
journey passes through the trading marts of India, the narrator

stops briefly to deplore the military strain between England and
France in India:

> Next Bengala's bay,
> On the vast globe the deepest, while the prow
> Turns northward to the rich disputed strand
> Of Cor'mandel, where Traffic grieves to see
> Discord and Avarice invade her realms,
> Portending ruinous war, and cries aloud,
> "Peace, peace, ye blinded Britons! and ye Gauls!
> Nation to nation is a light, a fire,
> Enkindling virtue, sciences, and arts";
> But cries aloud in vain. Yet, wise defence
> Against Ambition's wide-destroying pride,
> Madrass erected, and Saint David's fort,
> And those which rise on Ganges' twenty streams,
> Guarding the woven Fleece, Calcutta's tower,
> And Maldo's and Patana's . . .
>
> [4:322–36]

Acknowledging that trade grieves to see the effects of discord and
avarice, the narrator is innocent of any awareness that trade itself
might be the cause of these evils. The poet simply calls upon a
cliché in his approving account of the erection of forts at Madras
and Saint David and along the Ganges: they are "wise defence
against Ambition's pride." All along, of course, the narrator has
celebrated the strenuous, desperate energies that drive men across
the world's oceans. Surely these energies have some relation to
"Ambition's pride." Yet the narrator glosses over this difficulty in
his celebration of trade, just as he glosses over the uncomfortable
connection between luxury, which he deems a vice, and wealth, in
his eyes a virtue. Of course, it is just this uneasy sense that war and
luxury and corruption were deeply implicated in the growth of
England's wealth and power that led to the insights and the despair
of the great satiric literature of the age. But in his prosecution of
his effort to celebrate the new world of work and wealth Dyer wrote
a poem untouched by Virgil's tragic sense, though modeled on
Virgil's forms, and unencumbered by the satirist's uneasy insights.
Although there appear in Dyer's poem certain habitual attitudes

and tropes, like the praise of innocence and content, along with the conventional identification of the pastoral landscape with these virtuous states, Dyer fails to integrate such attitudes and expressive habits with his poem's celebrative enthusiasms. All that clashes with those enthusiasms still does not force upon Dyer the realization that his celebration of wealth and power needs to be qualified, treated with some measure of ambiguity. Though modeled formally on Virgil's *Georgics*, Dyer's poem is untouched by that sense of limits pervading Virgil's work and imparting a tragic dimension to his celebration of Roman civilization. None of Virgil's praise of Rome is expressed with the simple exuberance with which Dyer communicates his response to English wealth and power. Virgil's is a deeply religious poem; Dyer's reflects a kind of simple piety in its attempt to link the domains of God and the market, but its enthusiasm for the market grows into an infatuation with the possibilities, not the limits, of human achievement. Despite its piety, *The Fleece* is an unmistakably secular poem.

Undoubtedly, the piety Dyer associates with his celebration of industry, like the idyll of innocence into which he places his account of the woolgathering, makes it easier than it might otherwise have been for him to link his vocation as a poet with the commercial projects of English Society. In Goldsmith's *Deserted Village* one of the casualties of the new rural order is poetry itself, evicted from Auburn along with the men and women scattered about by the emergence of the new masters. The poet-narrator of Goldsmith's poem is unable to return to his home as he had hoped. But no such difficulty suggests itself to the narrator of *The Fleece*, whose poetic career is deeply involved with the growing new order he celebrates:

> For me, 'tis mine to pray that men regard
> Their occupations with an honest heart
> And cheerful diligence . . .
> For this I wake the weary hours of rest;
> With this desire the merchant I attend;
> By this impell'd the shepherd's hut I seek,
> And, as he tends his flock, his lectures hear
> Attentive, pleas'd with pure simplicity,

And rules divulg'd beneficent to sheep:
Or turn the compass o'er the painted chart,
To mark the ways of traffic, Volga's stream,
Cold Hudson's cloudy streights, warm Afric's cape,
Latium's firm roads, the Ptolemean fosse,
And China's long canals: those noble works,
Those high effects of civilizing trade,
Employ me, sedulous of public weal:
Yet not unmindful of my sacred charge;
Thus also mindful, thus devising good
At vacant seasons oft, when ev'ning mild
Purples the vallies, and the shepherd counts
His flock, returning to the quiet fold
With dumb complacence; for religion this,
To give our every comfort to distress,
And follow virtue with an humble mind;
This pure religion.

[2:494–96, 503–24]

The didactic task of the poet makes him part of the industrial community, indeed, its spokesman. Poetry's place is thus assured. It will teach the new methods of production and celebrate the wealth and power they create. In this assertion of poetry's intimacy with industry and wealth there is no evidence at all of the fears and doubts of the satirist, nor is there any intimation of the stance of the next generation, the romantics, who sensed a threat in the new order, and who set the spirit of poetry against the forces of industry— therefore, against the social forces with which Dyer in *The Fleece* so enthusiastically allies his vocation.[7]

Dyer was able to take this stance because he had no clear sense that the forces he was celebrating were inevitably part of a new

7. This is Raymond William's formulation: "A Romantic structure of feeling— the assertion of nature against industry and of poetry against trade; the isolation of humanity and community into the idea of culture, against the real social pressures of the time. . . . We can catch its echoes, exactly in Blake, in Wordsworth, and in Shelley" (*The Country and the City* [London: Chatto and Windus, 1973], p. 79). For Wordsworth on Dyer see his own note to *The Excursion* book 8, lines 82–116 (in *The Poetical Works of William Wordsworth*, ed. Thomas Hutchinson, 2nd ed. rev. [London, New York, Toronto: Oxford University Press, 1936, reset 1950 and reprinted 1953], p. 733) and also his sonnet "To the Poet, John Dyer" (1811). He expresses both affection and esteem.

order, very different from that sense of things which sustains the pastoral vision. In his penetrating critique of Goldsmith's attack against the forces of the new commercialism in *The Deserted Village*, Raymond Williams studies Goldsmith's use of the pastoral perspective as it intersects with social fact. Unlike Dyer, Goldsmith saw very clearly that England was moving unalterably away from the past, that the new world of work was not to be easily harmonized with the old order, or understood by old habits of judgment. Goldsmith, however, in his distress over the new, could not adequately deal with its accomplishments. His Auburn is decrepit, ruined, stinted, decaying. Nothing in that ruined landscape suggests the productive transformation the real countryside was experiencing at the urging of the agricultural reformers like Arthur Young. Thus Goldsmith's decrepit Auburn, his "desert landscape," is the creation of "the imaginative rather than the social process." And Goldsmith's assertion that poetry has been evicted from the new order is, in effect, an assertion that "to be a poet is . . . to be a pastoral poet: the social condition of poetry . . . is the idealized pastoral economy. The destruction of one is, or is made to stand for, the destruction of the other."[8] To the imagination of the pastoral poet the new countryside will seem to be the ruined landscape of Auburn, not the improved fields of Young's bustling Norfolk.

Dyer's poem exhibits a similar flaw, though its intention is quite the opposite of Goldsmith's. More accurate than the *Deserted Village* in its account of the appearance of events, *The Fleece* does seem to express the simple wonder and pride one might feel in looking about him at the spectacular effects of England's growth. But Dyer's enthusiasm, like Goldsmith's despair, in the end also produces an imaginative result which is inadequate to the historical moment. In order to celebrate his new world of profit and delight Dyer had to gloss over those very real problems which discerning observers had long noted: like Goldsmith, Dyer also essentially believes that to be a poet is to be a pastoral—and a

8. Williams, *Country and the City*, p. 78.

georgic—poet. The pastoral economy and social order are somehow in the back of his mind even as he celebrates activities which
could not possibly be contained within them. Dyer's optimism
comes from his ability to tame England's new and brazen energies,
fitting them within that old order. In that way he never needed to
confront the terrors hidden in the machines he so easily placed in
his gardens. Dyer's use of bucolic tradition helped him to feel at
ease with the new forces around him; Goldsmith's use of the same
tradition helped him express his despair. In each case the imagination is not adequate to the historical moment the poet dwells in.
For Dyer, wealth could exist without luxury, power without war,
finance without corruption, and the poet could reside in the center
of his society as its spokesman.

All of which justifies our judging his work naive in its interpretation of the events and energies of its time. To some extent, of
course, this naivete is a perfectly appropriate and honest response
to an awesome spectacle of power and possibility. To some extent
it may be seen as the inevitable result of Dyer's choice of the georgic
form, which committed him to a celebration of England. But
though Dyer chose to work within that form, he also eliminated
the tragic tone always present in his Virgilian model, always
qualifying Virgil's enthusiasm for Roman power. If *The Fleece* is
inadequate, its inadequacy is not merely a formal matter but the
result of Dyer's lack of interest in certain expressive possibilities
present in his model. But, then again, the tragic sense present in
Virgil's poem, though it qualifies Virgil's enthusiasm, never
threatens to subvert it. His faith in the Roman political order is
never, in that poem, undermined by his awareness of its fragility,
or its cost, or its corruptions, though that awareness is real and
sustained. In the *Georgics*, as in some versions of tragedy, the faith
in order persists; it thus becomes possible for Virgil to translate the
terms of politics into the terms of a celebrative poetry. The countryside can be confidently put forth as the emblem of the empire. And
this assertion is all the more authentic for Virgil's insistent communication of how rough and chaotic the country life had been
and could be again.

Not so much the georgic or pastoral forms, but the underlying attitude invigorating them, was the real issue at stake during that period of deceptive calm amidst radical change, the later eighteenth century. As we have seen, Pope was already able to sense the terms of a subversive, radical inquiry into the nature of society, an inquiry keenly sensitive to the darker implications of the power and wealth which later astonished Dyer. Though undeveloped, the implications of the *Epistle to Bathurst* suggest a view of society of a totally different order from that of the bucolic modes, which respond to corruption and complication as temporary aberrations of art in a world to which nature's measure is always applicable if only it will be recognized. That the inadequacy of *The Fleece* results from more than formal considerations will be evident as we turn to Cowper, whose *The Task* is a composition considerably freer in form than Dyer's careful imitation of Virgil, though it is founded on similar attitudes; these in the end drive Cowper back from all that he sees as he attempts unsuccessfully to contain his analysis of the town, the countryside, and the state within the limits of his pastoral attitude. The point is that in sensing the new energies and quality of the economic and social environment, these poets nevertheless chose to interpret the new world in traditional terms with traditional forms. The result was not that they were wrong, but that their work became internally inconsistent or simply incomplete. And this was so whether their attitude was optimistic, like Dyer's, or despairing, like Goldsmith's. Beyond despair or naive optimism a third alternative—enhancing the expressive range of the bucolic forms, as in the past they had been enhanced by Virgil for Rome, and later by Renaissance poets into a vehicle adequate to the exploration of the pressing concerns of the Christian life—was beyond the reach of the poets—and projectors—who were trying to find their way into the moral world of the commercial and industrial spirit in the later eighteenth century.

IV

William Cowper: State, Society, and Countryside

The idiosyncrasies of William Cowper's poetic career create an obvious difficulty for a study dealing with his work in a context wider than that provided by the man's life and work themselves. Cowper's life was tormented by a set of symptoms, habits, and fears which his poetry in many places reflects. It seems perfectly reasonable to maintain that whatever can be explained about Cowper's poetry will need to be carefully qualified by referring to his peculiar biography, particularly when we consider that Cowper turned to poetry for reasons intimately connected with the torment his life at times became for him.

The importance of Cowper's biography cannot be denied, but its significance diminishes when we take for our subject those segments of his poetry which are avowedly public in their expression and intention. I am concerned not with Cowper's personal needs or peculiarities as they are reflected in his writing of *The Task*, but with the stance and purpose that shape the public form of the poem. And an insistent note in *The Task* is the poet's claim that he is a normal man who can speak meaningfully to other men about public issues.

> 'T were well, says one sage erudite, profound . . .
> 'T were well, could you permit the world to live
> As the world pleases. What's the world to you?—
> Much. I was born of woman, and drew milk,
> As sweet as charity, from human breasts.

I think, articulate, I laugh and weep,
And exercise all functions of a man.
How then should I and any man that lives
Be strangers to each other?

[3:191, 194–201][1]

Furthermore, in *The Task*, the chief subject of this chapter, we can perceive a shift in emphasis away from those religious fears which so devastated Cowper's mind, and have so often served as the focal point upon which critical discussion of Cowper's work has turned. For Hoxie N. Fairchild, Cowper was the "laureate of Evangelicalism," and from this source Fairchild sees springing, in the ruminative poems and satires preceding *The Task*, the scolding and threatening vein which is Cowper's mode of expostulation. But between these poems and *The Task* Fairchild perceived a shift in tone—wit and urbanity replacing scolding and threatening—a shift which, without indicating any radical transformation in Cowper, nevertheless indicated that he was looking out on the world as would a poet, not a preacher.[2] Moreover, the peculiar terrors with which Cowper invested his communication with his God, terrors stemming from his conviction that he was singled out by God as an "object of special detestation," are in general not to be found in *The Task*. In other places Cowper frequently expressed his religious fears in poems about castaways, about the terrible manifestations of God in the awful motions of the natural world, and about the arbitrary cruelty of the rulers of the world, but little of all this is in his manner in *The Task*.

To be sure, Cowper in reflecting upon the devastation caused by the volcano in Sicily (2:75–160), can attribute that fearful event to the anger of God at a corrupt race, but the poet chooses to draw from the event a moral for all of England, and does not interpret the catastrophe as a sign of the wrath specifically intended for

1. All extracts of Cowper's poetry are from *The Poetical Works of William Cowper*, ed. H. S. Milford, 3d ed. (London: Oxford University Press, 1926). References to "Heroism" are to line numbers; extracts from *The Task* are cited by book and line numbers.

2. Hoxie N. Fairchild, *Religious Trends in English Poetry*, 5 vols. (New York: Columbia University Press, 1939–62), 2:184.

himself. Indeed, the God that reveals himself in the world of nature
in this poem is a God whose major mode is his gentler one, whose
daily miracles are more impressive than his occasional, sublime
spectacles:

> What prodigies can pow'r divine perform
> More grand than it produces year by year,
> And all in sight of inattentive man?
> Familiar with th' effect we slight the cause,
> And, in the constancy of nature's course,
> The regular return of genial months,
> And renovation of a faded world,
> See nought to wonder at. Should God again,
> As once in Gibeon, interrupt the race
> Of the undeviating and punctual sun,
> How would the world admire! but speaks it less
> An agency divine, to make him know
> His moment when to sink and when to rise,
> Age after age, than to arrest his course?
> All we behold is miracle; but seen
> So duly, all is miracle in vain.
>
> [6:118–33]

And as for the uneasiness which Cowper often expressed towards
figures of earthly authority—an uneasiness which some have seen
as another reflection of the poet's peculiar relation with his God—
certainly we see that in *The Task* the princes, kings, and queens of
the world come in for their share of the poet's mistrust and anger;
but again, as the following passage on paternal authority would
seem to indicate, Cowper is making an effort to temper impulses
which are peculiar to him in order to speak to the common
experience of mankind:

> How readily we wish time spent revok'd,
> That we might try the ground again, where once
> (Through inexperience, as we now perceive)
> We miss'd that happiness we might have found!
> Some friend is gone, perhaps his son's best friend,
> A father, whose authority in show
> When most severe, and must'ring all its force,
> Was but the graver countenance of love;

Whose favour, like the clouds of spring, might low'r,
And utter now and then an awful voice,
But had a blessing in its darkest frown,
Threat'ning at once and nourishing the plant.
We lov'd, but not enough, the gentle hand
That rear'd us.

[6:25–38]

Because much of the best Cowper scholarship has been biographical, *The Task* has not often received close analytical scrutiny.
Even so fine a critical biography of Cowper as Maurice Quinlan's
offers only rather general descriptions of *The Task;*[3] Quinlan's
criticism of the hymns and the shorter poems is more successful
because these more personal compositions can be fruitfully approached in terms suggested by Cowper's life. But *The Task* is
composed in a public voice and needs to be studied as a public
poem. Morris Golden's study does indeed recognize the public
nature of the poem, but proceeds to interpret Cowper's treatment of
public themes in the light of the poet's well-known maladies.[4]
Despite some interesting observations about Cowper's attitude
toward civilization, and despite his devotion of a full-length book
to *The Task*, Golden adds rather little to previous sketches of that
poem because he refers his observations on the poem's public
concerns back to the story of Cowper's nervous disorders. The
poem, once more, is treated as the peculiar product of a tortured life.

In his brief introduction to his selections from Cowper in *The
Late Augustans,* Donald Davie acknowledges how significant Cowper's biography is to our understanding of his poetry, but adds a
needed corrective to the biographical emphasis of much Cowper
scholarship, and also to the commonplaces about the poet's preromanticism. Davie writes that in Cowper's "very conservative and
late Augustan expressions of Horatian urbanity . . . he resolutely

3. Maurice Quinlan, *William Cowper: A Critical Life* (Minneapolis: University
of Minnesota Press, 1953).

4. Morris Golden, *In Search of Stability: The Poetry of William Cowper* (New
York: Bookman Associates, 1960). For a balanced discussion of the personal and
public elements of *The Task* see William N. Free, *William Cowper* (New York:
Twayne Publishers, 1970), pp. 104–12.

turns his eye away from his private world, and we go to him for the fullest image in poetry of the public life of his times." Lodowick Hartley's excellent study of Cowper has made sufficiently clear how deeply the man was concerned with many of the pressing social and political issues of his time, but Hartley's work does not deal with Cowper's poetry as art.[5] Norman Nicholson's fine study begins to combine an awareness of the public nature of *The Task* with a recognition of that poem's roots in the classics. But Nicholson takes a fairly superficial view of Cowper's treatment of public matters, emphasizing the ideal of retirement as a simple criticism of London life.[6] To date the best study of Cowper's art seems to me to be Patricia M. Spacks's essay in *The Poetry of Vision* (1967), and though her study only touches on Cowper's attitudes towards public experience, focusing instead upon the character of Cowper's visual imagination, it will become obvious in the next chapter how helpful her observations on the theme of nature and art were to me.

My purpose in this chapter and the next is to examine *The Task* critically as a public poem—to study its complex judgments of the public world in relation to the bucolic art of the poem. This chapter will discuss some of the leading themes of Cowper's social outlook; the next will examine the bucolic art of *The Task* as it gives expression to those themes.

❦

Probably no line of *The Task* stays more firmly in the reader's mind than the curt and simple formula: "God made the country, and man made the town." It is, of course, a commonplace in Cowper scholarship that the poet's total attitude towards the proper life for man is somewhat more complex than that formula would seem to allow. That the polarities of urbanity and rusticity were not, perhaps, so absolute in the poet's mind as the well-known formula would imply, is clear from an apparent qualification made

5. Lodowick Hartley, *William Cowper, Humanitarian* (Chapel Hill: University of North Carolina Press, 1938).

6. Norman Nicholson, *William Cowper* (London: Longmans, Green, 1960).

in another section of the poem: "The town has ting'd the country: and the stain/Appears a spot upon a vestal's robe,/The worse for what it soils" (4:553–55). The onus remains with the town, but Cowper evidently intends to see clearly, to avoid sentimental simplicity. He will use bucolic themes, but he will not indulge in pastoral sentimentality. Furthermore, *The Task* skirts every fashion of contemporary rural sentimentalism, and yet avoids the total plunge; it is an extensive and serious treatment of public problems; its perspective and norms owe much to bucolic tradition. Yet, if it refuses to risk sentimentalizing the country, by avoiding the risk, the poem also fails to raise the country into that symbolic and imaginative fact which it must become in order to evoke from its bucolic elements the full richness of metaphoric statement. We see in *The Task* the elements of bucolic tradition used in a way which marks a crisis in that tradition. My object in this chapter and the next is to determine how Cowper's ideas about the nature of the social bond affected his intention to work with the bucolic topics of retirement, nature, and art—topics which he used to organize his criticism of contemporary English life.

About two years before he began to write *The Task,* Cowper composed a poem of ninety lines to which he sardonically gave the title "Heroism." Touching upon the poem in his study of Cowper, Lodowick Hartley sees it as an expression of some of the poet's thoughts on the enterprise of war. As such, the poem appears to bring in an indictment against the monarchs of the earth, who are likened to the volcano in Sicily, erupting periodically to ravage their unsuspecting and industrious neighboring states in order to plunder their riches. Hartley mentions in passing the presence in the poem of a realistic insight into the economic motives of aggression, motives regularly camouflaged by such rubrics as national honor and justice, which help to blow the shrill trumpets.[7] The poem ends with a breath of praise blown in the direction of the English king, who, according to the poet, manages to keep both himself and his island innocent of such barbarism.

This much is an adequate summary of the poem, but a closer

7. Hartley, *William Cowper, Humanitarian,* p. 151.

investigation yields some interesting questions about the evaluation of the nature and purposes of the social and political community implied in the poem. The arrangement of the poem is symmetrical; the first forty lines are devoted to an account of the eruption
of Aetna's once "silent fire" and its disastrous effects upon the
cultivated fields that had lain on "the mountains sloping sides."
The second half of the poem develops a moral from that catastro-
phic event, showing how an envious monarch whose appetite is
excited by the rich harvests of his neighboring state erupts in war
against his neighbor in order to plunder his wealth. Of particular
note is the poet's use of pastoral language to depict the unsuspecting fields on the mountainside and the similarly unsuspecting
lands to be invaded by the greedy king: the mountain "tow'r'd a
cloud capt pyramid of snow."

> No thunders shook with deep intestine sound
> The blooming groves that girdled her around.
> Her unctuous olives, and her purple vines,
> (Unfelt the fury of those bursting mines) . . .
>
> [5–8]

until the eruption, when

> In dazzling streaks, the vivid lightnings play.
> But, oh! what muse, and in what pow'rs of song,
> Can trace the torrent as it burns along?
> Havoc and devastation in the van,
> It marches o'er the prostrate works of man—
> Vines, olives, herbage, forest, disappear,
> And all the charms of a Sicilian year.
>
> [18–24]

Similarly, in the peaceful neighboring kingdom, "Earth seems a
garden in its loveliest dress" in front of the invading army, but in
the army's train it is "a wilderness" where "Famine, and pestilence,
her first born son,/Attend to finish what the sword begun." There
is nothing remarkable in this definition of the landscape to express
moral as well as natural states of being, but the contrast between
the cultivated fields and the wilderness serves at least to show that,
for Cowper, as for many others, it is the landscape of cultivated

nature—the emblem of nature's harmony with art in optimal civilization—that defines the moral center of his span of vision. There is only one instance in all of his work in which he momentarily adopts the more radical norms implicit in the primitivist rather than the cultivated landscape; it is in the opening lines of book two of *The Task,* a moment of special stress when the poet reacts to the crueler facts of human life:[8]

> Oh for a lodge in some vast wilderness,
> Some boundless contiguity of shade,
> Where rumour of oppression and deceit,
> Of unsuccessful or successful war,
> Might never reach me more.
>
> [2:1–5]

But if the moral landscape of "Heroism" includes the vision of the wilderness, it is centered, nevertheless, in the little picture of the cultivated country, the emblem of civilization. Cowper never begins with the intention of judging human civilization as irredeemable, and it is only after considerable struggle that his posture as a public poet relaxes in disillusionment with civilization into the acceptance of God's peace in retirement. His initial effort is to judge the works of man on the basis of the norms implicit in the cultivated landscape, not the wilderness. And the cultivated landscape suggests that human civilization can create itself, with the resources and powers God has given to man, as a harmonious resolution of nature and art.

In likening the depredations of warlike monarchs to the periodic eruptions of Aetna, the poem expresses the familiar theory of history as a cyclical process which witnesses the growth, decay, and subsequent rebirth of civilizations. Thus, following the eruption of the volcano, the cultivated landscape is in time restored; Cowper associates the process of restoration with pastoral feelings, here evoked by mention of the myrtle, the shade, the flocks. Time, not work, is emphasized as the agent of restoration, making us think of the process as nature's own, wholly consonant with pastoral expectations:

---

8. Quinlan, *William Cowper,* pp. 205–6.

> Yet time at length (what will not time achieve?)
> Clothes it with earth, and bids the produce live.
> Once more the spiry myrtle crowns the glade,
> And ruminating flocks enjoy the shade.
>
> [29–32]

A similar process takes place in the restoration of the conquered and plundered lands; the poetry here, however, is cast in a georgic vein, thus acknowledging, without hardening, the distinction between the restorative processes of nature (suggested in the passage above) and those of human work. Time was the agent of restoration in the first passage; the volcano was the destroyer. Here it is human work that restores, warfare that destroys. But the poem in these two passages works to link these two kinds of positive energy, time and work, to affirm that characteristic eighteenth-century blend of pastoral and georgic understanding:

> Yet man, laborious man, by slow degrees,
> (Such is his thirst of opulence and ease)
> Plies all the sinews of industrious toil,
> Gleans up the refuse of the gen'ral spoil,
> Rebuilds the tow'rs that smok'd upon the plain,
> And the sun gilds the shining spires again.
>
> Increasing commerce and reviving art
> Renew the quarrel on the conq'rors' part;
> And the sad lesson must be learn'd once more,
> That wealth within is ruin at the door.
>
> [67–77]

Yet, in this last account of the reestablishment of civilized industry in the once plundered lands, certain problems suggest themselves. At the center of the poem Cowper concluded his account of the eruption of Aetna by introducing the subject of war as an evil to be understood with the help of the example of "Aetna's emblematic fires" (45)—emblematic, that is, of the havoc caused by the ambitious pride of kings (46). However, a subtle shift in emphasis considerably complicates the problem in those lines which describe the renewal of the cycle of war (73–77). A portion of the burden of guilt is shifted from the shoulders of the ambitious and proud monarchs and comes to rest upon their victims. This sad lesson that must be learned once more is not the schoolwork of the predator; clearly it is the victim who needs the new instruction—and what he is to learn is that "wealth within is ruin at the door." Certainly, the victimized state is not responsible for the greed of its rapacious neighbor, but here there is a suggestion of a more problematic connection between the internal and external causes of international violence than had perhaps been implied earlier in the poem. Thus, in his account of the renewal of the once plundered region, Cowper attributes the georgic energy that "plies all the sinews of industrious toil" to man's "thirst of opulence and ease." Although in Cowper's thought industrious toil is always a virtue, opulence is often depicted as vicious in itself and in its effects. However, as these lines associate the pastoral quality of ease with the vicious condition of opulence, a measure of ambiguity slips into this apparently straightforward poem, disturbing its effort to link the pastoral and georgic ambiences. We perceive that the land of industrious toil, whose wealth invites the aggression of its neighbors, harbors within itself some of the seeds of evil: "wealth within is ruin at the door." The volcano, which had hitherto been a somewhat unsatisfactory emblem for external aggression, takes on added significance as we see that the real issue is not aggressive greed by itself, but aggressive greed as it is provoked by a less obvious, but nonetheless festering, fault within the victim of that aggression: his thirst for opulence and ease. Luxury once again is the vicious mole of nature, festering within, realistically and un-comfortably associated with the pastoral virtue of ease. More—unlike Dyer, Cowper fitfully perceives that industrious toil, too, is somehow implicated with ruinous luxury, and both with war.

"Heroism" is not a perfect poem. Its central device, the volcano, is not a very precise emblem for external aggression; furthermore, the poem raises a problem it fails to resolve by suggesting that the victim of greed is in some measure responsible for the devastation he suffers, because the very wealth which invites attack upon him is the product of his own morally ambiguous industry. The hint arises that the volcano is perhaps more appropriately the emblem of the lurking evil of wealth within the victimized nation than it is

of the aggressive depredations of his neighbor state. But Cowper
concludes the poem without developing that possibility.

> What are ye, monarchs, laurel'd heroes, say—
> But Aetnas of the suff'ring world ye sway?
> Sweet nature, stripp'd of her embroider'd robe,
> Deplores the wasted regions of her globe;
> And stands a witness at truth's awful bar,
> To prove you, there, destroyers as ye are.
>
> [78–82]

In these lines he returns to his original position, overlooks the
subtle qualifications of that position which had crept into his
verse, and repeats the essential polarity between the cultivated
landscape of peace (sweet nature's embroidered robe) and the
wilderness created by warlike greed.

The poem concludes with a curious burst of patriotism:

> Oh, place me in some heav'n protected isle,
> Where peace, and equity, and freedom smile;
> Where no volcano pours his fiery flood,
> No crested warrior dips his plume in blood;
> Where pow'r secures what industry has won;
> Where to succeed is not to be undone;
> A land that distant tyrants hate in vain,
> In Britain's isle, beneath a George's reign.
>
> [83–90]

As patriotic rhetoric these lines are not especially noteworthy; but
considered within the context of bucolic reference they raise some
fundamental questions. For example, is the wish for refuge in
"some heav'n protected isle" merely an example of easy, unthink-
ing rhetoric, or does it express the poet's longing to escape the
vicious cycle of a politics which has failed to function healthily
within the moral possibilities defined by the domains of nature (the
pastoral fields, the volcano) and civilization (increasing commerce,
war)—to escape, that is, to some "heav'n protected isle" where the
functioning of nature and civilization is controlled within the
overarching and protective dominion of grace? Furthermore, the
fact that the conclusion tempers its patriotism with the yearning

for retreat suggests that the important aspect of the haven is not so much that it is England but that it is an island. This aspect of England's geography becomes significant in the context of the moral geography of the poem, so to speak, when we consider the earlier lines about the relations between neighboring states. Cowper addresses the warring monarch, about to pounce upon the pastoral domains of his neighbor:

> Fast by the stream that bounds your just domain,
> And tells you where ye have a right to reign,
> A nation dwells, not envious of your throne,
> Studious of peace, their neighbours', and their own.
> Ill-fated race! how deeply must they rue
> Their only crime, vicinity to you!
>
> [47–52]

These lines recall others from the opening section of book two of *The Task,* where again Cowper contemplates the ironies and cruelties of power:

> Lands intersected by a narrow firth
> Abhor each other. Mountains interpos'd
> Make enemies of nations, who had else,
> Like kindred drops, been mingled into one.
>
> [16–19]

In each instance the fact of power generates its own realities, makes its own influence felt, in ways that challenge the limits implied by nature. Power makes a mockery of the idea of proper bounds and just domains. The worlds of nature and power conflict with each other, so that the only haven is an island, the only peace is in isolation. To the moral geography defined by the wilderness on the one side and the cultivated landscape on the other, Cowper has added in his poem "Heroism" a third ground, the island; but this addition to the landscape is not a place where the political experience of man is manageable and comprehensible within the dialectic of nature and civilization; it is a heavenly isle, and in its isolation from the vicious drama of power, the domains of nature and civilization are successfully harmonized only under the dominion of grace. It is as if civilization is helpless to find within its own proper resources the power to preserve itself. Not surprisingly, this uncomfortable possibility has been expressed in disruptions within the poem's system of bucolic allusion.

❦

If the curiously unresolved ambiguities of "Heroism" stem in part from the poet's serious reservations about the value of society's foremost activity, industry, we can see in *The Task* Cowper wrestling with similar difficulties in his attempt to understand the general nature of the social bond. The perspective finally asserted is that of rural retirement, which, in Cowper's treatment, takes on a meaning significantly different from its metaphorical substance as a topic of pastoral. In Cowper's work retirement is presented finally as an option, not as the emblem of a psychological moment of positive political significance, as, for example, in Pope's *Epistle to Burlington*, where the experience of rural pleasure is intrinsically linked to the poem's vision of a good public and political order. It is the development of the concept of retirement from an emblem to a simple life option that I am concerned with here, together with the implications this process entails for the expression, in bucolic themes, of serious social criticism. I have begun with a consideration of "Heroism" because that poem, in its establishment of the isolated island as an alternative source of norms to the cultivated middle landscape, prefigures a similar development of the concept of retirement in *The Task*. In *The Task* retirement is no longer a poetical idea working as a catalyst to resolve the strains between nature and art inside a poem and inside the mind experiencing the poem. Instead, it serves as a suburban option signifying a failure to resolve the antinomy between nature and art in a poem, and of the poet's need to escape, to isolate himself from the battleground of nature and art in life in order to comprehend nature morally as a creature of grace. The world of art is, in the end, left outside of the realm of redemption.

The Task is structured like a rondo; we can enter the poem at almost any point and before long find ourselves at its thematic center, the virtues of rural retirement. The topics that alternate with the central theme either arise from it or lead back to it. The narrative progress in itself embodies no observable climactic direction. The six separate books of *The Task* are not easily distinguishable in terms of their concerns: each major division is about retirement; whatever distinctions exist are noticeable not in the treatment of that central theme, but in the subsidiary themes which alternate with it. Thus, book two weaves its way about the thematic center through the subsidiary topics of clerical corruption and educational abuses; book four defines the virtues of retirement by engaging the problem of the nature of the social bond; book five works its way around a discussion of political liberty, only to return at the end to the praise of retirement as the seat of the only trustworthy freedom, spiritual rest; and book six amplifies the discussion of God's peace as it is experienced in the retired life. Book one serves to introduce the theme of retirement by establishing the polarity between country and town; book three deals with the activities that make retirement useful and valuable.

In book four, "The Winter Evening," the life of retirement is studied in symmetrical juxtaposition with the active life, the thrust of the poet's thought pointing towards a theory of the social bond upon which can be founded an apology for the life of retirement. Book four aims at a balanced statement of the worth of retirement, an evaluation arrived at by a fair consideration of the active life, which is, in the end, renounced. The work begins with the arrival of the eagerly anticipated post, carrying with it the news from the outside world; the early sections of the work describe the retired man's relations with the outside world by depicting his use of the weekly news sheet: he prepares for it with relish, careful at the same time to define his delight as the pleasure arising from the distance separating him from the objects of his interest:

> The grand debate,
> The popular harangue, the tart reply,
> The logic, and the wisdom, and the wit,
> And the loud laugh—I long to know them all;
> I burn to set th' imprison'd wranglers free,
> And give them voice and utt'rance once again.
> . . . .

'Tis pleasant through the loop-holes of retreat
To peep at such a world; to see the stir
Of the great Babel, and not feel the crowd;
To hear the roar she sends through all her gates
At a safe distance, where the dying sound
Falls a soft murmur on th' uninjur'd ear.

[4:30–35, 88–93]

The vicarious pleasure, however, is a complex one. The narrator can imitate in his eager anticipation of the news the very motions of the souls who make the news. He *"longs* to know them all"; he *"burns* to set th' imprison'd wranglers free" (italics added). At the same time, he has the advantage of a critical perspective, the advantage of distance. Although he speaks of his almost intemperate eagerness to hear the news of the world, nevertheless "Thus sitting, and surveying thus at ease/The globe and its concerns, I seem advanc'd/To some secure and more than mortal height,/That lib'rates and exempts me from them all" (4:94–97). In this way he defines a middle ground. Unlike the postboy, "the light-hearted wretch,/Cold and yet cheerful" who brings the news and yet is incapable of being touched by it, he nevertheless avoids the lack of consciousness of the other sort, of those who do not understand what they do precisely because of their involvement. Retirement is thus a middle ground, psychologically and morally: it is, in fact, proper participation, since the only alternatives depicted are frenetic involvement or cloddish insensibility. "I behold the tumult, and am still" (4:99–101). Cowper does not, at first, present the picture of retirement as a kind of isolation. It is "with a kindred heart" that the narrator suffers the woes and shares the escapes of the active man (4:116–17).

Still, the perspective of retirement is not productive merely of sympathetic motions; one of its fruits is criticism. Indeed, criticism is the very process which helps to locate and define the moral ground which the happy man of the country inhabits, as the following passage makes clear:

Now stir the fire, and close the shutters fast,
Let fall the curtains, wheel the sofa round,
And, while the bubbling and loud-hissing urn

Throws up a steamy column, and the cups,
That cheer but not inebriate, wait on each,
So let us welcome peaceful ev'ning in.
Not such his ev'ning, who with shining face
Sweats in the crowded theatre, and, squeezed
And bor'd with elbow-points through both his sides,
Out-scolds the ranting actor on the stage. . . .

[4:36–45]

The country pleasures define and are defined by the urban irrita-
tions. This passage is typical of the manner in which the theme of
retirement is woven into the fabric of the poem; it arises from, and
gives rise to, reflections on the outer, active world. Critical perspective is created by the constant juxtaposition of the two options.
Another passage from book four substantiates this point. The
narrator launches into a description of one of the pleasures of
retirement, the delight to be had from the exercise of the fancy. He
writes of a fireside reverie, inspired by the glowing of the red
cinders in the hearth; we cannot miss here the note of pastoral
otium:

Me oft has fancy, ludicrous and wild,
Sooth'd with a waking dream of houses, tow'rs,
Trees, churches, and strange visages, express'd
In the red cinders, while with poring eye
I gaz'd, myself creating what I saw.

[4:286–90]

These lines, however, are not their own justification; they are
introduced by a glancing thrust at those for whom so simple a
pleasure is contemptible:

Laugh ye, who boast your more mercurial pow'rs,
That never feel a stupor, know no pause,
Nor need one; I am conscious, and confess,
Fearless, a soul that does not always think.

[4:282–85]

The larger section of the poem to which these lines belong is itself
built upon two sets of juxtaposed images: on the one hand, there is
the dim, but suggestive light of the glowing rural hearth, on the
other is the brilliant light of the fashionable urban salons from

which the narrator is measuring his moral as well as physical
distance. The entire passage on the happy enjoyment of the pleasures of the imagination, some forty lines long, is introduced by six
lines depicting the activities of the corresponding hour in the
fashionable world.

> Just when our drawing-rooms begin to blaze
> With lights, by clear reflection multiplied
> From many a mirror, in which he of Gath,
> Goliath, might have seen his giant bulk
> Whole, without stooping, tow'ring crest and all,
> My pleasures, too, begin.
>
> [4:267–72]

Here the lighting is brilliant, not glowing, and multiplied in the
outsized mirrors of the salon, it produces its own phantasmagoric
effects. The reference to Goliath is significant. Although the idea is
not thoroughly worked out in the verse, the narrator seems to have
in mind a contrast between two kinds of imaginative experience:
the one is restful and restorative, the other is deceptive and irritat-
ing, deceptive as was the size and apparent strength of Goliath,
whose bulk could easily be contained within the dimensions of the
blazing mirrors of the fashionable drawing rooms. In contrast, the
retired man's otiose fancy is not merely a reflection of a delusion, as
is clear to him when his revery is abruptly ended by the banging of a
shutter:

> 'Tis thus the understanding takes repose
> In indolent vacuity of thought,
> And sleeps, and is refresh'd . . .
> Thus oft, reclin'd at ease, I lose an hour
> At ev'ning, till at length the freezing blast,
> That sweeps the bolted shutter, summons home
> The recollected pow'rs: and, snapping short
> The glassy threads, with which the fancy weaves
> Her brittle ties, restores me to myself,
> How calm is my recess; and how the frost,
> Raging abroad, and the rough wind, endear
> The silence and the warmth enjoy'd within!
>
> [4:296–98, 302–10]

He calls attention here to the healthful effect of his revery: his understanding refreshed, the man is restored to himself, and the abrupt ending of the revery does not leave his mind a poor shrunken thing, the product of pleasing delusions, but rather creates in him a serene appreciation of his happy situation as he is aroused into awareness of the silence and the warmth he enjoys inside the house. The retired life is contrasted with the fashionable life in terms of the health and heightened awareness of reality available to the one, and denied to the other. The cottage is a kind of pleasance.

This is Cowper's manner—to define the nature and virtues of retirement by constantly juxtaposing with it the corresponding activities of the larger world. In its treatment, therefore, of its central theme, retirement, the poem accomplishes a corollary purpose, the criticism of the active world. It is his judgment of the active world, the milieu of society at large, that concerns us here, because in the end, Cowper's concept of retirement is developed in response to his sense of the nature of social experience, and grows into something rather more like alienation and not the emblematic opportunity for the experience of *otium*—either the Epicurean or Horatian kind.

In book four Cowper presents a panoramic picture of the various elements of English society: we have touched upon (and will return later to) the life of the retired man, and its counterpart, active involvement, seen so far in two of its aspects, the world reflected in the newspaper and the world of the drawing rooms. The experiences of involvement and of retirement are the poles upon which much of book four turns. There appears, also, a third set of experiences in this section of the poem, represented by such figures as the postboy, the laborer, and the industrious poor. These figures do not come into focus as subjects of the poet's attention when it is turned towards the criticism of society: the laborer, like the postboy, represents that order of life which is committed neither to active involvement nor retirement, but connected to nature in the simplest of ways: rugged nerves.

> Oh happy; and, in my account denied
> That sensibility of pain with which
> Refinement is endued, thrice happy thou!

Thy frame, robust and hardy, feels indeed
The piercing cold, but feels it unimpair'd.

[4:357–61]

The teamster of these lines shares with the postboy that low
metabolism whose chief blessing is insensibility, a quality which
distinguishes these figures from both the fashionable and the
retired.[9] Insensibility is not, however, the blessing of the industrious poor. They suffer, and the narrator extends to them his com-
passion and charity. Nevertheless, their poverty is not one of the
narrator's *social* concerns: it does not enter into the system of
concerns which structure his indictment of society. It is rather the
"undeserving poor" who open for Cowper an entrance into the
arena of social criticism, and it is interesting to see the route he
takes. The industrious poor he praises for preferring honest poverty to the degradation of beggarship, often, as the narrator says, a
well-rewarded beggarship, since knaves in office are "lib'ral of their
aid/To clam'rous importunity in rags,/But oft-times deaf to sup-
pliants, who would blush/To wear a tatter'd garb however coarse
. . ." (4:413–16). But Cowper has no explanation for the suffering of
the industrious poor: nowhere does he suggest which fault or flaw
in the economic organization of society bears the responsibility for
their plight. And thus their only appeal is to private charity and
the hopefully fortunate changes that may come with time.

These figures—the postboy, the teamster, the industrious poor—
people the landscape of *The Task* and suggest the presence of
modes of experience that Cowper wishes to acknowledge although
his real attention is elsewhere, as is clear from his treatment of the
undeserving poor. The narrator may be at a loss to explain the
suffering of the worthy poor, but the plight of the unworthy is a
different matter: gin. The narrator's analysis of the poverty of the

9. Cowper's lack of interest in these figures—he simply does not develop them
beyond this acknowledgment of their existence—illustrates, as does the social and
psychological distinction he immediately asserts between them and him, how
difficult it was for an eighteenth-century poet to imagine a world of Theocritean
tranquility and song. Yet Cowper's interest in the psychological experience of
otium is obvious; to embody it in a metaphoric idea with social implications was
nevertheless inconceivable to him.

rural thief and drunkard leads him abruptly away from the contemplation of the happy insensibility of the teamster and the
grinding poverty of the decent poor and back into his central
subject—the corruption of the world at large and the contrasting
virtues of retirement.

Cowper's study of the rural thief is not an impressive achievement: it supports Donald Davie's assertion that no poet understood
what was happening in the English countryside during these years
of momentous change in the practice of agriculture. We are presented with a caricature—the chicken stealing wastrel whose sole
concern is not to feed his wretched family but rather to raise money
for drink. This poverty, the narrator asserts, is the "effect of laziness
or sottish waste" (4:431), and to see their results we are ushered into
a neighborhood tavern where sitting or reeling in debauch is, not
only the nightly thief, but also the lackey, groom, smith,
cobbler, joiner, shepherd, and baker, virtually the entire range of
rural employment.

Once we are taken inside the tavern, however, the range of the
narrator's perspective widens and the spectacle of rural debauchery
is placed within a wider context:

> Dire is the frequent curse, and its twin sound
> The cheek-distending oath, not to be prais'd
> As ornamental, musical, polite,
> Like those which modern senators employ,
> Whose oath is rhet'ric, and who swear for fame!
> Behold the schools in which plebeian minds,
> Once simple, are initiated in arts
> Which some may practise with politer grace,
> But none with readier skill!—'tis here they learn
> The road that leads, from competence and peace,
> To indigence and rapine; till at last
> Society, grown weary of the load,
> Shakes her encumber'd lap, and casts them out.
>
> [4:487–99]

These lines depict the tavern scene as a kind of rural analogue to
the activities of the great world without: what distinguishes the
swearing of the boors from the rhetoric of senators is merely style,

and to Cowper's mind style does not redeem. If, as Empson suggests, the pastoral form is one way of expressing the possibility that a beautiful relation exists between noble and peasant so that the noble can celebrate himself in shepherd's dress, the preceding passage can be read as a kind of parody of that idea: the vices of each class are precisely mirrored in their respective styles of debauchery, the rhetoric of senators and the drunken oaths of boors. The passage continues with a crucial elaboration of the manner in which the country louts, in their debauchery, live in harmony with the interests of a corrupt state:

> But censure profits little: vain th' attempt
> To advertise in verse a public pest,
> That, like the filth with which the peasant feeds
> His hungry acres, stinks, and is of use.
> Th' excise is fatten'd with the rich result
> Of all this riot; and ten thousand casks,
> For ever dribbling out their base contents,
> Touch'd by the Midas finger of the state,
> Bleed gold for ministers to sport away.
> Drink and be mad, then; 'tis your country bids!
> [4:500–509]

We come back, in these lines, to the unresolved antinomies of Pope's *Epistle to Bathurst*, in which the Mandevillian formula for the relation between private vices and public benefits is examined. Cowper's tone here is caustic and sarcastic, and his point is a serious one, for he can see only a perverse harmony between the larger purposes of the English nation and the private vices which support those purposes. Cowper's recognition of the country's participation in national corruption is expressed in a striking simile likening the manuring of the fields to the fattening of the treasury. The evil of drink, a "public pest . . . like the filth with which the peasant feeds/His hungry acres, stinks, and is of use." The simile concentrates its vituperation into the metaphor identifying the "hungry acres" of the farmer with the excise, "fatten'd with the rich result/Of all this riot." In this crucial passage we have clear evidence of Cowper's unsentimental observations of the countryside, of his sophisticated recognition of its participation in the economy of the nation. The rural fields themselves become an emblem, for the moment, of the treasury, and share in its corruption. Cowper's striking use of the manured fields as a simile for the corrupted treasury is a thoroughly antipastoral apprehension. It indicates how realistic observation and appraisal begin to hamper full imaginative commitment to bucolic habits of expression, and may be usefully contrasted with Pope's richer figure in *The Epistle to Bathurst,* a poem whose social realism has not thoroughly disrupted its thematic and figurative bucolic system:[10]

> Wealth in the gross is death, but life diffus'd,
> As Poison heals, in just proportion us'd:
> In heaps, like Ambergrise, a stink it lies,
> But well-dispers'd, is Incense to the Skies.
>
> [233–36]

Yet Cowper was a patriotic Englishman. *The Task* reflects in many places the poet's effort to discover "public virtue," and to praise it. In these passages of caustic observation, he has not yet expressed that complete disaffection from the national life which later in book four places him clearly apart from it, driving him to accept rural retirement in its most radical form as a totally critical stance. In these realistic passages on the countryside Cowper still asserts the presence of forces which oppose the drift toward corruption. The drunken louts of the country taverns, whom he has compared with "modern senators," continue in the debauchery until "Society, grown weary of the load,/Shakes her encumber'd lap, and casts them out" (4:498–99). This observation reflects the narrator's fundamental sense of the possibility of public virtue; underlying his criticism of the national corruption is his sense that the corrupt are yet "outcasts" of society, so that the drunkard may be said to be one of the "signatories" of a kind of unspoken pact; he tacitly rejects the community of the virtuous sober who accept his rejection. This community of virtue Cowper labels as "society," and society is the term he often uses to describe that good union of men within the environment of optimal civilization. But

10. I owe this point to Paul Alpers.

the passages we have been considering include within the range of their criticism more than the merely antisocial habits of the drunkards. Cowper is studying, and attacking, the relation between the vices of the antisocial and the political institutions which are the formal expression of social union. Thus, if it is society which casts out its drunken load, it nevertheless is "the Midas finger of the state" (4:507) which creates revenue, through the excise, from the vicious habit. "Drink and be mad, then; 'tis your country bids!" At this point in the poem the narrator seems to distinguish between the state, the power that levies the excise tax and benefits from private debauchery, and society, that community of virtue which seems to have no clear connection to the state, and seems, indeed, to function in opposition to it. The excise tax, the swearing ministers, the drunken louts—all of these are sanctioned by, or at least clearly and formally connected with the political body, the state. But in what relationship does "society" exist with the state? By which mechanism does society rid itself of its dangerous and useless members, who are yet so useful to the state, and who, indeed, are among its senators? Certainly the narrator seems to distinguish between society and the state, locating virtue in the one and vice in the other. The result is that the criticism of corruption is never assimilated to a vision of the essential virtue of the English polity. Virtue is the characteristic of society (a term never clearly defined); vice is the business of the state. The implication is that virtue cannot be an element of the political order. And this, of course, suggests that, for all of his patriotism, Cowper will find no way to express his public themes in a celebrative mode.

Following immediately the section on the drunkenness of the country workmen is a passage lamenting the loss of the pastoral dream of an innocent countryside, a loss accompanied by the disappearance of an age that favored such a dream, "in days like these/Impossible, when virtue is so scarce" (4:529–31). "The town has ting'd the country" (4:553), laments the narrator, and he proceeds to examine the reasons for this unhappy change. The first approach to the problem is the familiar analysis of luxury. Indeed, the evils of luxury are never far from Cowper's thought; thus, in

book two, where the poet's attention turns to the collapse of
discipline in the schools, the source of even that plague is traced
back to luxury: "Profusion breeds them; and the cause itself/Of
that calamitous mischief has been found: Found, too, where most
offensive in the skirts/Of the rob'd pedagogue!" (2:820–23). And, in
book four, where Cowper's subject is not the schools, but the
nation in general, this same familiar analysis of social decay is the
explanation. However, although luxury is presented here as the
chief symptom of a corrupt polity, the cycle of decay begins first
with power: "Increase of pow'r begets increase of wealth;/Wealth
luxury, and luxury excess" (4:580–81). It is, then, the unhappy
confluence of power and wealth that the narrator suggests as the
root of England's plight. The first victim of these subversive forces
is order:

> The rich, and they that have an arm to check
> The license of the lowest in degree
> Desert their office; and themselves, intent
> On pleasure, haunt the capital, and thus
> To all the violence of lawless hands
> Resign the scenes their presence might protect.
> Authority herself not seldom sleeps,
> Though resident, and witness of the wrong.
>
> [4:586–94]

The argument here is complex; we may notice that "authority" is,
in this passage, a term of value. It seems to represent power exerted
properly, because exerted by the proper guardians of social order.
But in England's present plight "authority herself not seldom
sleeps." This is because the rich have themselves become lost in
England's new world of power, wealth, luxury, and excess. The
power that may be properly used "to check/The license of the
lowest in degree" is thus something different from the power that
generates wealth, luxury, and excess. This new form of power,
Cowper implies, is utterly unlike the power emanating from the
proper authority of the formerly virtuous polity. And the passage
clearly suggests that the once virtuous polity was characterized by a
social order based upon subordination. In this virtuous polity the

social order reflected, indeed maintained, the political order. Society and state were inextricably involved with each other. But in the new polity of power and wealth, the polity of the aggrandized state, the moral basis of politics is destroyed along with the old order of society because the former guardians also now join in the new riot of luxury. So that in Cowper's analysis of the effects of the power of the aggrandized state, the very growth of that state destroys that system of human communal identity, society, which had been the basis of the state's legitimacy. In the new England, this moral order, which Cowper calls society, exists with no formal connection to the new apparatus of power, the state, so that the power of England is real but illegitimate. Cowper's social thought does not, any more than that of earlier figures like Pope and Swift, conceive of the possibility that the organization of society creates, rather than reflects, the purposes of the state. A certain kind of order, therefore, Cowper assumes as a good, and this order he understands as a creature of moral rather than political desiderata, though under the right conditions moral and political order can be linked. But power and order can also come to cross purposes, as have the new state and that other, now unpolitical entity, society. In the new state "society" is an undefined mechanism (though it is a term of value), and the power which now emanates from the state is not linked with "society" in a necessary relation. So that private vices like the drunkenness that fills the treasury through the excise tax are not simply public benefits, because Cowper implies a distinction between the political institutions of the state and the moral structure of society.

These points are substantiated by the poet's attack on universal soldiership, which immediately follows the passage on power and luxury. In the narrator's search for the causes of the debauchery of the countryside, the attack on power and luxury is the prelude to his discussion of what seems to him to be the major cause of the countryside's fall from grace.

> But faster far, and more than all the rest,
> A noble cause, which none who bears a spark
> Of public virtue ever wish'd remov'd,

Works the deplor'd and mischievous effect,
'Tis universal soldiership has stabb'd
The heart of merit in the meaner class,
Arms, through the vanity and brainless rage
Of those that bear them, in whatever cause,
Seem most at variance with all moral good . . .
                                                    [4:613–21]

The thought here is peculiar, attributing to an instrument of the state's power, the military, the major responsibility for the state's contribution to the decline of rural order. This shift of emphasis from cause to apparent symptom permits Cowper to invent a short narrative detailing the progress of the country bumpkin from a simple, useful member of the rural order to a superfluous though gorgeous adjunct of the state—a soldier. The narrative is based upon the poet's critical treatment of such ideas as heroism and the nobility of arms, and echoes the poem "Heroism" in its revaluation of those ceremonial standards of worth—a revaluation marked by the narrator's awareness of the intimate connection between such traditional measures of value and the corrupt purposes of power which, in fact, they simultaneously serve and disguise. Thus, we find the "noble cause" of soldiership (4:614) to be at odds with "public virtue" (4:615), even as the military splendor of the recruit is at odds with his former rural identity, the recruit who,

his three years of heroship expir'd,
Returns indignant to the slighted plough,
He hates the field, in which no fife or drum
Attends him . . .
To be a pest where he was useful once;
[Is] his sole aim, and all his glory now!
                                            [4:644–47, 657–58]

Nobility, heroism, and glory are the terms which emerge unfavorably from Cowper's scrutiny here, but the important point is that his scrutiny is in the name of public virtue (4:615), whose traditional emblems are nobility, heroism, and glory. Once again, however, public virtue, like that undefined mechanism by which society casts out the rural drunkards, is a quality whose place in the public order is not clear. The state, armed with power, is corrupted by power; nobility, glory, heroism do not survive Cowper's analysis of their connection with power. How then, and through which public mode of action, does public virtue express itself, removed as it necessarily is from the seat of power which is the state?

The Task supplies no answer to this question; the only virtuous life portrayed is the life of retirement, and this option, as it is developed in the poem, can hardly be understood as the stage for the exercise of public virtue. But public virtue, like that undefined entity, society, is a crucial aspect of Cowper's thought, just as society is a more complex idea in *The Task* than we might be led to believe from the poet's habit of citing the vices of society in order to define the virtues of retirement.

The desire to strike a balance between retirement and involvement is in evidence throughout the poem, although the effort, finally, is not successful because of the poet's inability to discover that aspect of the world at large in which he might move. Thus, in the opening lines of book four, where the narrator described the eager anticipation with which he awaits the post, among the several objects of his curiosity about the doings of the world are the success of the war effort in the American colonies and the condition of India:

> But oh th' important budget! usher'd in
> With such heart-shaking music, who can say
> What are its tidings? have our troops awak'd
> Or do they still, as if with opium drugg'd,
> Snore to the murmurs of th' Atlantic wave?
> Is India free? and does she wear her plum'd
> And jewell'd turban with a smile of peace,
> Or do we grind her still?

> [4:23-30]

These are curious thoughts, particularly when considered in the light of the later section on the evils of soldiership and power. Here the retired man expresses, on the one hand, his patriotic disgust for the failure of the English war in the American colonies, a subject which receives more extended consideration in a passage of bitter sarcasm in book five, where the failure of English power at war is attributed to English weakness and moral decline at home; on the other hand, the imperial adventure in India is here the object of a different kind of censure: it is an example of power ruthlessly applied. The whole passage is incompletely realized; no measured indictment or justification of the use of power emerges: more vigor from the troops in the colonies, less from those in India, are equally desirable alternatives. The passage seems to rest on the assumption that there is such a thing as English honor, for that is what is degraded by the drugged behavior of the troops in the colonies (and, as the passage in book five makes clear, by the shameful failure of that war); but the implication here is that English honor would be reflected in the success of English power, a position inconsistent with the concern for India's freedom, and with those passages in *The Task* attacking the brutality of war and conscription, and those others which attack commercial enterprise and luxury for their intimate connection with power and empire. It would seem that the poet is not thinking seriously or systematically here about the problems of power as it is wielded by the English state, but rather that his attention is focused on that portion of honor belonging to English society. The troops in America and the troops in India seem, then, emblems in these lines not of English power, but of English honor, not of the state, but of the society, the term that Cowper does not define but which, in his usage, seems to stand for the communal and moral identity of the English people. It thus becomes possible for the narrator to despise warfare and soldiership as activities of the state, and to praise them as emblems or metaphors of the social identity of the English nation. And it is only with this vague concept of the social order as opposed to the political, that the retired man admits some personal connection.

The troubled distinction between society and state is not a subject of systematic discussion in *The Task*, but it is central to the poet's attempt to define a perspective for himself as a judge of English life. Book four concludes with an assertion of the perspective of retirement, but not before the narrator makes a final attempt to clarify his position on the moral nature of society. In this attempt the following passage is crucial, placed as it is immediately after the attack on the military as the corrupter of the rural order and immediately before a long concluding passage defining the virtues of retirement:

> Man in society is like a flow'r
> Blown in its native bed: 'tis there alone
> His faculties, expanded in full bloom,
> Shine out; there only reach their proper use.
> But man, associated and leagu'd with man
> By regal warrant, or self-join'd by bond
> For int'rest sake, or swarming into clans
> Beneath one head for purposes of war,
> Like flow'rs selected from the rest, and bound
> And bundled close to fill some crowded vase,
> Fades rapidly, and, by compression marr'd,
> Contracts defilement not to be endur'd.
> Hence charter'd boroughs are such public plagues;
> And burghers, men immaculate perhaps
> In all their private functions, once combin'd,
> Become a loathsome body, only fit
> For dissolution, hurtful to the main.
> Hence merchants, unimpeachable of sin
> Against the charities of domestic life,
> Incorporated, seem at once to lose
> Their nature; and, disclaiming all regard
> For mercy and the common rights of man,
> Build factories with blood, conducting trade
> At the sword's point, and dyeing the white robe
> Of innocent commercial justice red.
> Hence, too, the field of glory, as the world
> Misdeems it, dazzled by its bright array,
> With all its majesty of thund'ring pomp,
> Enchanting music, and immortal wreaths,
> Is but a school where thoughtlessness is taught
> On principle, where foppery atones
> For folly, gallantry for ev'ry vice.

[4:659–90]

The passage repeats Cowper's implied distinction between society and state, and proposes a more radical criticism of man's political life than has hitherto appeared in the poem. To this point in the poem there have been many criticisms of the corruptions of the English body politic; what we see here is a destructive analysis of union itself in all the forms it takes when sanctioned by the state: political, mercantile, military.

The first third of the passage (4:569–670) is based upon a simile which suggests a harmonious resolution of the forces of nature and art: man, like the flower growing in its native bed, grows to his fulfillment in society: he "blooms" there. Here again we see that society to Cowper is not merely the object of his criticism, though in general the larger world has served as the foil for the retired life. But as the passage continues with a consideration of the purposes served by the different forms of union within human society, the simile shifts from man as the flower in its native bed (man in society) to man as the flower plucked and arranged for ornament (man leagued with man in politics, in business, in war). The possibility of harmonizing the forces of nature and art thus vanishes in the new vision of the ornamental vase, with its plucked flowers, fading rapidly, stunted in their growth, ("by compression marr'd," 4:669), defiling their neighbors. The ornamental vase, the image of art, represents not man in society, but man leagued with man to exercise power in its various forms. The passage, coming as it does immediately after the attack on soldiership, compares a state-sanctioned organization like the military to the kind of bond typified by the rotting flowers of art in the ornamental vase (al-though the figures here are not carefully managed, since the precise metaphor for the military is that of swarming insects [4:666], so that man joined with man in war is like a "clan" of swarming insects, which are like the bundled flowers of the crowded vase). All kinds of formal human organization sanctioned by the state are the objects of the poet's attack here: associations created by regal warrant, or by mutual consent "for int'rest sake." The passage, indeed, goes on to include within its attack such forms of political and commercial organization as the chartered borough and the commercial corporation, whose members "lose their nature" though "unimpeachable of sin/Against the charities of domestic life." It is "incorporated man" whom Cowper attacks for such abuses as factories built with blood and the conduct of trade at the sword's point. Indeed, if by "politics" we mean the systematic organization of men into groups that can exert power and respond to it, then what emerges from this passage is a radical criticism of the political impulse itself, in all of the forms it assumes, from state to corporation.

But it is an incomplete criticism. Cowper insists upon the essential decency of human nature in its private mode: the incorporated merchant at home with his family is quite another fellow from the same merchant in league with his business associates. Nothing in the passage evokes the satirical tone which would suggest that the private and inner intensities of the merchant are implicated in his public, corporate behavior. Similarly we are told that there is such a thing as "innocent commercial justice" (4:683): its robe is white; but we are not told on what political power innocent commercial justice might be founded and by which private energies it may be sustained. We *do* learn which political process stains its robe, but Cowper does not say by which political institutions innocent commercial justice might be supported. In short, we see in this passage the epitome of the poem's failure as a document of consistent social thought: there is no theory to explain, no central emblem to express, the relations between power and justice, between state and society. Cowper demands the fruits of justice but rejects every source of political power, every type of political organization, for it is in the very process of political incorporation that he locates the source of injustice and corruption. What we have is a forthright recognition of the corruptions of the social order set forth in a way that precludes the discovery within politics of a remedy for those corruptions. When Cowper proposes retirement in book four, therefore, it is not man he withdraws from, only the institutions, inexplicably evil, created by men who are in themselves good.

Nevertheless, we must keep in mind the complexities of Cowper's outlook on the public world. His social criticism does not involve him in sentimentalizing the rural life as a scene removed from the corruptions of the larger life of the nation. Furthermore, despite his critical insight into the meaning of such terms as honor, nobility, and glory—an insight arising from his awareness of their often intimate connection with the brutal realities of power—they still remain for him terms of value, as we have seen in his concern for English honor as it is exemplified in English military success. But by the end of book four, it has become impossible for him to identify his sense of virtuous community with any of the institutions formally sanctioned by the state. Yet Cowper draws back: at the end of book four, instead of pursuing his critical thoughts as far as they might go, he chooses the option of retirement as a personal solution to the public dilemma he has defined.

> Some must be great. Great offices will have
> Great talents. And God gives to ev'ry man
> The virtue, temper, understanding, taste,
> That lifts him into life; and lets him fall
> Just in the niche he was ordain'd to fill.
> To the deliv'rer of an injur'd land
> He gives a tongue t' enlarge upon, an heart
> To feel, and courage to redress her wrongs;
> To monarch's dignity; to judges sense;
> To artists ingenuity and skill;
> To me an unambitious mind, content
> In the low vale of life, that early felt
> A wish for ease and leisure, and ere long
> Found here that leisure and that ease I wish'd.
>
> [4:788–801]

In these concluding lines to book four, Cowper retreats to a position which, in fact, his analysis of political union ought to have precluded. Once again he admits the possibility of a virtuous politics, though he removes himself from any participation in it. Once again he speaks of the dignity of monarchs, the sense of judges and the eloquence of freedom fighters, all filling the places ordained for them in the order of things by God. But it is an unsatisfactory conclusion, a private wish parading as a cosmic vision.[11] These lines indicate, at least, that despite his choice of

11. "Superficially, the conventional praise of rural life balances the satire of the town. But the shift in tone and argument, from vituperation of man's institution-

rural retirement, it was not without great effort that Cowper relinquished the posture of the public poet. *The Task* needs to be understood, not as a simple and sentimental statement of the pleasures of retirement, but as a tortured, and often self-contradictory attempt to speak in a public voice. The elements of bucolic tradition in the poem can best be understood in the light of that attempt, to which they contribute, and by which they are shaped. Cowper's use of bucolic tradition in his complex interpretation of public life is the subject of the next chapter.

---

alized greed to an affirmation that society reflects the divine order of things, is as strikingly unusual as the conjunction in this passage of the generalization 'everything has its place' with the personalized rejection of ambition. . . . What happens in the final lines is that personal feeling takes the place of moral concern" (Free, *William Cowper*, p. 109).

V

Art Divorced from Nature: *The Task* and Bucolic Tradition

The pastoral and georgic elements appearing in *The Task* need to be studied in relation to Cowper's thoughts on society and state. In his use of bucolic topics Cowper undoubtedly shows the influence of several currents of thought running through eighteenth-century writing: a complete picture of his work would have to take into account, among others, such influences as physicotheology, such topics as the happy man of the "beatus ille" tradition, and such effects as Cowper's evangelicism may have had upon his apprehension of the natural world about him. Certainly Cowper's religious experience and its connections in his mind with the phenomena of rural nature contribute a major subject to *The Task*.[1] Nevertheless, despite the contribution each of these perspectives makes to the whole poem, the striking feature of *The Task* is its own emphasis on contemporary problems of power. To be sure, the poem as a whole moves towards a vision of things which

1. For a discussion of Cowper's religious attitudes as they are reflected in his depiction of natural scenery see Roderick Huang, *William Cowper: Nature Poet* (London: Oxford University Press for the University of Malaya, 1957), chaps. 3 and 4. Huang offers a good account of the pertinent intellectual and religious background, but not much in the way of critical study. Patricia M. Spacks's *The Poetry of Vision* (Cambridge: Harvard University Press, 1967), chap. 8 presents the best critical discussion of the meaning the natural world had for Cowper as a literary artist.

transcends the realms of power and politics: the direction of the poem is always towards the revelation of the realm of grace as the only alternative to the broken world; but if that is the direction of the poem, its starting point, nevertheless, is in the realm of art. As a document of its time *The Task* is remarkable for the extent of its concern with the issues and conditions of contemporary life; its failure to achieve a resolution, within the domains of nature and art, of the problems it raises, is a measure of the unsentimental clarity of Cowper's statement of those problems.

The Task presents itself as a poem of social comment and criticism; from that initial purpose the poem moves in several directions in response to the pressure of its observation of contemporary life. Finally unable to reconcile the fact of an inherently corrupt political corporation with the normative idea of a healthy community for which his poem envisions no political home, Cowper posits for the good man the alternative of rural retirement with an ultimate aim of religious peace. Even when, as in book five, the subject, political liberty, admits of some praise for the English polity in contrast to the French, Cowper permits his focus to shift from political to spiritual freedom; spiritual freedom, he asserts, is the final and only real object of man's devotion, the British freeman's or the French slave's.

In organizing his criticism of society and state Cowper has recourse to certain leading themes or topics of bucolic tradition. The theme of nature and art is constantly in his mind, as we have seen already in his use of the metaphor of flowers blown in their native bed to represent healthy community; in contrast are the flowers plucked, arranged and rotting in a vase, which represent man leagued with his neighbor in any of the forms of political union—corporation, guild, military. However, although Cowper's themes and topics—nature and art, retirement, active man and contemplative—derive from bucolic tradition, there is throughout *The Task* an insistent social realism that we feel in the poet's aversion to rural sentimentality, both in life and in literature. In book three, for example, where his subject is the activity proper to rural retirement, Cowper's well-known contempt for hunting is expressed in part as an attack on those "self deluded nymphs and swains/Who dream they have a taste for fields and groves" (3: 316–17), but who, in reality, were they deprived of the violent sport, the pageantry, dance, feast, and song of their summer retreat, would be impatient for the town. The mockery in Cowper's use of the words "nymphs" and "swains" is as clear as his allusion to the kind of poem peopled by such shadows, mere projections of an urban dream. In book four, introducing the passage I have discussed on the corruption of the countryside, Cowper makes some observations about the pastoral mode itself. He laments, even as he acknowledges, the passing of the pastoral dream, vanished in the corruption of the countryside which, in days of earlier virtue, could nourish the pleasing pastoral delusions of Virgil and of Sidney, "warbler of poetic prose." No longer possible as a vehicle for serious expression is the literary type, with its nymphs and shepherds, and its root assumption that these figures could serve as metaphors of the active lives of the nobles they are surrogates for:

> Nymphs were Dianas then, and swains had hearts
> That felt their virtues: innocence, it seems,
> From courts dismiss'd, found shelter in the groves;
> The footsteps of simplicity, impress'd
> Upon the yielding herbage, (so they sing)
> Then were not all effac'd. . . .
> Vain wish! these days were never: airy dreams
> Sat for the picture; and the poet's hand
> Imparting substance to an empty shade
> Impos'd a gay delirium for a truth.
> Grant it:—I still must envy them an age
> That favour'd such a dream; in days like these
> Impossible, when virtue is so scarce . . .
>
> [4:517–22, 525–31]

Cowper here demonstrates his awareness of the literary nature of the pastoral mode, recognizing it as a "gay delirium." He does not lament the passing of a time when life was in reality as it is pictured in Sidney's romance; rather he laments the passing of an age which could seek its ideal image in those pages: "I still must envy them an age/That favour'd such a dream . . ." (4:529–30).

Cowper acknowledges, in effect, the insufficiency to his time of the pastoral as a literary form.

It is important, I think, to emphasize that Cowper had no sentimental illusions about the countryside. Nevertheless, he uses bucolic tradition in developing his theme of retirement, so that what emerges from his work is a crucial set of problems inherent in his attempt to write unsentimentally about the country while, at the same time, proposing the rural perspective as the measure of the vices of the England of his time. Despite his employment of traditional ideas and topics, his work emerges as an essentially modern poem in its definition of issues and dilemmas arising from his observation of a rapidly changing world.

We have seen in book four the direction in which the poem tends in its treatment of retirement: the poet's ruminations on society and state effectively preclude the development of retirement as an emblematic concept serving to help the contemplative man back to his active life in society. Yet we have seen also that the poet, in his introduction of the theme of retirement in book four, did not necessarily preclude this traditional development of the idea. Book four begins, after all, with the arrival of the eagerly anticipated post carrying its news of the great world; the narrator admits his distant kinship with that world. It is the subsequent analysis of the political component of social union that, in the end, leaves him no role to play within the community.

A similar pattern emerges in book three of *The Task*, "The Garden." In this section of the poem, devoted to the activities of man in rural retirement, the poet works his thought through the possibilities presented by the topic of nature and art as he sets forth the moral quality of the life of retirement.

> How various his employments, whom the world
> Calls idle; and who justly, in return,
> Esteems that busy world an idler too!
> Friends, books, a garden, and perhaps his pen,
> Delightful industry enjoy'd at home,
> And nature in her cultivated trim

Dress'd to his taste, inviting him abroad—
Can he want occupation who has these?
Will he be idle who has much t'enjoy?

. . . .

He that attends to his interior self,
That has a heart, and keeps it; has a mind
That hungers, and supplies it; and who seeks
A social not a dissipated life;
Has business; feels himself engag'd t'achieve
No unimportant, though a silent, task.

[3:352–60, 373–78]

In this passage, a kind of proem to the detailed account of his rural labors, the poet emphasizes his "business"; it is an important point to him, this insistence upon the link with society available to the retired man. To be sure, he distinguishes between the fruits of retirement and those of active life ("wisdom is a pearl with most success/Sought in still water" [3:381–82]), but he does not emphasize any sense of isolation from the general pursuits of mankind. The great theme of this section of his poem is the happy blend of nature and art in the healthy activities of rural retirement. These activities, furthermore, are social in nature, a kind of "business." The appropriate landscape of retirement is, accordingly, "nature in her cultivated trim," emblematic of the civilized achievements of proper industry.

Cowper's model of the country life has, on occasion, been seen as a kind of refined sentimentality itself, all of a piece with his general preference for the familiar, as opposed to the sublime, landscape. But it is precisely his effort in much of *The Task* to depict nature not only as it is, but also as it might be; his taste for nature in its cultivated trim creates those moments in *The Task* where the poet shows himself closest to the bucolic literary heritage, both in its pastoral and georgic aspects. Thus, if we examine at length a passage which might offend for its lack of robust primitivism, we may perhaps discover some excessive gentility, but to stop there would hinder us from grasping the poet's real purpose. As a kind of proem to the famous georgic interlude in "The Garden," Cowper tells us of the retired man's attitude toward garden labor:

Nor does he govern only or direct,
But much performs himself. No works indeed
That ask robust tough sinews, bred to toil,
Servile employ; but such as may amuse,
Not tire, demanding rather skill than force.
Proud of his well-spread walls, he views his trees
That meet (no barren interval between)
With pleasure more than ev'n their fruits afford,
Which save himself who trains them, none can feel:
These therefore, are his own peculiar charge;
No meaner hand may discipline the shoots,
None but his steel approach them. What is weak,
Distemper'd, or has lost prolific pow'rs,
Impair'd by age, his unrelenting hand
Dooms to the knife: nor does he spare the soft
And succulent, that feeds its giant growth,
But barren, at th'expense of neighb'ring twigs
Less ostentatious, and not studded thick
With hopeful gems. The rest, no portion left
That may disgrace his art, or disappoint
Large expectation, he disposes neat
At measur'd distances, that air and sun,
Admitted freely, may afford their aid,
And ventilate and warm the swelling buds.
Hence summer has her riches, autumn hence,
And hence ev'n winter fills his wither'd hand
With blushing fruits, and plenty, not his own.
Fair recompense of labour well bestow'd
And wise precaution; which a clime so rude
Makes needful still, whose spring is but the child
Of churlish winter, in her froward moods
Discov'ring much the temper of her sire.

[3:403–34]

The great theme of this passage—the possible harmony of nature and art—is anticipated in the gentility of the first few lines, which distinguish between simple toil and the work of the gardener: the distinction is, of course, in the exercise of art, skill; the passage goes on to focus attention repeatedly on the successes of art: a line of trees is a "wall" and the walls are "well spread"; the trees are "trained," disposed neatly at "measured distances" so that "no portion may disgrace his art." Not only are the efforts of art praised here, but they are shown to withstand the defects of nature and complement its insufficiencies. It is in union with the efforts of art that summer and autumn produce their "riches," and that winter, an *unnatural* parent, is prevented from killing her infant, the spring. "Assistant art/Then acts in nature's office, brings to pass/The glad espousals, and ensures the crop" (3:541–43).

These are the thoughts that frame the famous georgic passage on the cultivation of the cucumber and introduce the lengthy account of the care and disposition of the greenhouse and garden. Behind them lie some two thousand years of familiar repetition, and their essential direction is toward the union of nature and art. When, however, Cowper adopts a critical perspective on the works of man and civilization, he is likely to interpret the relations between the paired terms more simply, to understand them as conflicting choices rather than blended forces. For example, the poem on several occasions introduces the term "art" to clarify or to structure its thoughts on nature and God. In book one the calm rapture over the beauties of nature finds expression, in part, through the idea of God, the artist, fashioning nature as his "artifact." But, though the paired terms, nature and art, help Cowper to make a point about God's works, the thrust of his thought is not towards a clarification of certain problems of the Christian life, but rather towards a confrontation with the absurdities of civilized life:

> Strange! there should be found,
> Who, self-imprison'd in their proud saloons,
> Renounce the odours of the open field
> For the unscented fictions of the loom;
> Who satisfied with only pencil'd scenes
> Prefer to the performance of a God
> Th' inferior wonders of an artist's hand!
>
> [1., 413–419]

Helping to organize the thought here, the theme of nature and art appears in its simplest form as the vehicle for the praise of simplicity. Closer to the poet's intention than an elaboration of some aspect of the Christian life is the criticism of excessive civilization—the preference for artifact over immediate experience. Art in its simpler sense becomes the term of lesser value; nature, bearing in this instance the burden of meaning implied in the concept of God as artist, becomes the norm against which the vain inclinations of man as artist are measured. The famous aphorism towards which Book I leads—God made the country, man made the town—develops in part from this very simple application of the paired terms to social experience and expresses an essentially social criticism, rather than a religious theme. In this context, art is placed in simple contrast with nature.

Still, we have noted earlier that Cowper's thinking about politics and society is more complex than the famous aphorism suggests. In book four his search into the distinction between society and state leads to a more thorough consideration of the claims of society, and perhaps a more adequate account of the source of man's difficulties in society, than is implied in the formula with which book one concludes. But in book one, too, despite the finality with which he asserts the absolute distinction between country and town, the poet spends considerable effort laboring to establish a more conplex evaluation of the opposing claims. In this effort the terms *nature* and *art* become very important.

If, as we have seen, the idea of God as artist is useful to Cowper in establishing the moral authority of nature over the works of man, nevertheless, much of the thought in book one probes the limits of nature and asserts the powers of human art. There is, for example, the encounter with Kate, the mad woman, who "roams the dreary waste" (1., 546–547), and the wretched misery of the peasant's nest. These are aspects of the rural landscape which qualify the idyllic virtues of the countryside whose rural sights and sounds more usually "lull the spirit while they fill the mind" (1., 187). There is, furthermore, the description of the gypsy band. Repulsed—almost horrified—by the bestial details of their forest life, the narrator is pushed towards an acknowledgment of the value of art, of society, and, indeed, of commerce:

> A vagabond and useless tribe there eat
> Their miserable meal. A kettle, slung

> Between two poles upon a stick transverse,
> Receives the morsel—flesh obscene of dog,
> Or vermin, or, at best, of cock purloin'd
> From his accustom'd perch.
>
> . . . .
>
> Strange! that a creature rational, and cast
> In human mould, should brutalize by choice
> His nature; and though capable of arts
> By which the world might profit, and himself,
> Self-banish'd from society prefer
> Such squalid sloth to honourable toil!
>
> [1., 559–564, 574–579]

But even these wretches

> Can change their whine into a mirthful note
> When safe occasion offers; and, with dance,
> And music of the bladder and the bag,
> Beguile their woes, and make the weeds resound.
> Such health and gaiety of heart enjoy
> The houseless rovers of the sylvan world;
> And, breathing wholesome air, and wand'ring much,
> Need other physic none to heal th'effects
> Of loathsome diet, penury, and cold.
>
> [1:583–91]

Here it is human art that redeems nature, for certainly what we see of the forest life is not the work of God the artist. As soon as the narrator has perceived that the gypsies are capable of some scraps of art ("the music of the bladder and the bag"), his tone changes. The change is reflected in the diction: the "vagabond and useless tribe" now become the "houseless rovers of the sylvan world," words which recall some of the stylized expressive habits of the formal pastoral.

Such an acknowledgment of art's virtues which we see briefly in these sections of book one is an element of the larger effort of Cowper's imagination: an attempt not merely to acknowledge the virtues of art, but to resolve the antinomy between art and nature. We had noticed this before in the proem to the georgic interlude of book three, and we may observe it again in book one, where the

poet directly praises the works of civilized man. But Cowper's effort
to harmonize in his imagination the claims of nature and of art can
be observed also in places where the praise of art is not the poet's
primary topic. For example, there is his description of an enclosed
field, formerly part of a forest:

> Ye fallen avenues! once more I mourn
> Your fate unmerited, once more rejoice
> That yet a remnant of your race survives.
> How airy and how light the graceful arch,
> Yet awful as the consecrated roof
> Re-echoing pious anthems! while beneath
> The chequer'd earth seems restless as a flood
> Brush'd by the wind.
>
> [1:338–45]

Here, in fact, the ostensible subject of the lines deals with the
ravages perpetrated on nature by man, the cultivator. Yet the
diction and the imagery which express the poet's praise of the
destroyed trees are of towns, temples, and architecture: avenues,
arch, roof. Conversely, in another section of the poem dealing with
the virtues, limited as they may be, of the city, the narrator slips
into the language of agriculture in his discussion of the art of
sculpture:

> Nor does the chissel occupy alone
> The pow'rs of sculpture, but the style as much;
> Each province of her art her equal care.
> With nice incision of her guided steel
> She ploughs a brazen field, and clothes a soil
> So sterile with what charms soe'er she will,
> The richest scen'ry and the loveliest forms.
>
> [1:705–11]

In these lines it is the figure of the chisel as plow that generates the
extended metaphor likening sculpture to the tilling of a field.

   If, then, some of Cowper's imaginative energy works throughout
the poem to express the possible harmony between art and nature,
we need to inquire into the causes of his final failure to achieve a
sustained vision of that harmony. It is in the face of evidence

emerging from lines such as those quoted above that the simple and abrupt formula distinguishing between the works of man and the works of God, art and nature, town and country, becomes a problem. "God made the country; man made the town."

If that simple formula does not express the full complexity of Cowper's social thought, neither does it contradict the final implications of his social thought. We have seen in book four how Cowper, thinking of the entity "society" seems to include it among the phenomena of nature, whereas he places the state within the realm of art. As a social critic, therefore, Cowper maintains the absolute distinction between the two realms. He can conceive of the possibility of a good society in which man is leagued with man like flowers in their native bed, but he can see no evidence of it in the political world around him. In book one the split between nature and art is expressed in simpler terms as a split between town and country, but the division is just as absolute as in book four, despite those undercurrents which suggest that Cowper's imagination can construct an image of the possible harmony between the two realms.

The problem of *The Task* as a poem of social criticism referring to certain aspects of bucolic tradition for its normative attitudes is thus squarely raised by these observations about book one. We see nothing less than an unresolved conflict between the poet's imagination, whose impulse is to express a vision of the harmony possible between nature and art, and the social critic's observations, which force upon him the recognition that harmony between the two realms is impossible.

By the end of book one Cowper puts the term "art" through a tortuous development, finally reducing the word to its simplest signification: corruption and artificiality. That the poet had been aiming at a more complex statement than he finally gives us can be seen, not only in those passages studied above, but also in the concluding movement of "The Sofa" where Cowper attempts an evaluation of London life. It is from that section that the lines on sculpture come, and it is that section which is introduced by the picture of the South Sea native pining as he remembers his London experiences. "I cannot think thee yet so dull of heart/And spiritless as never to regret/Sweets tasted here, and left as soon as known" (1: 651–53). If we remember everything the notion of the noble savage meant to the popular imagination in Cowper's day, perhaps no lines in *The Task* will strike us so clearly as do these with Cowper's effort to avoid contemporary sentimentality about the virtues of simplicity. That he is dealing with a complex problem, and that he is aware of it, is plainly evident in the tortured syntax which reflects, in the following lines introducing his judgment of London, a totally honest attempt to see what the city means, independent of the clichés and formulas so readily available to him:

> But, though true worth and virtue in the mild
> And genial soil of cultivated life
> Thrive most, and may perhaps thrive only there,
> Yet not in cities oft: in proud and gay
> And gain-devoted cities.
>
> [1:678–82]

This short passage once again makes use of the diction of the land to express its vision of the virtues of civilization. The syntactical play around the verb *thrive* expresses the poet's effort to come to a judicious, not a simple, statement: most in cities, perhaps only in cities, yet not often in cities do true worth and virtue thrive. It is his attempt to avoid simple judgments that he displays here in a very effective line.

Yet this acknowledgment of the possibilities of good in civilization will give way easily and immediately to that other, simple and censorious manner so characteristic of Cowper. The final vision of book one is one of doom, doom attributed to the corruption spreading from the cities through English life. It is a vision inconsistent with the poet's effort to make a judicious judgment of the matter, an effort expressed in the very lines which introduce his censure of London.

> She [London] has her praise. Now mark a spot or two,
> That so much beauty would do well to purge;
> And show this queen of cities, that so fair
> May yet be foul; so witty, yet not wise.
>
> [1:725–28]

The implication here is that a balanced judgment is possible, that the world of art is open to redemption. He invites us merely to "mark a spot or two." But that hint does not survive the force of Cowper's observations of the dark side of the town, observations centering largely on the political corruption that is companion to luxury, and the slackness of religious discipline, which is the chief symptom of all else that is wrong with the city and the nation. Scarcely twenty-five lines after the promise of a balanced judgment ("Now mark a spot or two,/That so much beauty would do well to purge . . . ") comes the famous line which announces the impossibility of that balanced judgment. "God made the country, and man made the town." In the light of the unqualified judgment stated in that line, we may wonder how seriously the poet meant to be taken when he acknowledged, not many lines earlier, that virtue may perhaps thrive only in cities. The conclusion to book one is entirely dominated by the force of the poet's social criticism, expressed in the apocalyptic vision which marks the failure of his imagination to achieve that other vision of art harmonized with nature:

> Folly such as yours,
> Grac'd with a sword, and worthier of a fan,
> Has made, what enemies could ne'er have done,
> Our arch of empire, stedfast but for you,
> A mutilated structure, soon to fall.

[1:770–74

***

As if disregarding the virtues of civilization he had labored to express, Cowper, in the concluding lines of book one, establishes a picture of retirement drawn entirely in response to the corruption of urban life. The conclusion of book one, therefore, offers a simple alternative to that corruption. If urban civilization has been "Advancing fashion to the post of truth,/And centr'ing all authority in modes/And customs of her own" (1:744–46), then this ancient problem is not to be resolved within society, but away from it.

> Possess ye, therefore, ye, who, borne about
> In chariots and sedans, know no fatigue

But that of idleness, and taste no scenes
But such as art contrives, possess ye still
Your element; there only can ye shine. . . .

　　Your songs confound
Our more harmonious notes; the thrush departs
Scar'd, and th' offended nightingale is mute.
　　　　　　　　　　　　　　　[1:754–58, 766–68]

This condemnation of art with which book one concludes expresses Cowper's judgment of society and forms his idea of retirement at that point in the poem. Picking up for fuller treatment some of the hints dropped in book one on the virtues of art and civilization, the poet in book three returns to the same problem, attempting a more complex approach to it. The lines on the cucumber, the greenhouse, and the garden are perhaps the most imaginatively rich section of the poem. Here rural labor and the gardener's skill are not at first set forth as modes of action distinct from and opposed to man's activities as a member of the social order. We have noted already that Cowper calls attention to his garden work as his "business," and is quick to justify it in terms which link it with the business of the larger world. At the same time, we can glean suggestions in his gardening of some of the prelapsarian magic of Adam's work in Eden. The retired man at work in his garden is engaged in something like the magical labor which was Adam's lot before the fall—work that is not quite work, but a kind of praise for the abundance of created nature. Milton's Eden comes to mind here, because Milton, too, was concerned with the distinction between abundance and excess, between that art which is corrupt and associated with luxury, and that art which is in harmony with nature. In *Paradise Lost* the abundance of Eden's plant life is without excess, and Milton tells us that, for all its profusion, it is "wrought mosaic."

Cowper's account of his greenhouse displays for us his most forthright statement in praise of the labors of art; further, it is in this section of his poem that he attempts to fuse into an imaginative whole his thoughts on the good social order with his praise of the efforts of art.

Who loves a garden loves a green-house too.
Unconscious of a less propitious clime,
There blooms exotic beauty, warm and snug,
While the winds whistle and snows descend.

. . . .

 All plants, of ev'ry leaf, that can endure
The winter's frown, if screen'd from his shrewd bite,
Live there, and prosper. Those Ausonia claims,
Levantine regions these; th' Azores send
Their jessamine, her jessamine remote
Caffraia: foreigners from many lands,
They form one social shade, as if conven'd
By magic summons of th' Orphean lyre.
Yet just arrangement, rarely brought to pass
But by a master's hand, disposing well
The gay diversities of leaf and flow'r,
Must lend its aid t'illustrate all their charms,
And dress the regular yet various scene.

           [3:566–69, 580–92]

We may hear, perhaps, in this passage some of the epic sonorities
of Milton's Eden: the place names, the geographic sweep represented by the various plants together with the exotic quality of the
display, contribute to an effect unusual in Cowper. But the whole
scene is carefully limited and controlled; it is not God's, but man's
art which is the subject of the passage. It is "just arrangement,"
and not sublimity, which the passage celebrates. Here, the efforts of
art are brought together with the energies of nature to form that
characteristically pastoral vision of man engaged in healthy, which
is to say, magical, songlike labor. The flowers "form one social
shade, as if conven'd/By magic summons of th' Orphean lyre."
Cowper's gardener is something less than Milton's Adam, and
something more than Dyer's merchant: his skill is akin to that of
Orpheus, and the efforts of his art yield "one social shade." In a
moment of unusual poetic concentration Cowper has succeeded in
fusing together three essential strains of feeling underlying the
bucolic attitude: the sense of society as a healthy harmony; the
sense of art as nature, at once creating and exemplifying the work

of the good society; and the idea of magical labor whose essence is the praise of its materials, not their exploitation.

That the greenhouse and garden can serve as emblems of the good social order is an idea reinforced by the repetition in the garden section of several images of harmony, all of them unified in the reference they bear to social order.

> He, therefore, who would see his flow'rs dispos'd
> Sightly and in just order, ere he gives
> The beds the trusted treasure of their seeds,
> Forecasts the future whole; that, when the scene
> Shall break into its preconceiv'd display,
> Each for itself, and all as with one voice
> Conspiring, may attest his bright design.
> Nor even then, dismissing as perform'd
> His pleasant work, may he suppose it done.
> Few self-supported flow'rs endure the wind
> Uninjur'd, but expect th'upholding aid
> Of the smooth-shaven prop, and, neatly tied,
> Are wedded thus, like beauty to old age,
> For int'rest sake, the living to the dead.
> Some clothe the soil that feeds them, far diffus'd
> And lowly creeping, modest and yet fair,
> Like virtue, thriving most where little seen:
> Some, more aspiring, catch the neighbor shrub
> With clasping tendrils, and invest his branch,
> Else unadorn'd, with many a gay festoon
> And fragrant chaplet, recompensing well
> The strength they borrow with the grace they lend.
> All hate the rank society of weeds,
> Noisome, and ever greedy to exhaust
> Th' impov'rish'd earth; an overbearing race,
> That, like the multitude made faction-mad,
> Disturb good order, and degrade true worth.
>
> [3:648–74]

Cowper's garden is designed to shine with "contrasted beauty" (3: 635); as a garden it is a tribute to elegance and taste. However, as the passage develops, the virtues of elegance and taste are woven into a larger fabric of meaning, just as the garden itself, the product of elegance and taste, begins to resonate to larger ideas. The passage as a whole suggests that the elegance and taste which go into the making of a garden have, as their characteristic effect, that harmonious tension which is also the underlying principle of good social order. As the images of harmony begin to collect, it becomes clear that Cowper's garden, in its elegance and taste, is also an emblem of a good society: the flower unable to stand self-supported is "wedded" "for int'rest sake" to a prop; the low plants clothe the soil that feeds them; the taller plants with their clasping tendrils fix themselves to a neighboring shrub, and the poet tells us that in so doing they recompense the strength they borrow with the grace they lend. Finally, even the weeds are brought into the scheme if only to contrast with it; the language here is perfectly clear in revealing Cowper's emblematic intention in the description of his garden: the weeds are a "rank society." They disturb "good order"; like the multitude, they are "faction-mad." Unlike the other plants, they exhaust the earth and contribute nothing to it. They live outside the harmony of opposing forces which gives the garden its character, and Cowper's description of them in political terms signals to us both the larger meaning of his garden as an image of good social order, and his definition of that order as the *concordia discors* which Pope spoke for in *The Epistle to Bathurst* and the *Essay on Man*. Cowper's garden is "one social shade" and in it the powers of art and the energies of nature are one.

The portrait of the garden complements the account of the greenhouse which had preceded it. There, too, the gardener's labors are made meaningful in reference to the theme of nature and art and the vision of the good society.

> Plant behind plant aspiring, in the van
> The dwarfish, in the rear retir'd, but still
> Sublime above the rest, the statelier stand.
> So once were rang'd the sons of ancient Rome,
> A noble show while Roscius trod the stage;
> And so while Garrick, as renown'd as he,
> The sons of Albion; fearing each to lose
> Some note of Nature's music from his lips,
> And covetous of Shakespeare's beauty, seen
> In ev'ry flash of his far-beaming eye.
>
> [3:593–602]

The floral display here has become a theater, the ordered rows of

blossoms an audience, the flowers of the gardener's art the specta-
tors of Garrick's and Shakespeare's. The combined efforts of Shakespeare and Garrick produce "nature's music," that art which is
nature, while Cowper's flowers, that nature which is art, are ranged
together as images of the "sons of Albion," a picture of what social
experience might be under the harmonized energies of nature and
art. The English nation is brought into focus alongside the Roman
model, "a noble show." This is an extraordinary moment in *The
Task*, perhaps the most concentrated expression of Cowper's intention as a pastoral poet. Cowper's writing here goes beyond those
effects of realistic observation which have often been taken for his
special contribution to literary history, his "preromanticism." In
his depiction of the greenhouse and garden, Cowper brings his
poem as close as it will come to elevating genre into metaphor. His
attention is applied to much more than what these scenes actually
look like; he is concerned with what they might mean. We discover
in this section of the poem what might be called the generic
attributes of bucolic poetry: a model of the good society developed
within the perspective created by the paired terms, nature and art.

For a sustained moment in *The Task,* the poem's representations
of created nature take on the quality of metaphor; they absorb into
themselves the poet's ideas about good social order. Emblematic of
that union of nature and art defining optimal civilization, Cowper's greenhouse and garden are the fullest achievement in the
poem of the imaginative impulse which had not been successfully
expressed in book one. For a long moment as the poem rises in
imaginative intensity, we can recognize in it that mode of social
celebration which is characteristic of the pastoral and the georgic.
We become aware in the garden and greenhouse of an imaginative
intensity working to fuse the several concerns of the poem into that
metaphorical apprehension of reality which the bucolic mode can
be. And when this happens we feel the poem functioning in a
celebrative manner.

But this manner cannot be sustained; the narrator of *The Task* is
far more a critic than a celebrant and his critical purpose often
overwhelms those other tendencies of the poem which reach their

height in the greenhouse and garden section. Fluctuating from celebration to criticism instead of generating celebration from criticism, the poem's design displays flaws not unrelated to those we have noted in Cowper's social and political thought. At the heart of Cowper's social thought is an unsatisfactorily examined assertion of the split between society and state; this is reflected in his poem's failure to establish a central tone or voice. Just as the poem fluctuates without controlled design between celebration and criticism, the voice of the narrator tends to shift from rapture, to reflection, to censorious and indignant attack.[2] An instance of this faulty control of tone was evident in the conclusion to the first book where the intention to express a judicious appraisal of London dissolves rapidly into the indignant tone of the speaker's categorical rejection of the urban world. More revealing as an example of the indecisive quality of his poem's imaginative design is Cowper's coda to the georgic interlude on the cucumber. That idyll of the happy man busily engaged in his virtuous work is abruptly shattered by the intrusion once again of the censorious manner.

> Grudge not, ye rich, (since luxury must have
> His dainties, and the world's more num'rous half
> Lives by contriving delicates for you)
> Grudge not the cost. Ye little know the cares,
> The vigilance, the labour, and the skill,
> That day and night are exercis'd, and hang
> Upon the ticklish balance of suspense,
> That ye may garnish your profuse regales
> With summer fruits brought forth by wintry suns.
>
> [3:544–52]

2. David Boyd has recently interpreted these oscillations in judgment as determined by a swing between pastoral and satirical impulses; Boyd understands the pastoral movement in *The Task* simply as the vehicle for Cowper's negative judgments on the town, giving to his presentation of rural retirement the character merely of "safe sterility." For Boyd, the pastoral serves Cowper as a "flight, not only from the corruption of the world, but also from the burdens of its moral responsibilities." "His garden is not a 'green world' but a garrison, the moral issues of the social world are not clarified, but rather vigorously excluded" ("Satire and Pastoral in *The Task*," *PLL* 10, no. 4 (Fall 1974): 375–76, 377. This seems to me to miss the complex mixture of attitudes evident throughout in Cowper's use of pastoral; it is not a simple vehicle for negative judgments on the town or on

These lines provide the transition from the cucumber passage to the section we have examined above on the greenhouse. Their effect is to interrupt the voice appropriate to the emblematic intention of these passages taken together. The intrusion of the censorious manner in this place is a symptom of the poet's failure to control his design, and a look at the lines explains once again what has diverted his attention. Whereas the preceding georgic on the cucumber had for its subject the good work of the happy man, the subject of the coda is the consumption of his labor's fruits by that corrupt world which is implacably there outside the boundaries of the fields of retirement. The labor that had been worthy of praise because it itself had been praise and not exploitation is suddenly placed in another context. The labor devoted to the cucumber cannot be considered apart from the luxurious, pampered consumption of "summer fruits brought forth by wintry suns." Thus, innocent country labor also plays its part in the consuming luxury, also contributes to the "profuse regales" of a nation which has lost its way. But we may ask whether it was necessary for these considerations to be injected into a passage of the poem that had been working to create a symbolic vision of innocent labor. The effect is to destroy the imaginative integrity of the georgic passage: the world of London breaks through the fences defining the symbolic locale of retirement's garden. The purposes of celebration give way to the pressure of criticism, but at considerable cost to the poem's design.

The pervading theme of the georgic interlude is the marriage of nature and art in the virtuous labor of retirement. It is a labor that sets the energies of art alongside the rougher aspects of nature; the relationship between the two worlds is expressed in complexity. It is when "November dark/Checks vegetation in the torpid plant/ Expos'd to his cold breath, the task begins." But it is not as an adversary that the retired man offers his labor, not as a triumph

---

civilization, but is capable of valuing both. When this effort finally proves unsuccessful, what we have is not a simple reliance on the pastoral as a standard of negative judgment, but instead a disintegration of its metaphoric complexity, in effect a dismissal of the pastoral as a useful structure of judgment.

over nature that he offers his fruits. For in working alongside nature he is deeply involved in her rhythms:

> Thrice must the voluble and restless earth
> Spin round upon her axle, ere the warmth,
> Slow gathering in the midst, through the square mass
> Diffus'd, attain the surface. . . .

[3:490–93]

Every step in the process of raising the unseasonable fruit is expressed, not as a triumph, but as a patient submission to those rhythms.

> Experience, slow preceptress, teaching oft
> The way to glory by miscarriage foul,
> Must prompt him, and admonish how to catch
> Th' auspicious moment, when the temper'd heat,
> Friendly to vital motion, may afford
> Soft fomentation, and invite the seed.

(3:505–10]

His seed is invited, not imposed, for his labor against November he does not understand as a struggle against nature. Consequently, his art does not loom larger than the forces which are its materials. Several times the habit of expression in the georgic interlude underlines the narrator's complex understanding of his task. He sees himself finally as the servant of his creations, not their master. "The crowded roots *demand* enlargment . . . *Indulg'd* in what they wish, they soon supply/Large foliage . . ." (3:532, 534–35, italics added). There is something far more subtle here than exultation over man's power to shape nature. When the poet tells us finally that under his care

> Assistant art
> Then acts in nature's office, brings to pass
> The glad espousals, and ensures the crop. . . .

[3:541–43]

we understand the complexity of that union of nature and art in the happy projects of retirement. Art acts in nature's offices only by submitting itself to nature's powers and demands. This is innocent labor because it is without pride; art's success is nature's praise.

This precisely expressed interlude is of a piece with Cowper's fine achievement in his presentation of his garden and greenhouse. These sections together mark the height of his poetic expression of the bucolic vision which serves as the normative foundation for his criticisms of his contemporary England. We have seen how the topic of nature and art is deeply involved in that vision; out of the greenhouse and garden, an imaginative locale is created in which the good work of the gardener, the marriage of nature and art, and a vision of the social potential of man all come together in a complex, emblematic fusion that celebrates the harmony a poet perceives in the natural and social orders of experience.

But we have seen also that the intensity of these heightened moments of imagination fusing genre into metaphor gives way and slackens as the poet's critical voice makes itself heard. Because the complex vision of optimal civilization is intruded upon by the censorious voice, the bucolic metaphor does not in itself express the total range of the poet's concerns. Much the same thing happens again at the close of the passages following those on the greenhouse and garden; once more the critical voice speaks out against those vulgar mansions, gardens, and estates which, blemishing the countryside, testify not to the marriage of nature and art, but rather to the conspicuous consumption exported to the land from London. Cowper's idyllic countryside, therefore, never becomes a poetic idea large enough to encompass everything he wishes to say about England; unlike Lord Burlington's estate, Cowper's garden and greenhouse, those emblems of the marriage of nature and art and the good social order, have not emerged as the poem's central vehicle of imaginative apprehension. Some part of England's life has been unassimilable within their emblematic range.

A metaphor contains within itself, or is the result of, a play of opposing energies; the metaphor, at best, expresses the resolution of those opposing forces. The bucolic metaphor tells us that the energies of nature and the powers of art are one. Hence the elegant shepherd or the soldier-farmer. But in *The Task* that metaphor is a lesser thing. Failing to culminate in the creation of an imaginative vision resolving the opposing forces of the poem's subject, the poem in fact uses the bucolic metaphor itself as only one of the elements of the dialectic actually pulsing through the work. The metaphor of the marriage of nature and art expresses Cowper's imaginative understanding of optimal civilization; if, as I have argued, there lies at the heart of the poem an implied distinction between society and state, then the bucolic metaphor serves to express Cowper's understanding of society as the term of value. His bucolic vision is expressed in a celebrative mode; it is not, however, the kingdom which he celebrates, but rather what the kingdom might be—were it to divest itself of all the appurtenances of political power: money, weapons, organization. Therefore, although the poem reaches its imaginative heights in those places where its subject is the marriage of nature and art, the larger subject, the irremediable split between society and state, forces the bucolic metaphor over to the periphery of the poem, not allowing it to become the poem's crown. The bucolic metaphor is useless as a means of apprehending or of expressing the meaning of the state. It expresses, in fact, everything which the state is not.

❦

When the poet's attention turns, as it does in book five, to an examination of the state, we may observe how the bucolic metaphor virtually disintegrates; its elements, nature and art, fly away from each other, each going off to reassume its simplest meaning, dissipating all the energy that had been needed to create their momentary fusion in the greenhouse and garden. In book five Cowper ranges over several topics: kingship, warfare, political liberty, the good state. The discussion begins within the bounds prescribed by the terms nature and art; by the end of book five, however, the term "art" drops out, having been reduced to its simplest meaning: artifice. The term replacing "art" to form a new dialectic with "nature" is "grace." And with the introduction of the order of grace into his system of social thought, Cowper moves beyond any possibility of integrating man's political experience with his larger purposes as a participant in God's sacramental order.

"The Winter Morning Walk" works into its discussion of king-ship through the account of the Russian czarina's ice palace. It is a palace of art and of ingenuity; the narrator is both fascinated and repelled by it. On the one hand, it provides him the chance to create a poem, to exercise the fancy, and he seizes the opportunity.

> In such a palace Aristaeus found
> Cyrene, when he bore the plaintive tale
> Of his lost bees to her maternal ear:
> In such a palace poetry might place
> The armory of winter; where his troops,
> The gloomy clouds, find weapons, arrowy sleet,
> Skin-piercing volley, blossom-bruising hail,
> And snow that often blinds the trav'ler's course,
> And wraps him in an unexpected tomb.
>
> [5:135–43]

But the meaning of the empress's ice palace is controlled by other intentions: it appears in the poem as a contrast to the fantastic designs in the fields of snow and frost astonishing the eye on a winter morning.

> Thus nature works as if to mock at art,
> And in defiance of her rival pow'rs;
> By these fortuitous and random strokes
> Performing such inimitable feats
> As she with all her rules can never reach.
> Less worthy of applause, though more admir'd,
> Because a novelty, the work of man,
> Imperial mistress of the fur-clad Russ!
> Thy most magnificent and mighty freak,
> The wonder of the North.
>
> [5:122–31]

Quite clearly the paired terms here carry their simplest meaning: art is the term of lesser value; it is used to signify the works issuing from human pride. The ice palace becomes for Cowper a conveni-ent emblem of impermanence, the implacable foe of pride; it is "a scene of evanescent glory, once a stream,/And soon to slide into a stream again" (5:166–68). These very familiar topics, presented in perhaps their most familiar shape, provide the foundation for the ruminations on statecraft which occupy the middle segment of book five.[3]

Using the term "art" to signify merely artifice, and identifying such art with human pride, Cowper's analysis of the institutions of government proceeds along a predictable path. Art, civilization, kingship, war, and political organization ultimately are to be understood together as the effects of pride: "the first smith was the first murd'rer's son" (5:219). Unlike Pope, Cowper offers no theory to account for the social, as opposed to the political instincts of man, and devotes merely a dozen lines to a sketch of the golden age which preceded the founding of civilization and political organization.

> When Babel was confounded, and the great
> Confed'racy of projectors wild and vain
> Was split into diversity of tongues,
> Then, as a shepherd separates his flock,
> These to the upland, to the valley those,
> God drave asunder, and assign'd their lot
> To all the nations. Ample was the boon
> He gave them, in its distribution fair
> And equal, and he bade them dwell in peace.
> Peace was awhile their care: they plough'd, and sow'd,
> And reap'd their plenty, without grudge or strife.
> But violence can never longer sleep
> Than human passions please.
>
> [5:193–205]

The golden age was one of agricultural harmony: to what human energy it owed its stability is not clear, nor is the poet much concerned with the question. On the other hand, the human energies which lie behind political civilization receive an inordinately larger share of the poet's attention as he enumerates the progress of the political arts from that first moment in which the natural violence of men broke forth. It is interesting that Cowper

---

3. Cf. Spacks, *The Poetry of Vision*, pp. 189–92.

has no explanation for the social cohesiveness of the golden age; but the psychology, so to speak, of violence and pride is his explanation of the political and economic institutions of civilization. It is a very familiar set of ideas; the analysis of the origins of political allegiance is sufficient to serve as an example. The masses

> know not what it is to feel within
> A comprehensive faculty, that grasps
> Great purposes with ease, that turns and wields,
> Almost without an effort, plans too vast
> For their conception, which they cannot move.
> Conscious of impotence, they soon grow drunk
> With gazing, when they see an able man
> Step forth to notice; and, besotted thus,
> Build him a pedestal, and say, Stand there,
> And be our admiration and our praise.
> They roll themselves before him in the dust,
> Then most deserving in their own account
> When most extravagant in his applause,
> As if exalting him they rais'd themselves.
>
> [5:250–63]

Cowper's use of the golden age fable, then, is instructive in its brevity. In fact, it has little meaning for him, and he has little to say about it. Whereas Pope offered a theory of the social bond which explained it, perhaps too simply, as the natural expression of certain human instincts, Cowper is at a loss, throughout his work, to discover a foundation in human nature for the phenomenon which he posits as a good: man as a social—as distinct from a political—animal. Therefore, Cowper draws all of his political lessons from the events subsequent to the age of innocence, although the fabled social experience of the age of innocence serves throughout his work as the standard against which the subsequent decline is measured.

The inevitable direction, therefore, of Cowper's analysis of the state is toward a religious transcendence of the political dilemmas he confronts. It would be a mistake, I think, to permit Cowper's biography to intrude here. Indeed, what we know of his life might suggest that the remarkable thing about his poem is that it turns to

God only after the poet has devoted considerable effort to come to grips with his subject in other ways, as we have seen. Most curious, in fact, is the shape of his discussion in book five; a long digression on the comparative merits of England and France—a discussion based upon the degree of political liberty each nation provides its subjects—is permitted to intrude between the conclusion of the mythical narrative on the progress of civilization and the final section of book five, in which the dilemmas of politics are transcended in a vision of grace. This digression is curious in several ways. For one thing, it adds little to the conclusions implicit in the mythical narrative, which tells us enough of the ravages of pride, violence, and artifice to preclude the possibility that these evils will be cured in nature or by art. That is, the mythical narrative itself points only to the realm of grace, in which natural and political evils are transcended rather than resolved.

The digression was probably important to Cowper for the specific direction it gave to his final ascent above politics towards God. It provides him with the theme of liberty. What is noteworthy is that the discussion of political liberty presupposes, indeed is based upon, a radically different pattern of history from that implied by the fable of the evil progress of civilization. The historiography of the fable is the familiar sequence of decline. It recalls the ancient myth of the succession of the ages of man, differing only in that it ignores the age of silver. In Cowper's myth the iron age follows immediately upon the golden, recalling in particular the sequence of history adumbrated in his poem "Heroism."

But, curiously enough, when the discussion shifts from myth to experience—that is, in the extended comparison of the governments of England and France—a very different theory of history is implied. The discussion of political liberty grows from Cowper's mythological account of the origin of kingship:

> Strange, that such folly as lifts bloated man
> To eminence, fit only for a god,
> Should ever drivel out of human lips,
> Ev'n in the cradled weakness of the world!
> Still stranger much, that, when at length mankind

> Had reach'd the sinewy firmness of their youth,
> And could discriminate and argue well
> On subjects more mysterious, they were yet
> Babes in the cause of freedom, and should fear
> And quake before the gods themselves had made!
> But above measure strange, that neither proof
> Of sad experience, nor examples set
> By some whose patriot virtue has prevail'd
> Can even now, when they are grown mature
> In wisdom, and with philosophic deeps
> Familiar, serve t' emancipate the rest!
>
>   [5:283–98]

This passage expresses a sense of history as progress, a kind of stage for the maturation of man—superimposed upon the quite contrasting pattern of moral decline adumbrated earlier in the myth of civilization's growth and man's decline. The lengthy paean to English liberty which follows contains within it a fine account of the peculiarly English institution of constitutional monarchy, and, once again, the poem approaches the celebrative mode, though highly qualified, in its praise of the poet's native land.

>   'Tis liberty alone gives the flow'r
> Of fleeting life its lustre and perfume;
> And we are weeds without it. All constraint,
> Except what wisdom lays on evil men,
> Is evil; hurts the faculties, impedes
> Their progress in the road of science; blinds
> The eyesight of discov'ry; and begets,
> In those that suffer it, a sordid mind
> Bestial, a meagre intellect, unfit
> To be the tenant of man's noble form.
> Thee therefore still, blame-worthy as thou art,
> With all thy loss of empire, and though squeez'd
> By public exigence till annual food
> Fails for the craving hunger of the state,
> Thee I account still happy, and the chief
> Among the nations, seeing thou art free
> My native nook of earth!
>
>   [5:446–62]

But Cowper's discussion of political liberty is inadequate. It is not worked into the poem on the energy of a poetic idea whose force is sufficient to play against the myth of civilization's prideful decline into barbarity and slavery. Therefore no imaginative dialectic is created out of the opposing forces of decline and progress, no metaphor emerges to express a new vision of a redeemed politics, a politics in which the energies of art and pride are molded to form the institutions of liberty. It is clear from the lines above that Cowper does not locate the sources of English liberty in the institution of the English state, but rather sees English liberty as existing somehow independently of the state, indeed, despite the state (5:456–59).

Not surprisingly, the discussion of political liberty is inconclusive. Yet, it testifies to a consistent pattern of failure in *The Task*, a pattern of failure rooted in the poet's attempt to include politics within the range of mankind's moral experience, all the while the imaginative ingredients necessary to such a synthesis fail to work for the poet. In a very few lines the pattern of decline reestablishes itself: "th' age of virtuous politics is past." English liberty, though real, is tenuous, and the importance of the contrast with French slavery diminishes. Liberty, too, is one of the works of men, of art. Cowper speaks of "the old castle of the [virtuous] state . . . so assailed/That all its tempest-beaten turrets shake . . ." (5:525–27). The products and the victims of pride,

> all our mightiest works
> Die too: the deep foundations that we lay,
> Time ploughs them up, and not a trace remains.
>
> [5:531–33]

The old castle of the state was once a virtuous edifice, but its fate is indistinguishable, finally, from that ice palace of the empress's pride. The next section of the poem goes on to speak of a different kind of liberty, "liberty of heart, deriv'd from heav'n; Bought with HIS blood who gave it to mankind . . ." (5:545–46). The purpose, then, of the digression on political liberty, to which Cowper devoted some one hundred sixty lines, is to remove from the poem any further consideration of politics and the state as morally significant aspects of human experience. "Grace makes the slave a freeman" (5:688).

Political experience having been identified as an aspect of art, the poem completes its pattern of meaning by establishing the terms nature and grace as the axis around which significant human experience circles. Cowper returns, near the end of book five, to the old terms, nature and art, in order to depart from them. Not merely the political institution, the state, but also its celebrant, the poet, are no longer relevant to the moral experience of spiritual liberty.

> Patriots have toil'd, and in their country's cause
> Bled nobly; and their deeds, as they deserve,
> Receive proud recompense. We give in charge
> Their names to the sweet lyre. Th' historic muse,
> Proud of the treasure, marches with it down
> To latest times; and sculpture, in her turn,
> Gives bond in stone and ever-during brass
> To guard them, and t'immortalize her trust:
> But fairer wreaths are due, though never paid,
> To those who, posted at the shrine of truth,
> Have fall'n in her defence. A patriot's blood,
> Well spent in such a strife, may earn indeed,
> And for a time ensure, to his lov'd land,
> The sweets of liberty and equal laws;
> But martyrs struggle for a brighter prize,
> And win it with more pain. Their blood is shed
> In confirmation of the noblest claim—
> Our claim to feed upon immortal truth,
> To walk with God, to be divinely free,
> To soar, and to anticipate the skies!
> Yet few remember them. They liv'd unknown
> Till persecution dragg'd them into fame,
> And chas'd them up to heav'n. Their ashes flew
> No marble tells us whither. With their names
> No bard embalms and sanctifies his song:
> And history, so warm on meaner themes,
> Is cold on this. She execrates indeed
> The tyranny that doom'd them to the fire,
> But gives the glorious suff'rers little praise.
>
> [5:704–32]

This passage sets three figures against each other: the patriot, the poet, and the martyr. The martyr, representing a kind of experience not rooted in pride, is curiously saved from the oblivion to which all the efforts of art are doomed, while the poet and patriot exist for each other as hero and celebrant, doomed to that oblivion their works are designed to conquer. Thus Cowper's poem brings us almost schematically to a crisis in an ancient tradition in the history of literature. Not only the subject of the bucolic kinds— nature and art—but also their positive possibilities for the celebration of human society are no longer adequate to the meaning of political experience. Cowper's own failures as an artist are the most cogent testimony to the exhaustion of the bucolic kinds. *The Task* attempts to confront the realities of a new kind of political experience—the secular state—with the imaginative devices appropriate to an earlier sense of political experience. The difficulties inherent in this attempt come to the surface in an almost logical pattern of failure. In the end, politics and art are divorced from nature, and the meaning of nature itself is radically changed to suit its new function as the antipode of grace.

Nature, no longer married to art, becomes a means of grace. As such, the idea of nature becomes a simpler thing than it had been in its other context. There is, in Cowper's conception of the axis of nature and grace, some ambiguity. If Cowper's religious position is the center of our interest, then the sequence of devotion implied in the connection between nature and grace will become an important problem. He seems to move somewhat carelessly between two attitudes. On the one hand there is the advice to "Acquaint thyself with God, if thou would'st taste His works" (5:779–80). On the other hand is the assertion that nature itself is the road to God. An observer sensitive to the changing seasons will understand that

> From dearth to plenty, and from death to life
> Is Nature's progress when she lectures man
> In heav'nly truth; evincing, as she makes
> The grand transition, that there lives and works
> A soul in all things, and that soul is God.
>
> [6:181–85]

However, whether grace makes nature available or nature, grace, is not a crucial problem to this study. In either case, nature means, simply, created nature. It is not that complex phenomenon whose full meaning grows from its relation with art. Cowper's poetry has often been designated as "preromantic" (which perhaps merely means that in places it contains scenes of nature "realistically" observed). But this aspect of his work, and it is only an aspect of it, is perhaps to be best understood as the style of thought and expression which inevitably arises when the complex bucolic metaphor disintegrates. Though there are many passages in *The Task* whose effects are merely descriptive, Cowper's interest in created nature and his descriptive powers find their appropriate expressive context only after the split between nature and art becomes irremediable. And this split, as we have seen, has its roots in the difficulties the poet encounters in assimilating the realities of political experience to the imaginative and moral context of the bucolic vision. In fact, there are two styles of nature poetry in *The Task*.

Ultimately, nature's new identity as a means of grace can be understood as a momentous new departure in cultural history. But all of this is only fitfully apparent in *The Task*. Perhaps it needs to be acknowledged here that *The Task*, considered as an eighteenth-century document, simply reflects an attitude whose roots are complex and whose history began much earlier. Newton's *Optics*, the aesthetics of the sublime—these have been shown to be intimately involved in the extraordinary history of the changing idea of nature in the eighteenth century.[4] Cowper's work, indeed, comes near the end of a line of poetry which had, in one way or another, responded to the force of that history. What is perhaps unique about *The Task* is the conflicting presence in the poem of both the new and the old conceptions of nature. It is the general quality of Cowper's work as a public poem incorporating a strong

4. To acknowledge fully the body of scholarship on this crucial subject would be impossible, but I want here to mention Marjorie Nicolson's *Mountain Gloom and Mountain Glory: The Development of the Aesthetics of the Infinite* (Ithaca: Cornell University Press, 1959); her *Newton Demands the Muse* (Princeton: Princeton University Press, 1946); and Ernest Tuveson's *The Imagination as a Means of Grace: Locke and the Aesthetics of Romanticism* (Berkeley: University of California Press, 1960) as having been generally helpful in suggesting an approach to Cowper.

element of social criticism and realistic social observation which distinguishes it from such poetry as Akenside's or the Wartons', and which places it meaningfully in the great bucolic tradition; that is, in the line of literary kinds which are concerned largely with the interplay of man's social order and his natural instincts. Thus the two formulations of nature—nature understood in relation to art, nature understood in its relation to grace—split apart in *The Task* because each serves a different purpose, and their purposes are incompatible.

Although the implications of nature's new identity are only fitfully apparent in *The Task,* certain directions can be gleaned. In the context of Cowper's political concerns, his understanding of nature as a means of grace permits him to think of nature as a means of transcending political experience. It would be foolish to suggest that, as such, nature for Cowper is reduced to a means of escape. In fact, Cowper's interest in created nature is not always limited to its potential as a subject for descriptive virtuosity; it can become a nucleus of ideas, as well. Created nature, seen through eyes which are opened by grace, is a means of health and mental harmony. It exists in a complex relation with the mind of man, becoming a psychological as well as a physical fact.

But Cowper is very much aware of the possibilities of nature as escape. Both in his poem *Retirement* and in *The Task* he devotes some space to this "sociological" phenomenon. We have already noted his expression of contempt for certain fashionable uses of the countryside—gorgeous, tasteless landscaping, hunting parties, urban vacationers masquerading as nymphs and swains. More interesting is the sympathetic attention he pays to another manifestation of mankind's pathetic response to the corrupting, stifling growth of its urban civilization.

> 'Tis born with all: the love of Nature's works
> Is an ingredient in the compound man,
> Infus'd at the creation of the kind. . . .
> It is a flame that dies not even there,
> Where nothing feeds it: neither business crowds,
> Nor habits of luxurious city-life;

Whatever else they smother of true worth
In human bosoms; quench it, or abate.
The villas with which London stands begirt,
Like a swarth Indian with his belt of beads,
Prove it. A breath of unadult'rate air,
The glimpse of a green pasture, how they cheer
The citizen, and brace his languid frame!
Ev'n in the stifling bosom of the town,
A garden, in which nothing thrives, has charms
That soothe the rich possessor; much consol'd,
That here and there some sprigs of mournful mint,
Of nightshade, or valerian, grace the well
He cultivates. These serve him with a hint
That nature lives. . . .
     Are they not all proofs
That man, immur'd in cities, still retains
His inborn inextinguishable thirst
Of rural scenes, compensating his loss
By supplemental shifts, the best he may?
The most unfurnish'd with the means of life,
And they that never pass their brick-wall bounds
To range the fields and treat their lungs with air,
Yet feel the burning instinct: over head
Suspend their crazy boxes, planted thick,
And water'd duly. There the pitcher stands
A fragment, and the spoutless tea-pot there;
Sad witnesses how close-pent man regrets
The country, with what ardour he contrives
A peep at nature, when he can no more.
                   [4:731–33, 743–59, 765–79]

Cowper stands at a distance from the objects of his attention here, but he is at once critical and sympathetic: critical of man's involvement with a corrupt and luxurious city, sympathetic to man's poor efforts to escape it through some pathetic appropriation of nature's effects: urban gardens, window boxes, suburban villas, all "supplemental shifts." These ornaments are observed by the poet with something like sociological detachment. That is, he "theorizes" about certain expressions of popular taste, the window box, for example. And what are these "supplemental shifts" but symptoms of the uneasiness that all levels of the population are experiencing with their urban environment, turning to nature in the simplest of ways, making of it a kind of escape. The point should not be unduly emphasized because the poem itself does not pursue it, but for a moment the narrator has paused to take notice of certain details in the societal environment, so to speak, and we may notice them for what they are—the growth of suburbs, the keeping of small city gardens, the dressing of window boxes—symptoms of that sense of nature as escape which we recognize as the sentimentalizing of nature: the pursuit of a month in the country, a suburban home, two weeks in a tent, all so familiar to us now. Has Cowper not noticed in these suburban villas and urban window boxes that sentimentalizing of nature which lies behind so many features of modern life, and which is a simplification and vulgarization of the earlier vision of nature's union with art, a vision expressing the complex, celebrative intention of the bucolic kinds in their confrontation with civilization. Cowper distances himself from these pathetic efforts of a humanity beleaguered by its civilization. For him nature as a means of grace is not nature sentimentalized. But the nature which is a means of grace for Cowper easily becomes the nature which is a means of escape for most of us— trees, brooks, rocks, and flowers merely. Our design is to commune with it temporarily, and the purity of the communion must be untainted by the intrusion of art.

Book six of *The Task* develops from the idea of nature as a means of grace a plan for virtuous retirement which takes the happy man forever out of the realm of politics. Retirement is no longer a metaphor for the creation of order and harmony which is the mind's task as it regularly organizes its experiences in the realm of nature and art. Retirement, for Cowper, is a suburban option. In book six Cowper returns to the theme of nature and art, but only to assert the limits of art. Cowper's interest in art in this section of his work is limited to a study of its symbiotic relation to human pride. The sustained attack of the "man praises man" section is directed entirely at the corrupt human uses of human art. This is not to say that for Cowper, as he approaches the end of his poem, human art is utterly valueless. He praises Handel's music, sees Handel's music as art properly devoted to the glory of God. But Cowper is not so much interested in the good possibilities of art as he is in its susceptibility to be fed upon by human pride. His lines on Garrick are in pointed contrast to the lines in book three where the flowers of his greenhouse suggested to him the stately scene of a theater, and the order of a good society.

> Man praises man; and Garrick's mem'ry next,
> When time hath somewhat mellow'd it, and made
> The idol of our worship while he liv'd
> The god of our idolatry once more,
> Shall have its altar; and the world shall go
> In pilgrimage to bow before his shrine.
> The theatre, too small, shall suffocate
> Its squeez'd contents, and more than it admits
> Shall sigh at their exclusion, and return
> Ungratified.
>
> [6:664–73]

In book six Cowper has passed beyond concern for the mutual redemptive powers residing in nature and art. Whatever else it is, the vision of the millenium, (which one critic has seen as the crucial center of the work)[5] is not a vision of the marriage of nature and art. It transcends—more accurately, ignores—politics, and its harmony owes nothing to the efforts of human art. The energies which create the millenium belong to God. To human art there is only the attention implied in the passing observation that the land under human cultivation has been "fertile only in its own disgrace" (6:767), a devastating denial of the bucolic assertion of agricultural labor as the virtuous work emblematic of the positive qualities of human civilization. For Cowper, therefore, retirement is escape from the scenes of pride, art, and politics; it is preparation for the millenium.

> He is the happy man, whose life ev'n now
> Shows somewhat of that happier life to come;

5. Morris Golden, *In Search of Stability: The Poetry of William Cowper* (New York: Bookman Associates, 1960), p. 152.

Who, doom'd to an obscure but tranquil state,
Is pleas'd with it. . . .

[6:906-9]

How far removed this is from the character of rural virtue established in Pope's praise of Lord Burlington's estate, an area of
dynamic retreat inhabited by the mind as it negotiates an accord
between the claims of culture and of the enhanced self.

❦

The disintegration of nature's union with art in the bucolic
metaphor inevitably follows from the poet's judgments of political
experience. But, as I have been arguing, the correspondence between the social and political orders and the corollary concept of
the body politic as a creature of art fulfilling the purposes of nature,
are crucial assumptions of the pastoral and georgic modes. To
envision such a basis for politics thus implies that politics is an art
concerned with more than art, that the state is not merely a creature
of art. Yet in the eighteenth century, competing theoretical formulations of the nature of the state and disturbing developments in its
behavior had increasingly been challenging these assumptions.
Perhaps, as Edward Tayler suggests, it is the secular thrust of
Hobbes's thought, leading to the blunt and devastating conclusion
that the state is merely a creature of art, which attacks most clearly
the attitudes upon which bucolic poetry is based and to which it
gives expression. Certainly Cowper's work, to the extent that it
concerns itself with the problems of society and state, displays
conflicting purposes: the poet writes with the bucolic tradition very
much in mind about a world to which that tradition has become
irrelevant. Nowhere is this clearer than in his difficulties in recon-
ciling the purposes of society and state. Cowper's poem begins to
reflect, therefore, one of the most salient features of modern
thought. The Hobbesian analysis of the state, identifying it entirely as a creature of art, understanding its chief function to be the
controlled use of violence, precludes the possibility of integrating
the moral and political ends of mankind in the manner of the
bucolic vision. In his *Essay on Man* Pope asserted the older tradi-

tion as he wrote his poem on man and society. But we have seen the strains imposed on his art when, in the *Epistle to Bathurst*, he attempted to confront certain characteristics of the modern state and to understand them within the older context.

Cowper's work also reflects these difficulties. It is a strange poem. Among all of its faults, critics have always noted its lack of logical rigor; but it is not a lack of logic that accounts for its failures. Its highest peaks of imaginative power are, in the end, at odds with certain of the purposes which the poet adheres to with both rigor and integrity. The marriage of nature and art, so carefully, precisely, and exquisitely expressed in book three, must give way to the force of the poet's utterly unsentimental confrontation of the facts of English political and economic life. We have studied some of the ways the poem fails; it is a familiar kind of failure, characteristic of periods when experience seems to be uncontrollable by the forms of thought and feeling which an artist must work with. But the poem's very failure is a kind of testament to the poet's integrity. There is no effort to impose upon the recalcitrant facts a resolution that is undeserved.

Most eighteenth-century bucolic poetry fails for us today because it seems to express nothing that can be seriously thought about within a larger context than that of contemporary fashion. But Cowper's poem, in the tradition of bucolic literature, addresses itself to the great questions of human political and social experience. It is not able to deal with these questions as a fully achieved poem because the sources of its very considerable imaginative power are not appropriate to its insights as a work of social criticism. Driven back and forth between celebration and criticism, working with two conflicting conceptions of nature's meaning, *The Task* is among the first of many works which, in their confrontation with modern experience, are forced into a search for a style. In *The Task* that search is not rewarded. Too much had changed in the world Cowper was writing about. *The Task,* examining that world from the perspective of the bucolic kinds, had to fail as a poem if it were to retain its integrity in confronting the evils of a world of power and art divorced from the world of nature.

Eighteenth-Century Endings, Romantic Beginnings

"Our enemy," commented Thomas Jefferson on the results of the War of 1812, "has indeed the consolation of Satan on removing our first parents from Paradise: from a peaceable and agricultural nation, he makes us a military and manufacturing one."[1] The rhetoric is by now familiar, and so is the dilemma. Earlier in his career, when he was leading a nation he had dreamed of as the home of sturdy, educated, noble husbandmen, Jefferson nevertheless had to make the choices which opened another path. Leo Marx has shown how Jefferson's writings exhibit in their rhetoric an ardent devotion to the rural ideal, and a cool, self-aware, pragmatic dismissal of it. "Recognizing that the ideal society of the middle landscape was unattainable, he kept it in view as a kind of model, a guide to long range policies as indispensable to intelligent political thought or action as the recognition of present necessities. Like certain great poets who have written in the pastoral mode, Jefferson's genius lay in his capacity to respond to the dream, yet to disengage himself from it."[2]

But the statesman, in moving between life and art, is not charged

1. Thomas Jefferson to William Short, 28 November 1814, as quoted in Leo Marx, *The Machine in the Garden: Technology and the Pastoral Ideal in America* (New York: Oxford University Press, 1964), p. 144.
2. Ibid.

with that absolute commitment to both that demands a steadiness of vision from the poet which, in the end, is proved only by the integrity of his expression. Jefferson could, like Adam Smith and Arthur Young, propose a rhetorical model of virtue in the shape of the rural ideal, and at the same time, although with genuine regret, urge or pursue policies which led to the development of an industrial economy. Sympathetically interpreting Jefferson's predicament, Marx observes that the "exultant pastoral wish-image [emerging from Jefferson's rhetorical praise of agriculture] may well emanate from a mind susceptible to the darkest foreboding. Looking to America's future, Jefferson anticipate[d] the tragic ambivalence that is the hallmark of our most resonant pastoral fables."[3]

Unlike Jefferson, Dyer saw no need to disengage himself from the rural dream. Exulting in, rather than fearing, the consequences of wealth and power, Dyer boldly, but too simply, interpreted them to be consonant with the bucolic ideal, and proceeded to celebrate the political and economic order which grew up with the new world of work. His celebration of England grew from his identification of her new industry and wealth with the ideal of virtuous work described by Virgil. And, unlike Cowper, Dyer had no difficulty in identifying the English state—its government, its army, its incorporated bodies—with the heroic and virtuous community of merchant-swains who participated in the adventure of wealth and power. If, as Marx suggests, Jefferson's tragic forebodings arose from his recognition of the necessity for choice—choice of a path for the nation to follow—then Dyer's poem preserves its simple celebrative mood thanks to a rhetoric which obscured the terms of that choice. The choice, of course, was made, and made by Dyer, but it does not shape the imaginative design of his poem; rather it disrupts it. The exultation over power and wealth and the conventional image of virtue in moderation clash with each other, each springing from a different imaginative impulse, each at odds with the other throughout the poem.

3. Ibid.

In *The Fleece* the bucolic themes of nature and art and virtuous work are employed in a traditional fashion to support the poem's celebration of its society. But Dyer's manner is to assert, not to demonstrate, the blend of nature and art in the acquisitive industry of his adventurous mariners. It became possible for him to bring the English political order within his celebrative ambit by evading the uncomfortable possibilities that England's new enterprises were indeed involved with the luxury and warfare, which he assumed, traditionally, to be evils. But Cowper in *The Task* faces these possibilities. Not wholly committed to celebration or to criticism, Cowper's poem participates in a major project of his age—the effort to come to an understanding of English civilization in other than satiric terms. In this effort, Cowper's employment of bucolic tradition is both critical and celebrative. Pastoral and georgic themes provide the basis for his approval of human civilization, as well as for his attack upon it. He takes more careful note of the uncomfortable facts than does Dyer, and his poem is not able to resolve in art the difficulties created by his observations of life. Luxury, corruption, warfare—these he understands to be inextricably connected with England's new enterprises, and his celebrative effort focuses, not upon the political corporation, the state, but rather upon a vaguely defined entity, which he tends to refer to as "society." It is in "society" that the possibilities of moral health reside; in "society," nature and art are blended and virtuous work is accomplished. We may note how Cowper's depiction of his gardening as virtuous work, though it takes on an emblematic significance referring outward to much more than the literal work of retirement, fails to incorporate within its emblematic significance all the energies of the harbor and the city so easily assimilated by Dyer to the rural ideal.

Cowper's poem tends to become overwhelmed by the poet's observations of the larger life of the English nation. He acknowledges, finally, that the realities of political power and economic wealth preclude a celebrative understanding of the state, the political embodiment of the English community. In this final assertion of criticism over celebration, the complex system of bucolic allusion, which, in those moments of the poem's greatest imaginative power, had held the balance between celebration and criticism, breaks apart. Nature and art come to be understood in their simplest terms as opposing values, and retirement becomes a literal option, not an emblem of mediation. We come to a crisis in the long history of the bucolic kinds.

Yet the breakdown in the design of Cowper's poem results from the steady gaze of the poet, his insistence that his art be accurate in its interpretation of life. Much more than Dyer's poem, *The Task* can speak to us today with some authority as a document of its time. The poet's uncertainties, even his failures, are themselves a kind of appropriate imaginative response to the feel of his age. We have seen how political economists and agrarian reformers and even a statesman like Jefferson were caught in a web of uncertainty as they tried to understand the nature of a public world which seemed to thrive on energies they all had learned to consider as evils. What we see in Cowper's poem—at least in its employment of bucolic tradition—is an accurate reflection in art of that uncertainty. Jefferson also found in an ancient rhetorical tradition that image of virtue which he sadly had to dismiss when he led his nation into new possibilities of power. Leo Marx senses a heroic quality in Jefferson's "capacity to respond to a dream, yet to disengage himself from it. To a degree, he exemplifies the kind of intelligence which Keats thought characteristic of men of achievement, especially in literature." That is, negative capability.[4]

But as Marx has also shown, Jefferson's writings demonstrate the characteristic contrast in styles which we have seen in Adam Smith and Arthur Young. Commenting on Jefferson's attitude toward agriculture, Marx defines it as pastoralism, not agrarianism, "for he does not conceive of the farm as a productive unit; he is devoted to agriculture largely as a means of preserving rural manners, i.e., rural virtue. . . . The reader is not warned, as he is in a poem, that he is crossing the boundary between life and art."[5] When, on the other hand, Jefferson writes seriously on economic policy, the style

4. Ibid.
5. Ibid., p. 129.

is as plain as Arthur Young's calculation of the cost of a fence.

Jefferson's steadiness in action, then, cannot be simply equated with that "negative capability" Keats claimed to be the essential element in the character of the artist. The artist cannot shift styles, cannot act pragmatically but at the same time judge morally. Expression is his only form of action and his poem must find itself in a style which accurately observes life, and in the process, judges it. What Jefferson could resolve in action, the poet cannot necessarily resolve in his expression. Virgil could in the *Georgics*, of course, but what Cowper saw of public life he could not interpret and express in a single style, neither the satirical nor the celebrative. We honor Jefferson both for his vision of the good society and for the difficult decisions he made in disregard of that vision. But we critically examine Cowper's poem for its faulty design. What he deserves to be honored for is the integrity he demonstrates in opening up his poem to include even those facts which his art could not absorb. He does, indeed, observe his environment realistically, but not in the simple sense usually intended in the epithet "preromanticism."

Cowper is, as Maurice Quinlan observes, a transitional poet. People generally mean by this that his poetry depicts the world of nature in close detail and in this respect anticipates Wordsworth's fuller development of that close observation. But much of what Cowper sought and found in nature becomes meaningful in relation to his frustrated commitment to society. It is when nature cannot be understood in harmony with art and is seen as a transcendent alternative to politics, as a means of grace, that its particular details become a subject of special interest for Cowper. This is clearest in book five where all the details of the snow-covered landscape are scrupulously observed in order that their fantastic and infinite effects may be contrasted with the poor efforts of human art, represented in the ice palace.

The transition from Cowper to Wordsworth, then, might be considered not only in terms of each poet's treatment of nature, but also in relation to each poet's treatment of public themes. *Michael*, which Wordsworth pointedly labeled "A Pastoral Poem," can be approached as a poem about nature and society. Indeed, MacLean suggests that in *Michael* Wordsworth "has fused . . . the sentimental and economic strands in his peasant poetry."[6] That is, not only are the figures in the poem close to nature (from which they derive their healthy affections), but they depend upon their property to maintain their relation with nature. The farm is the link between the family and nature. The disruption caused in their lives by the intrusion of the outside world can be understood as a form of the country-city theme which underlies both the pastoral and the georgic, and which is clearly enunciated in strikingly similar terms in Virgil's first eclogue, itself about an eviction from a farm. As in the best bucolic art, the relation depicted between nature and civilization is a complex one. Luke's misfortunes cannot be simply attributed to the town; indeed, his upbringing on the farm ought to have prepared him to enter the life in the city and to thrive, an *exemplum* of the healthy harmony achievable between nature and art. Michael makes this clear to the boy in his parting speech. Furthermore, there is evidence that just such a proper balance is possible; it comes from the history of Richard Bateman. Isabel remembers the poor parish boy, who, like Luke, went to seek his fortune and in the end "grew wondrous rich,/And left estates and monies to the poor./And, at his birthplace, built a chapel floored/With marble which he sent from foreign lands" (267–70).[7] Isabel takes comfort from this history of a boy who left the countryside and ended as its benefactor.

In a comparison of *Michael* with *The Task* or with *The Fleece*, what seems most obvious is the limited scope, the simpler texture, of Wordsworth's poem. Although the poem clearly avoids sentimental ruralism in its account of Luke's disgrace (and Richard Bateman's success), it is striking that the world of the city, where so much happens that affects the country, is entirely outside of the

6. Kenneth MacLean, *Agrarian Age: A Background for Wordsworth* (New Haven: Yale University Press, 1950), p. 98.

7. William Wordsworth, *The Poetical Works of William Wordsworth*, ed. Thomas Hutchinson, 2nd ed. rev. (1936; reprint ed., London, New York, Toronto: Oxford University Press, 1953). References to *Michael* are cited by line numbers; references to *The Prelude* by book and line numbers.

poem. Both Bateman's exemplary story, and Luke's, are merely mentioned, in the scantiest detail. In contrast, in *The Task* we are made to see the city in all of its detail: its salons, their mirrors, the card games, the arts, the sewers. Similarly, we are shown the details of rural corruption. Cowper's realism thus goes much beyond the depiction of nature. In part, it is a quantitative matter. We see too much of the city for us to sustain any simple wish that it may be harmonized with nature, and we see too much of the country's corruption for it to survive for us as an emblem of virtue. The landscape of *Michael* is more of an artifact than Cowper's neighborhood, because we are permitted to see less of it. *Michael* is a successful poem because its realism is carefully controlled to serve the purposes of the poet's pastoral design. The rich texture of social fact which Cowper brings into his poem is excluded from Wordsworth's. We can understand from *Michael* that country and city are not necessarily in simple conflict with each other, but the poem excludes entirely any attempt to demonstrate this by portraying the details of city life. Thus, Wordsworth's focus is entirely on the simplicity of rural manners and experiences, and his setting is limited to that aspect of rural nature which fits into his pastoral design.

In *Michael,* despite the concentrated focus in the country setting, nature has not yet emerged as the chief ingredient of a criticism of culture. Indeed, it may be maintained that in *The Task,* Cowper has moved further in that direction than has Wordsworth in *Michael.* But the lines on the shepherd in *The Prelude* rather clearly indicate the development of nature as a critical perspective. No more realistic than the elegant shepherd of the formal eclogue, Wordsworth's figure is totally a poetic idea, a symbol:

> In size a giant, stalking through thick fog,
> His sheep like Greenland bears; or, as he stepped
> Beyond the boundary line of some hill shadow,
> His form hath flashed upon me, glorified
> By the deep radiance of the setting sun;
> Or him have I descried in distant sky,
> A solitary object and sublime,
> Above all height! like an aerial cross

> Stationed alone upon a spiry rock
> Of the Chartreuse, for worship. . . .
> Far more of an imaginative form
> Than the gay Corin of the groves . . .

[8:266–75, 284–85]

This study can properly conclude with this image of the shepherd, "a power,/Or genius, under Nature, under God,/Presiding. . . ." He does not mediate between nature and art, but is rather an emblem of nature's divinity, an image of that power which serves us as

> a sure safeguard and defense
> Against the weight of meanness, selfish cares,
> Coarse manners, vulgar passions, that beat in
> On all sides from the ordinary world
> In which we traffic.

[8:318–22]

The shepherd of *The Prelude*, with his gigantic sheep, does not inhabit the bucolic landscape where nature and art are blended in man's virtuous and mundane work. He comes out of thick fog, or out of the radiance of the setting sun; he is seen on hill tops, "a solitary object and sublime." This awesome figure serves to remind us of the source of our best energies in nature. He is a defense against "the effective elements of society," not an embodiment of them.

Index

A

Addison, Joseph, 9
  Virgil and, 9
Aeneid (Virgil), 19
Agrarian Age: A Background for Wordsworth (MacLean), 198n
Agriculture (countryside)
  Balsamo on, 61-69
  cities and, 7-14, 27-30, 38, 59-69, 85-97, 100, 116, 117
  Cowper on, 125-30, 136, 140-43, 156-59, 164, 176, 179
  Dyer on, 7-8, 85-97, 100, 108, 194
  expansion of, 1, 2
  Jefferson on, 196-97
  Johnson on, 64n
  new methods of, 6
  Pope on, 33-35, 38
  Smith on, 27-29, 70, 73, 74, 76-81
  Virgil on, 22-27
  Young on, 51-69, 80-81, 113
"Agriculture" (Dodsley), 8n
Akenside, Mark, 187
Alexander Pope: The Poetry of Allusion (Brower), 43n
Alpers, Paul, 43n, 142n
Annals of Agriculture, 51-52, 61, 62n

Apocalypse, Pope and the, 39-41, 103
Aristotle, 3
Art, *see* Nature and art
Arthos, John, 48n
"Arthur Young, Traveller and Observer" (Middendorf), 54n

B

Balsamo, Paolo, 61-69, 82, 91
  on agriculture (countryside), 61-69
  on cities, 65, 66
  on luxury, 62-64
  significance of, 67
  on wealth, 90
  on work (labor), 67
  Young and, 61-69
Barrell, John, 56n, 94n
Blake, William, 116n
Boswell, James, 6n
Bovie, Smith Palmer, 20n
Boyd, David, 173n
Brissenden, R. F., 87n
Brower, Reuben, 43
Bucolic tradition
  Cowper, 155-92, 195-96

Bucolic tradition (*continued*).
  Dyer, 88, 91, 96, 195
  the good society and, 19-49
  Pope, 31-46
  Smith, 69-82
  Virgil, 19-31
  work (labor) and, 51-82
  Young, 51-69
Bull, John, 94n
Burke, Edmund, 47
Burlington, Lord, 176, 191

C

Capitalism
  Cowper on, 13
  Dyer on, 13
  work (labor) and, 68
  Young on, 54
Catastrophe, Cowper on, 122-23,
    127-29
Chalker, John, 86n, 94n
Chapman, R. W., 6n
Cicero, Marcus Tullius, 56
Cities, 4-5
  agriculture (countryside) and, 7-
    14, 27-30, 38, 59-69, 85-97, 100,
    116, 117
  Balsamo on, 65, 66
  Cowper on, 125-26, 136-37, 143,
    166-67, 173
  Dyer on, 85-95, 100
  Pope on, 33, 34
  Smith on, 73, 77, 78
  Young on, 59-69
Civilization
  Cowper on, 128, 131-33, 161-62,
    166, 176, 179, 183, 195
  Pope on, 31, 33
  Virgil on, 24, 30
Clare, John, 15
Clark, Sir Kenneth, 39

Commerce (industry-
    manufacturing)
  Cowper on, 129, 133, 151, 162-63,
    195
  Dyer on, 39, 86, 87, 89, 101, 104-
    106, 109-16
  expansion of, 1, 2, 28
  new forms of, 6
  new methods in, 6
  Smith on, 27-30, 70-74, 77, 80, 81
*Constitutional History of Modern
    Britain, The* (Keir), 47n
Corn Laws, 59
Corruption
  Cowper on, 141-43, 150, 156, 165,
    167, 168, 195
  Pope on, 41-43
Country and the City, The (Wil-
    liams), 3, 10-12, 27n, 82, 116n,
    117n
Countryside, *see* Agriculture
    (countryside)
Cowper, William, 2, 28, 81, 119,
    121-92, 195-99
  on agriculture (countryside),
    125-30, 136, 140-43, 156-59,
    164, 176, 179
  on artificiality, 165
  on authority, 132, 144
  bucolic tradition, 155-92, 195-96
  on capitalism, 13
  on catastrophe, 122-23, 127-29
  on cities, 125-26, 136-37, 143, 166-
    67, 173
  on civilization, 128, 131-33, 161-
    62, 166, 176, 179, 183, 195
  on commerce (industry-
    manufacturing), 129, 133, 151,
    162-63, 195
  on corruption, 141-43, 150, 156,
    165, 167, 168, 195
  on drunkards, 139-43, 146

Cowper, William (*continued*)
Dyer and, 130, 169, 194
on glory, 146, 152
on heroism, 146, 152
history and, 13, 140, 172
idiosyncrasies of, 121
on liberty, 181-84
on luxury, 130, 143-45, 168, 174, 195
Milton and, 168-69
mystification, 13
on nature and art, 123, 128, 129, 132, 133, 155-92, 196, 197
nervous disorders of, 124
on nobility, 146, 152
patriotism, 131-32, 147
on pleasure, 134-38
Pope and, 133, 141, 142, 145, 171, 179, 180, 191-92
on poverty, 139-40
on power, 132, 144-47, 155-56, 195
on public issues, 121-53
on public life, 30-31
on public virtue, 142, 143, 146-47, 166
on the realm of grace, 156, 183, 185, 189-90
religion and, 122-25, 128, 152, 155, 156, 161-69, 180-81, 185, 190
on retirement, 133-53, 156, 158-59, 167, 174, 189, 190
on the rural thief, 139-40
on society, 133, 134, 138-39, 142-45, 155-92
on the state (politics), 155-92
torments of, 121, 122, 124
as a transitional poet, 197
Virgil and, 157
on war, 126, 129-32, 148, 150, 179, 195

Cowper, William (*continued*)
on wealth, 130, 144-45, 195
Wordsworth and, 197-99
on work (labor), 130, 176, 195
Crabbe, George, 11, 82*n*

D

Danby, John F., 45*n*
Davie, Donald, 1-2, 124-25
Deserted Village (Goldsmith), 11, 81, 115, 117
Diderot, Denis, 43, 45
Discovery of the Mind, The (Snell), 16
Dobrée, Bonamy, 86*n*
"Dr. Johnson as Hero" (Hart), 6*n*
Dodsley, Robert, 8*n*
Drunkards, Cowper on, 139-43, 146
Dryden, John, 19*n*, 41
Dunciad, The (Pope), 30, 41, 103
Dyer, John, 1, 2, 30, 68, 83-119, 194-96
on agriculture (countryside), 7-8, 85-97, 100, 108, 194
bucolic tradition, 88, 91, 96, 195
on capitalism, 13
celebrative tone of, 83, 86, 90, 103-106, 110-17
on cities, 85-95, 100
on commerce (industry-manufacturing), 39, 86, 87, 89, 101, 104-106, 109-16
conservative aspect of, 7-8
Cowper and, 130, 169, 194
Goldsmith and, 115-19
history and, 4, 13, 103
on innocence, 98-103, 106-108, 115
on luxury, 113, 118, 195
Milton and, 86
on moderation, 97

Dyer, John (*continued*)
  mystification, 13
  on nature and art, 88-90
  Pope and, 90, 103, 119
  on power, 83, 86, 93-94, 107, 110,
    116, 118, 194
  Smith and, 90-91
  Virgil and, 7-8, 86, 87, 90, 96, 97,
    114, 115, 118, 119, 194
  on wealth, 83, 86, 87, 93-94, 107,
    111, 113, 116, 118, 194
  on the wool industry, 83-119
  on work (labor), 4, 83-119
  Young and, 113

E

Eclogues (Virgil), 16-17
Edwards, Thomas R., Jr., 35*n*, 40*n*,
  46, 47
Ehrenpreis, Irvin, 11
Eliot, T. S., 7-8
Empson, William, 14, 26, 141
Enclosure movement, 52, 58
"English Lord and the Happy
  Husbandman, The" (Sam-
  brook), 27*n*, 87*n*
Enjoyment, Pope on, 35-36
Epilogue to the Satires (Pope), 39
Epistle to Bathurst (Pope), 32*n*,
  35*n*, 36, 41-44, 68, 119, 141,
  142, 171, 192
Epistle to Burlington (Pope), 33-
  44, 133
Essay on Man (Pope), 42, 171, 191-
  92
Excursion, The (Wordsworth), 79-
  80

F

Fairchild, Hoxie N., 122

Farmers, *see* Agriculture (country-
  side)
Fielding, Henry, 83-86
  on wealth, 83-85
Fitzgerald, F. Scott, 95
Fleece, The (Dyer), 1, 30, 83-119,
  195, 198
  See also, Dyer, John
"Further Thoughts on Agricul-
  ture" (Johnson), 64*n*

G

*Garden and the City, The: Retire-
  ment and Politics in the Later
  Poetry of Pope 1731–1743*
  (Mack), 5*n*, 33*n*, 38*n*, 39*n*
Garrick, David, 172, 190
Gentleman Farmer (Kamers), 48
"Georgian Background, The"
  (Watt), 40*n*
Georgics (Virgil), 16-17, 19-31, 41,
  46, 55, 94*n*, 97, 115, 118, 197
  See also Virgil
Golden, Morris, 124, 190*n*
Goldsmith, Oliver, 11, 62, 81, 82*n*,
  115, 117
  Dyer and, 115-19
Green Cabinet, The (Rosenmeyer),
  17*n*

H

Handel, George Frederick, 190
*Happy Man, The: Studies in the
  Metamorphosis of a Classical
  Ideal* (Røstvig), 31*n*
Hart, Jeffrey, 6*n*
Hartley, Lodowick, 125, 126
"Heroism" (Cowper), 122*n*, 126-33,
  146, 181
Hesiod, 21, 26

Hill, G. B., 5n
History
  Cowper and, 13, 140, 172
  Dyer and, 4, 13, 103
  Johnson and, 6
  Pope and, 39, 40, 103
  two different attitudes of, 8-9
Hobbes, Thomas, 191
Hollander, Samuel, 75n
Horace, 56
Huang, Roderick, 155n
Hutchinson, Thomas, 198n

I

Idylls (Theocritus), 17n
*Imagination as a Means of Grace:
  Locke and the Aesthetics of
  Romanticism, The* (Tuveson),
  186n
*Imagination and Power: A Study of
  Poetry on Political Themes*
  (Edwards), 46n, 47n
"Importance of London to the Na-
  tional Husbandry" (Young),
  61n
*In Search of Stability: The Poetry
  of William Cowper* (Golden),
  124n, 190n
*Industrial Revolution in the Eigh-
  teenth Century, The* (Man-
  toux), 81n
Industry, *see* Commerce (industry-
  manufacturing)
Innocence, Dyer on, 98-103, 106-
  108, 115

J

Jefferson, Thomas, 193-94, 196-97
  on agriculture (countryside),
  196-97

Johnson, Samuel
  on agriculture (countryside), 64n
  history and, 6
  Pope and, 5
Johnsonian Studies (ed. Wahba),
  6n
Jonson, Benjamin, 12
  Pope and, 38
Journal of a Voyage to Lisbon
  (Fielding), 83-86
Juvenal, 3-4

K

Kames, Lord, 48
Keats, John, 196, 197
Keir, David Lindsay, 47n
Kermode, Frank, 14
Kernan, Alvin, 3-4

L

Landscape into Art (Clark), 39n
Langhorne, John, 82n
Late Augustans, The (Davie), 2n,
  124-25
Life of Johnson, The (Boswell), 6n
Lives of the English Poets (ed.
  Hill), 5n
London (Mack), 5
Luxury
  Balsamo on, 62-64
  Cowper on, 130, 143-45, 168, 174,
    195
  Dyer on, 113, 118, 195
  Mandeville on, 63
  Virgil on, 24

M

*Machine in the Garden, The: Tech-
  nology and the Pastoral Ideal
  in America* (Marx), 15-16, 193n

Mack, Maynard, 4-5
  Pope and, 4-5, 33*n*, 38, 39, 42
  Walpole and, 4
MacLean, Kenneth, 52*n*, 65, 74, 77,
  79, 80, 81, 198
Mandeville, Bernard
  on luxury, 63
  notorious formula of, 6, 46
  on the public good, 69
  significance of, 67
  Smith and, 70*n*
  on work (labor), 67
Mantoux, Paul, 81*n*
Manufacturing, *see* Commerce
  (industry-manufacturing)
Marvell, Andrew, 14
Marx, Leo, 15-16, 91, 193, 194, 196
Michael (Wordsworth), 197-99
Middendorf, John, 52*n*, 54*n*, 76
Miles, Josephine, 86*n*
Milford, H. S., 122*n*
Milic, Louis, 11*n*
Milton, John, 22
  Cowper and, 168-69
  Dyer and, 86
*Modernity of the Eighteenth Cen-
  tury, The* (ed. Milic), 11*n*
Moore, C. A., 5
*Mountain Gloom and Mountain
  Glory: The Development of
  the Aesthetics of the Infinite*
  (Nicolson), 186*n*
"Muse of Mercantilism, The"
  (Spate), 87*n*
Mystification, 10, 13

N

Nature and art
  Cowper on, 123, 128, 129, 132,
  133, 155-92, 196, 197
  Dyer on, 88-90
  Pope, 32-34, 37

Nature and art (*continued*)
  Tayler on, 14-16
  Toliver on, 15
  Virgil on, 69
  Young on, 55
*Nature and Art in Renaissance Lit-
  erature* (Tayler), 14
Newton Demands the Muse (Nicol-
  son), 186*n*
Nicholson, Norman, 125
Nicolson, Marjorie, 186*n*

O

Otis, Brooks, 17, 19*n*

P

Paradise Lost (Milton), 22, 168-69
Pastoral Forms and Attitudes (Toliver), 15*n*
Physiocrats, 71-74, 76
"Pleasures of Agriculture, The"
  (Young), 54-58
Poems of John Dyer, The (ed.
  Thomas), 4*n*
*Poetical Works of William Cow-
  per, The* (ed. Milford), 122*n*
*Poetical Works of William Words-
  worth, The* (Hutchinson),
  198*n*
Poetry of Vision, The (Spacks),
  125, 155*n*
Pope, Alexander, 3-5, 31-46, 103
  on agriculture (countryside), 33-
  35, 38
  the apocalypse and, 39-41, 103
  bucolic tradition, 31-46
  celebrative tone of, 36-37, 39, 41
  on cities, 33, 34
  on civilization, 31, 33
  on corruption, 41-43

Pope, Alexander (*continued*)
  Cowper and, 133, 141, 142, 145, 171, 179, 180, 191-92
  Dyer and, 90, 103, 119
  on enjoyment, 35-36
  history and, 39, 40, 103
  imaginative response of, 39
  imperial theme of, 37-38
  Johnson and, 5
  Jonson and, 38
  Mack and, 4-5, 33*n*, 38, 39, 42
  on nature and art, 32-34, 37
  on relaxation, 35
  satire of, 38, 39, 41, 103
  Smith and, 71
  on society, 31-46
  Virgil and, 9, 31, 32
  Walpole and, 4-5
  on wealth, 90
  on work (labor), 31, 33, 68
Population, new patterns of, 6
"Poverty and Poetry: Representations of the Poor in Augustan Literature" (Ehrenpreis), 11*n*
Power
  Cowper on, 132, 144-47, 155-56, 195
  Dyer on, 83, 86, 93-94, 107, 110, 116, 118, 194
Prelude, The (Wordsworth), 199-200
Public Virtue (Dodsley), 8*n*

Q

"Queries on the Irrigation of Land Answered" (Young), 57
Quinlan, Maurice, 124, 197

R

Rameau's Nephew (Diderot), 45

Religious Trends in English Poetry (Fairchild), 122*n*
Retirement (Cowper), 187
Rosenmeyer, Thomas G., 17*n*
Røstvig, M. S., 31*n*

S

Sambrook, A. J., 27*n*, 87*n*
Seasons, The (Thomson), 94*n*, 97
Shakespeare, William, 14, 45*n*, 172
Shakespeare's Doctrine of Nature (Danby), 45*n*
Shelley, Percy Bysshe, 116*n*
Short, William, 193*n*
Smith, Adam, 2, 27-30, 49, 52*n*, 69-82, 194, 196
  on agriculture (countryside), 27-29, 70, 73, 74, 76-81
  bucolic tradition, 69-82
  on cities, 73, 77, 78
  on commerce (industry-manufacturing), 27-30, 70-74, 77, 80, 81
  on the division of labor, 74, 90-91
  Dyer and, 90-91
  Mandeville and, 70*n*
  on the martial spirit, 75
  on the monopolistic spirit, 77
  moralizing of, 70-71
  on the physiocrats, 71-74, 76
  Pope and, 71
  on productivity, 69-70
  Virgil and, 75, 80
  on work (labor), 28, 69-82, 90-91
Snell, Bruno, 16
Society
  bucolic tradition and, 19-49
  Cowper on, 133, 134, 138-39, 144-45, 155-92
  Pope on, 31-46
  Virgil on, 19-31

Some Versions of Pastoral (Empson), 14
Spacks, Patricia M., 94*n*, 125, 155*n*
Spate, O. H. K., 87*n*
Spenser, Edmund, 14
Swift, Jonathan, 145

T

Task, The (Cowper), 1, 119, 121-92, 195-99
See also Cowper, William
Tayler, Edward W., 14-16, 191
Theocritus, 17*n*
Theory of the Moral Sentiments (Smith), 70*n*
This Dark Estate: A Reading of Pope (Edwards), 35*n*, 40*n*
Thomas, Edward, 4*n*
Thomson, James, 5, 9, 94*n*, 94*n*, 97
"Thoughts on Great Cities" (Balsamo), 62*n*, 65*n*
To Penshurst (Jonson), 12, 38
Toliver, Harold, 15
Tories, 7, 8
Travels in France (Young), 52-53
Tull, Jethro, 8*n*
Tuveson, Ernest, 186*n*
"Two Historical Aspects of the Augustan Tradition" (Watt), 7*n*, 40*n*

U

Usury, 67

V

Veblen, Thorstein, 67
Virgil, 7-9, 16-31, 41, 46, 55, 94*n*, 197, 198
  Addison and, 9

Virgil (*continued*)
  on agriculture (countryside), 22-27
  bucolic tradition, 19-31
  on civilization, 24, 30
  Clark on, 39
  Cowper and, 157
  Dyer and, 7-8, 86, 87, 90, 96, 97, 114, 115, 118, 119, 194
  on luxury, 24
  on nature and art, 69
  Pope and, 9, 31, 32
  on the public good, 69
  satire of, 30
  Smith and, 75, 80
  social intention of, 19
  on society, 19-31
  style of, 19
  on the virtue and destiny of heroic Rome, 25-26, 68-69
  on work (labor), 21-25, 67-69, 87
  Young and, 55, 56
Virgil: A Study of Civilized Poetry (Otis), 17
Virgil's "Georgics": A Modern English Verse Translation (trans. Bovie), 20*n*

W

Wahba, Magda, 6*n*
Walpole, Sir Robert, 4-5
  Mack and, 4
  Pope and, 4-5
War, Cowper on, 126, 129-32, 148, 150, 179, 195
War of 1812, 193
Warton, Joseph, 187
Warton, Thomas, 187
Watt, Ian, 7, 39, 40*n*
Wealth
  Balsamo on, 90

Wealth (*continued*)
  Cowper on, 130, 144-45, 195
  Dyer on, 83, 86, 87, 93-94, 107,
    111, 113, 116, 118, 194
  Fielding on, 83-85
  Pope on, 90
  Young on, 113
Wealth of Nations (Smith), 27-30,
  69-82
  leading theme of, 69-70
  See also, Smith, Adam
"Whig Panegyrical Poetry"
  (Moore), 5*n*
Whigs, 5, 7, 8, 9
William Cowper (Nicholson), 125*n*
William Cowper: A Critical Life
  (Quinlan), 124*n*
William Cowper: Humanitarian
  (Hartley), 125*n*, 126*n*
William Cowper: Nature Poet (Hu-
  ang), 155*n*
Williams, Ralph M., 86*n*
Williams, Raymond, 3, 10-12, 27*n*,
  81, 82, 116*n*, 117
Wool industry, Dyer on, 83-119
Wordsworth, William, 15, 79-80,
  116*n*, 197-200
  Cowper and, 197-99
Work (labor)
  Balsamo on, 67
  bucolic tradition and, 51-82
  capitalism and, 68
  Cowper on, 130, 176, 195

Work (labor) (*continued*)
  Dyer on, 4, 83-119
  Mandeville on, 67
  Pope on, 31, 33, 68
  Smith on, 28, 69-82, 90-91
  Virgil on, 21-25, 67-69, 87
  Young on, 51-69

X

Xenophon, 56

Y

Yeomanry, 58*n*
Young, Arthur, 2, 49, 51-69, 91,
  194, 196, 197
  on agriculture (countryside), 51-
    69, 80-81, 113
  Balsamo and, 61-69
  bucolic tradition, 51-69
  on capitalism, 54
  on cities, 59-69
  Dyer and, 113
  on the enclosure movement, 52,
    58
  on free trade, 54
  on nature and art, 55
  on speculative politicians, 61, 62
  on the state (politics), 53-54
  Virgil and, 55, 56
  on wealth, 113
  on work (labor), 51-69